Absentees

Absentees

On Variously Missing Persons

Daniel Heller-Roazen

ZONE BOOKS · NEW YORK

2021

ZONE BOOKS
633 Vanderbilt Street
Brooklyn, NY 11218

Printed in the United States of America.

Distributed by Princeton University Press,
Princeton, New Jersey, and Woodstock, United Kingdom

Library of Congress Cataloging-in-Publication Data
Names: Heller-Roazen, Daniel, author.
Title: Absentees : on variously missing persons / Daniel Heller-Roazen.
Description: New York : Zone Books, 2021. | Includes bibliographical references and index. | Summary: "From missing persons to disenfranchised civil subjects, from individuals tainted with infamy to the dead, Absentees explores the varieties of 'nonpersons,' human beings all too human, drawing examples, terms and concepts from the archives of European and American literature, legal studies, and the social sciences." —Provided by publisher.
Identifiers: LCCN 2020021857 (print) | LCCN 2020021858 (ebook) | ISBN 9781942130475 (hardback) | ISBN 9781942130482 (ebook)
Subjects: LCSH: Missing persons. | Disappeared persons.
Classification: LCC HV6762.A3 H45 2021 (print) | LCC HV6762.A3 (ebook) | DDC 362.88—dc23
LC record available at https://lccn.loc.gov/2020021857
LC ebook record available at https://lccn.loc.gov/2020021858

Contents

Preface

There are many ways not to be someone. Were one to attempt an enumeration, one would need to consider at the very least: being a lifeless thing of nature, such as a rock, a mineral, or a lake; being a living thing, such as a plant, an insect, or an animal; and being an artifact, such as an artwork, a machine, or an instrument. Each of these inhuman existences has been and will doubtless continue to be studied in detail. Yet there is also a different way not to be someone, a way that is open to human beings alone. It is to become a nonperson.

Who or what is such a being? The question might be judged of marginal importance were nonpersons rare or of a single sort or were they excluded according to a common rule. The question might be considered secondary were their eventuality, in number or in nature, merely one. The truth, however, is that nonpersons are legion. Whenever someone lays claim to a particular mask, a function, or an identity, they make their presence felt. There is no dwelling that their specters do not haunt. In every community, society, and assembly, nonpersons are lesser ones — where "lesser" points not to a quantity, but to a quality, which is intensely variable in kind.

For nonpersons can play many parts. They are always in some sense "missing," yet the forms of their absence and absenting are diverse. Nonpersons may be separated from others. They may be confined. They may be those not represented as the members of a certain group, although, visibly or invisibly, audibly or inaudibly, they move in their midst, disenfranchised in the societies to which they belong. Their dispossession may be limited to a certain interval or extended without reprieve; it can last a season, but it may also stain a lifespan, if not the expanse of memory and forgetting that succeeds it. Those who are legally declared as missing from their place of residence; those who have "disappeared" without any official recognition; servants, serfs, and slaves; foreigners and visitors; native people; convicts; those of a gender considered out of place; the disabled; the very old; infants and children; the ailing; the dead—they, and not only they, compose an unruly multitude. Their number challenges any simple reckoning. In certain cases, they defy comparison.

It might be argued that among human beings, there are mainly, so to speak, such lesser ones. This book's wager is that one can nonetheless distinguish some of their many kinds. To that end, a rudimentary tripartition will here be proposed.

A first variety of nonperson comes into being through unexplained disappearances. When persons remove themselves from a place of residence or fail to return as expected and when their departure is declared as such according to the procedures of civil law, persons give way to the nonpersons who are in technical terms "absentees": subjects of rights defined by lacking a present body. They persist, for a time, in a legal regime distinct from that of ordinary life and death.

A second type of nonperson results from an inverse configuration. In this case, individuals remain physically present in the societies to which they belong, yet their rights and prerogatives are reduced to the point at which their social, legal, and civil personalities may be nullified. These are people tainted and degraded, who may be judged to be dead even while alive.

A third variety of nonpersons, finally, results from the event of physical decease. In passing into the condition of the cadaver, a person ceases to be someone, without, for that matter, becoming any ordinary thing. Every society, people, and culture encounters that remaining being. It poses an almost insuperable challenge to the powers of naming and representation, even as it incites them.

The missing person, the diminished individual, the deceased: all are nonpersons in a sense that requires elucidation. The logic of the concept's name demands an initial commentary. Like any term prefixed by *not-* or *non-*, "nonperson" is equivocal. Its obscurity has been a spur to thinking at least since Aristotle, in *On Interpretation*, took the expression "nonman" or "nonperson" (*ouk anthrōpos*) as the paradigm of "infinite names" without lingering on the being that it signified.[1]

The term may be defined in several ways. A first set of understandings reflects the customary belief that the "nonhuman" must evoke something distinct from human beings: lifeless, living, or artificial things, variously distinct from the people who we are. In an initial sense, "nonperson" may thus be grasped as shorthand for the negation of "person": the denial that the word "person" applies. This reading is difficult to refute, yet it can also scarcely be developed. One might also aspire to give a more positive characterization. A second possibility is to grasp "nonperson" as meaning the contrary of "person." This thesis, however, assumes that whatever is designated by "person" admits of a contrary and of one contrary alone. Neither of these claims is certain. There is also a third possibility, which doubles the first, rendering it affirmative. "Nonperson" can be grasped as the positive expression of anything — animate or inanimate, good or bad, real or imaginary — that "person" is not. For this usage to be coherent, however, one must concede that such things that are not persons can be represented as a unity, forming a concept. That is also contestable.

There is also, however, a fourth reading. It is the most troubling of the glosses that one might propose, but it is also the one closest to ordinary speech. In this sense, a "nonperson" is a person exactly as a "nonstarter" is a starter, a "nonevent" an event, or a "nonentity" an entity. It is, in short, not external to the category of person, but internal to it. This "nonperson" names the depletion of the notion to which it is bound. If one grants such an understanding of the term, the first and third interpretations of the word will need to be tempered, if not set aside. "Person" and "nonperson" will no longer refer to two complementary classes, which, when combined, compose the totality of what there is. Their relations become far more difficult to define. In the concept of the person, the perilous possibility of the nonperson will lie enclosed. Of any "nonperson" it will then be impossible to state either of these contradictory propositions: "It is a person" or "It is not a person." The realities of an inhumanity all too human will defy this partition.

In exploring the conditions of the missing person, the diminished civil subject, and the dead, this book aims to bring into focus nonpersons of the last and most disquieting variety. Absentees in ways both restricted and extended, they are persons who, in different settings, yet each time anew, fail to be, demanding of our attention.

PART ONE

Vanishings

CHAPTER ONE

The Removal

"In some old magazine or newspaper," one of Hawthorne's unnamed narrators finds a "story, told as truth," from which he draws the matter of a work. Published in 1835, Hawthorne's tale concerns a man—"let us call him Wakefield"—who becomes the agent of "the strangest instance, on record, of marital delinquency; and, moreover, as remarkable a freak as may be found in the whole list of human oddities." The action is simply stated:

> The man, under pretence of going a journey, took lodgings in the next street to his own house, and there, unheard of by his wife or friends, and without the shadow of a reason for such self-banishment, dwelt upwards of twenty years. During that period, he beheld his home every day, and frequently the forlorn Mrs. Wakefield. And after so great a gap in his matrimonial felicity—when his death was reckoned certain, his estate settled, his name dismissed from memory, and his wife, long, long ago resigned to her autumnal widowhood—he entered the door one evening, quietly, as from a day's absence, and became a loving spouse till death.[1]

In the first decades of the nineteenth century, this "strangest instance . . . of marital delinquency" could scarcely have been imagined in the towns of the New World. Wakefield, conceived in Massachusetts, had to be a man of the European metropolis. Submerged in "the great mass of London life," unseen in its crowded streets, he enjoys a newly urban opportunity: that of absenting himself "for a long time, from his wife" while remaining in secret proximity to her.[2] The great city alone allows him to hold fast to the place of his vanishing, going missing without ever going far.

The years of Wakefield's "self-banishment" are almost entirely without incident. After "ten years or so" spent in the vicinity of his house, "without once crossing the threshold," "faithful to his wife, with all the affection of which his heart is capable, while he is slowly fading out of hers," Wakefield happens to encounter her "amid the throng of a London street." By this point, the narrator remarks, "she has the placid mien of settled widowhood."[3] The scene is set before the reader's eyes: "Their hands touch; the pressure of the crowd forces her bosom against his shoulder; they stand, face to face, staring into each other's eyes." Whether the "sober widow" registers the identity of the man who brushes up against her is a question. She proceeds along her way to church.

Ten more years pass. Now,

> Wakefield is taking his customary walk towards the dwelling which he still calls his own. It is a gusty night of autumn, with frequent showers, that patter down upon the pavement, and are gone, before a man can put up his umbrella. Pausing near the house, Wakefield discerns, through the parlor-windows of the second floor, the red glow, and the glimmer and fitful flash, of a comfortable fire. On the ceiling, appears a grotesque shadow of good Mrs. Wakefield. The cap, the nose and chin, and the broad waist, form an admirable caricature, which dances, moreover, with the up-flickering and down-sinking blaze, almost too merrily for the shade of an elderly widow.

Suddenly, "at this instant, a shower chances to fall." Wakefield is soon wet. An instance suffices for him to decide: "He ascends the steps—heavily!—for twenty years have stiffened his legs, since he came down." The door opens. Wakefield returns to his wife and home, but "we," the reader learns, "will not follow our friend across the threshold."[4]

Variously ingenious men inhabit Hawthorne's tales. Many are talented lovers or scheming husbands whose ambitions remove them, knowingly or unknowingly, from the women to whom they are attached. Young Goodman Brown leaves his Faith at home in Salem, venturing into the woods with his demonic companion, to behold her again at the congregation of the wicked at which he least expected to find himself in her company. Aylmer, the "man of science" in "The Birth-Mark," dedicates his art to excising the Crimson Hand imprinted on the face of his Georgina before glimpsing that the two are one and that his wife, rendered immaculate at last, must die. Unwitting Giovanni Guasconti, in "Rappaccini's Daughter," aims to cure his beloved Beatrice of her poisonous second nature, thus becoming the instrumental cause of her unexpected death. In mad pursuit of "the spiritualization of matter," in the words of his beloved Annie, Owen Warland, "the artist of the beautiful," succeeds only in assuring his lasting solitude, living to see the fruit of his labors crushed in the curious hand of Annie's inarticulate child.

Wakefield, for his part, embarks on a project that, "without the shadow of a reason," remains singularly unreadable, being, so to speak, markedly indeterminate. "He had contrived," the narrator explains, "or rather he had happened, to dissever himself from the world—to vanish—to give up his place and privileges with living men, without being admitted among the dead."[5]

This "contrivance" sets the scene for a tale of unprecedented blankness in which the only event that may be said to occur is a nonoccurrence: the unexpected and unregistered meeting of man and wife. "The twenty years of Wakefield's vagary" become those of a nineteenth-century *Odyssey*, which is too brief to constitute an epic, yet long enough to be emptied of all significant events.[6] Odysseus spent two decades journeying with his men from Ithaca to the siege of Ilium and back again before recovering his devoted Penelope, Telemachus, and his island kingdom. Wakefield leaves his wife's hearth alone, unbidden and to travel nowhere, and along his way, he encounters neither foes nor friends. He lives out his years away in solitude. Odysseus, when in duress, once claimed for himself the name of *Outis*, or No One, a pun or nickname, to outwit a monstrous host. His act of self-renaming and self-unnaming became one of the deeds that he would recount to those he later met. Wakefield, in stubborn silence and the absence of any interlocutors, makes himself into a No One of a different kind. He is an undistinguished *Outis* who has no adventures, being denied even the "great negative adventure" that Henry James would grant John Marcher in "The Beast in the Jungle."[7] "Forlorn" and "good Mrs. Wakefield," identifiable by the "grotesque shadow" of her "admirable caricature," is a childless Penelope who neither weaves by day nor unweaves by night. Far from any court, she waits for a while, untroubled by suitors, before surmising, in the absence of any news, that her erstwhile spouse will not return.

Hawthorne's narrator presents his tale, in conclusion, as "food for thought," of which a "portion" alone suffices to "lend its wisdom to a moral": "Amid the seeming confusion of our mysterious world, individuals are so nicely adjusted to a system, and systems to one another, and to a whole, that, by stepping aside for a moment, a man exposes himself to a fearful risk of losing his place forever. Like Wakefield he may become, as it were, the Outcast of the Universe."[8]

"A man" might do so, but the one named Wakefield does not. His disappearance is only transient. Like the archaic Greek hero, he leaves and he returns; however indeterminate, his vanishing, delimited because concluded, thus becomes the subject of a complete narrative. The specter of the "Outcast of the Universe" is at once summoned and safely set aside.

Other scenarios, however, are also imaginable. Were Wakefield to "dissever himself" without doing so solely in relation to his spouse, his deed would amount to something other than an act of strange "marital delinquency." Were he to "absent himself," moreover, not for twenty years, but for some unmeasured duration, setting forth "under pretence of going a journey" without returning, his tale would not be that of any voyage. His departure would mark the inception of a disseverance without orient or end. The possibilities are as numerous as the wiles of Odysseus or the reasons for the "little joke" that Wakefield, according to his censoriously attentive narrator, plays "at his wife's expense" in the tale that bears his name. The only certainty is that "amid the seeming confusion of our mysterious world," the event of absenting and self-absenting is one of uncovering. The removal clears a space. Vanishing gives way to visitation, and where there was an "I," some No One inexorably appears. In what ways, to what effects, and with what consequences are questions to which every community responds in terms and practices at once legal and literary, mythological, ritual, and imagistic.

CHAPTER TWO

Laws of Leaving

Civil law reckons with a variety of nonbeing that is unfamiliar to ordinary speech. It pertains solely to persons, defined as those who may speak and lay claim to rights. In technical parlance, it is generally known as "absence." To be "absent," in everyday language, is to be missing from a place or function. People not found where they are expected to be, whether at home, at school, or at work, are commonly called "absent" in this sense. Yet as Marcel Planiol long ago remarked, "in the science of the law" and, consequently, in legislation and in legal theory, "'absence' has a technical sense different from its vulgar one."[1] "For the law," it has been noted, "one who is absent is not at his legal domicile, but he is not just away from home. He has left no clue as to his whereabouts and it is impossible to ascertain whether he is alive or dead."[2] In such cases, absence is not a state definable with respect to some point of orientation ("absent from . . ."). It is, as it were, an absolute condition that characterizes the state of someone who has gone missing without any further specification, someone whose continued life or conceivable death remains, therefore, unknown.

Legal scholars have presented this distinction in a variety of forms. A nineteenth-century exposition of the French civil code draws a sharp line between persons who are merely "nonpresent" (*non-présents*) and persons who may "more properly" be viewed by the law as "absent" (*absents*).[3] Similarly, the scholars of Islamic law distinguish between two expressions: *ghā'ib*, which denotes the "person who is nonpresent at his residence, but whose existence is not in doubt," and *mafqūd*, which signifies the person who is absent "in the strict legal sense," that is, who has disappeared from his residence and whose life has therefore become a matter of doubt. Islamic jurists define the *mafqūd* as "the missing person of whom one does not know whether he is alive or dead" or as "the missing person of whom one does not know either the location or whether he is alive or dead."[4] According to a lapidary formula attributed to an eminent twelfth-century jurist, such a human being is deemed to be "alive with respect to his own rights, yet dead with respect to those of others" (*ḥayy fī ḥaqq nafsihi mayyit fī ḥaqq ghayrihi*).[5]

There are various grounds for the establishment of such a legal category. In his 1860 *Treatise on Absence*, once a standard reference work in France, Charles Demolombe argues that there are three "types of interest" in the vanishing of persons, each of which demands the utmost solicitude of the law. First, there is the particular interest of the person who has absented himself. "Even if it is true in general that everyone is expected to care for his affairs at his risk and peril, the law nonetheless owes its protection to the incapacity of those who cannot govern their fortune on their own"; hence the universal statutes regarding the guardianship of minors and variously incompetent persons. Second, there is the "interest of third parties, above all those possessing rights to which the decease of the absentee would grant access." Finally, there is the interest of society, "which demands that goods not remain long abandoned, without representative and master, in a kind of stagnation, and that the normal and regular course of their transmission not be indefinitely interrupted," access to property "barred," so to speak, by a missing man.[6]

Despite the reasons for the institution of such a special status, absentees have been known to cause difficulties in judicial processes. Referring to the situation in the United States, Jeanne Louise Carriere argues that "they create a morass of legal problems":

> Questions may arise concerning the security of transactions with the missing person's estate, such as the disposition of his land, the right to proceeds of insurance policies on his life and pensions, the right to a cause of action, the necessity of providing for his dependents, the marital status of his spouse, the paternity and legitimacy of children of his spouse's second marriage, the conservation of his property from possible waste, the devolution of succession rights that would pass to him, the release of property from a life tenancy, the requirement of his consent to certain transactions, the merchantability of land titles from his estate, and claims of inheritance from him.[7]

Such predicaments derive from the missing person's legal character, which is in certain respects unique. "Though the absentee has been likened to the minor and the interdict," Carriere notes, alluding to arguments such as Demolombe's,

> he differs from them in ways that make the system of administering their property inapplicable to them. The goal of these regimes is to protect and further the interests of individuals who are present and able to enjoy their estates, but incapacitated from managing them. No incertitude exists as to who should be protected and why. In contrast, whether the absent person is still able to enjoy the rights he obtained when present, whether he has created unknown claims upon his estate, and whether he will return to profit from the protection given to him are mysteries.[8]

Laws, statutes, and judgments have long aimed to order and accommodate such "mysteries" while also envisaging the possibility that they may never be dispelled. The Roman legal corpus suggests that the Latin jurists developed a set of rules to treat the questions pertaining to the estates and legacies of vanished persons. "Absence undoubtedly belongs to the circumstances that must have been more frequent in antiquity than today," Ernest Levy observes. "One need think only of the lesser valuation of human life, the dangers of a major trip, the more exiguous habitation of known land, the irregularity and solitude of means of transport, and the lack of a regular means of communication."[9]

Such factors may account for the lack of any single term, in the lexicon of Roman civil law, for the state of legal "absence."[10] Nonetheless, the Roman jurists could encounter cases of missing men in several branches of their law. The most flagrant among them may be that of *postliminium*, which treats the aftermath of war and the modifications in legal claims that result from captivity. Following a battle, a man might go missing, leaving his wife and children in a state of uncertainty as to "where he is and whether he is" (*ubi sit et an sit*). Starting with Plautus, Latin authors showed a lively interest in such predicaments. The jurists, however, hardly mention them. It seems that far from being exceptional, such situations were to them ordinary perturbations in relations of legal possession. Legal authorities would be expected to resolve the questions raised by missing persons on the basis of available evidence, without recourse to any special statutes. In Roman law, Levy comments, the absence of a spouse "does not mean the presumption of life or of death, but rather, the inaccessibility of one spouse by the other. It is a relative state of affairs, rather than an absolute one, and a state of affairs of the law of property, not the law of proof. Its analogy lies not in the modern law of 'absence,' *Verschollenheit*, *absence déclarée*, and so forth, but in the loss of property."[11]

Other ancient codes contain more detailed guidelines regarding absentees. The fifth-century "Syro-Roman Law-Book," which was originally written in Greek before being translated into Arabic, Armenian, Georgian, and Syrian, contains an explicit rule for cases in which husbands, in particular, go missing:

> When a man marries a woman and leaves her for a definite time, without providing for her maintenance and paying the king's taxes, the woman should wait for him for seven years. If, however, he has been taken by enemies or has (in any other way) fallen into captivity, then the law commands her to wait ten years, or fifteen years if he has fulfilled his duties to the king or has sons. But if she has no children, she should wait seven years and then, by the law of the judge, if she so wishes, she may be freed [from duty toward her absent

> husband]. And if the inheritance of her husband is in her possession, she gives all that is his to the sons of his family and his brothers.[12]

Such stipulations were hardly new in the legislation of the ancient world. The Assyrian code, which dates to the end of the second millennium BCE, already establishes that in the absence of her husband, a woman is to wait five years without changing residence while providing for any children she may have. If her erstwhile spouse does not return during this period, she may remarry in the sixth year of his absence, joining her new spouse in his household. Should her former husband then return, he will not be permitted to approach her, for she will by then have become "the untouchable property of her latter spouse."[13] The Code of Hammurabi, which is some five centuries older, contains similar stipulations, although they do not mention either children or the legal effects of the length of a husband's absence:

> § 133. If a man has been taken captive and there is the (necessary) maintenance in his house, his wife [so long as] her [husband is delayed] shall keep [herself chaste: she shall not] enter [another man's house]. If that woman has not kept herself chaste but enters another man's house, they shall convict that woman and cast her into water.
> § 134. If a man has been taken captive and there is not the (necessary) maintenance in his house, his wife may enter another man's house: that woman shall suffer no punishment.[14]

The missing person most often evoked in Jewish law is also a husband. The Rabbis' code, like the Romans', refuses to grant that after some period, an absent man may be presumed to be dead. Reuven Yaron writes that in cases of disappearance, "there is even a presumption pointing in the opposite direction."

> One might call this a presumption of continuity or *inertia*: a given state of affairs will be assumed to continue indefinitely. Since when last heard of the husband was alive, he is presumed to continue to be alive, as long as there is

> no evidence of his death. In the sphere of marriage this leads unavoidably to the ruling that lack of news does not affect the relationship. Jewish marriage terminates only in one of two manners, either by death or by divorce.[15]

In Jewish law, divorce requires the consent of both man and wife. When a husband vanishes, his wife therefore becomes *agunah*: "anchored" or "chained" to him. "Her remarriage is permanently prohibited."[16] The grounds for that stricture have been found in the perilous position in which remarriage would place a woman and her children. Since Jewish law does not grant a woman the right to two husbands at once, her offspring, to be legitimate, must be fathered by her sole living spouse. If a woman remarried some years after her first husband's vanishing and later gave birth, she and her children would be threatened by her first husband's return: in such a case, she would be judged an adulteress, and the children of her second union would be declared "illegitimate" (*mamzerim*).[17]

Being "chained" to an indefinitely missing man is an unfortunate condition. "To avoid *'aginuth*, the practice grew up of handing the wife a conditional deed of divorce (*get*) or of leaving instructions for the execution of the *get* in case the husband, about to go on a voyage or to join the army, etc., did not return within a specified time."[18] Should a husband not reappear within thirty days, or twelve months, after departing, the conditional divorce would take effect, and the woman would regain the right to remarry. The jurisprudence of preventive divorce contracts raises a host of questions of its own, amply cataloged and discussed in the Talmudic Tractate Gittin.[19] Other solutions to the problems posed by missing men were also envisaged, although they demanded precisely defined conditions of disappearance. Where a man was seen falling into water, for instance, without being observed to reach the shore, his wife might under some conditions be freed from matrimony. If the body of water in question was small, "so that all its shores were visible, and it could be observed that the man did not emerge from it anywhere," he was presumed to have drowned; his wife would become a widow and might thus remarry.

Were the man, however, to fall into "water that has no [visible] end," such as the open sea, no one could exclude the possibility that he reached a safe shore. In such cases, the wife would remain "anchored" to her absent spouse.[20]

The jurists of Islam built on such regulations and distinctions. That a properly "missing person" (*mafqūd*) is to be rigorously distinguished from a merely "nonpresent person" (*ghā'ib*) is a point that all classical authorities of Islamic law grant. In certain branches of Islamic jurisprudence, however, scholars go further, distinguishing between variously missing persons. The scholars of the Maliki school of Sunnite Islam take pains to specify four categories of absentees: those gone missing in Muslim territories; those gone missing in non-Muslim territories or, as is often said, hostile territories (*dār al-ḥarb*); those gone missing in battle, be it against Muslims or against Muslims and non-Muslims; and, finally, those gone missing in times of plague and epidemics.[21]

From the principle that an absentee is to be considered as "alive with respect to his own rights, yet dead with respect to those of others," several consequences follow. The first clause of that classical adage ensures that a missing man retains the full legal personality that he possessed when vanishing. As Émile Tyan explains, the absentee "remains the holder of his rights, be they patrimonial or extra-patrimonial; his estate may not be administered; the contracts that he concluded, such as marriage, rents, and mandates, are, in principle, not annulled. This is an application of the principle of the rule known as *iṣtisḥāb*, which stipulates that a legal situation existing in one moment rightfully extends in its own state."[22] At the same time, being "dead with respect to the rights of others," the missing person may not enter into any new contracts or receive goods deriving from an inheritance transmitted after his disappearance, nor is he bound by any deeds administered on his behalf during his absence. Roman law was familiar with the figure of the guardian (*curator*); such a person would be appointed to protect the interests of those, such as children and the insane, who could not manage them on their own.

Islamic law holds that a judge (*qaḍī*) may designate a ward to represent the missing person's rights. Yet such a representative's powers are to be limited to acts of "conservation" (*ḥifdh*) of the absentee's estate.

In Islam, legal "absence" is not interminable. Unlike the Roman and the Jewish jurists, the Muslim scholars grant a formal presumption of death: after a certain number of years, a missing person is judged, for all legal purposes, to be deceased. For such a decision to be made, "the most diverse of opinions are put forward concerning the length of the period that must have elapsed from the birth date of the absent man: 120, 100, 90, 80, 70, 60, even 30 years."[23] According to a different rule, an absentee may be deemed dead "when all persons of his generation and from his place of origin" are deceased.[24] Most authorities concur, however, on a probable span of time. Once the ninetieth birthday of the missing man has been reached, the absentee is considered to have died. According to some Muslim jurists, marital contracts are to be annulled at a quicker pace. In the Shafiʿi and Maliki branches of Islamic jurisprudence, a marriage to a missing man may be dissolved, following the wife's request, after four years.[25] Yet the effects of such measures are not absolutely definitive. "If the absent man reappears, the goods that had been passed on to the heirs and that have not been consumed while in their hands must be returned to him. His remarried spouse will be his again; but any children who will have come from the new union will belong the second husband."[26]

Such stipulations are in several respects close to those proposed by the medieval Christian jurists. As Rudolf Hübener observes, in the Middle Ages, it was common for there long to be no tidings of "one who had left his country; for traveling consumed much time and was dangerous, and the possibility of sending messages was slight. Especially one who was compelled to journey over sea as merchant, pilgrim, or crusader, often lost for a long period communication with his home."[27] In early Germanic law, as in classical Rome, legal authorities resolved questions pertaining to missing persons on the basis of extant evidence, without granting any presumptions of life or death.

"Under the theory of formal proof," however, the Italian lawyers introduced a new practice. A missing person could be viewed as alive until the end of the hundredth year from his birth; after that time, he would be taken to be deceased.[28] The lawyers of the Saxon courts adapted this rule, lowering the presumed life span of the absentee to seventy years, in accordance with the Psalmist's dictum.[29] In Silesia, a different expedient was adopted. It was to be the duration of absence, rather than life, that counted for the law: after thirty, twenty, or as few as ten years of being missing, an absentee could then be deemed dead.[30] Yet such assumptions remained susceptible to rebuttal, were the missing person ever to appear again.

When the absentee was married, special difficulties, of course, arose. In the last decades of the twelfth century, a number of women tied to such persons turned to the bishop of Saragossa for assistance in these situations. Their husbands had been missing for more than seven years, and although no certain news concerning them could be established, the women requested the right to enter into new marriages, on account of either "their young age or the fragility of their flesh" (*pro iuvenili aetate seu fragilitate carnis*). Pope Clement III intervened directly, pronouncing himself in terms that left little room for doubt. Not only did he recall that according to canon law, the sacrament of marriage retains its full force "as long as no certain news of the death of the living has been received"; he also bade the Spanish bishop not to waver before such a request.[31] A few years earlier, Pope Lucius III had defended a similar position, which Pope Gregory IX ratified in 1237 by the papal decree "On Second Marriages." Nothing less than the "firm certainty" (*firma certitudo*) of a man's decease sufficed for a woman to be released from her uxorious obligations.[32]

It appears that by the early fifteenth century, however, the masters of medieval canon law had begun to develop other means to treat such cases. Documents held in Regensburg, Bavaria, indicate that on February 20, 1489, "Walburga, wife [*uxor*] of one Antonius Koch of Weyern," appeared together with one Petrus Ziegler of Mainburg before the diocesan tribunal.

> Walburga declared that she had contracted a thirty-two-year-long marriage with the aforementioned Antonius Koch, who, however, went missing [*remotus*] after two years, then remaining continuously absent for the following thirty years. She thus assumed that Antonius had died and, despite her doubts in regard to the question, had resolved upon and performed a marriage to Petrus Ziegler. Petrus Ziegler confirmed Walburga's declaration and, together with Walburga, requested recognition of their marital union.

The archive contains almost four hundred proceedings of this kind, all dated to the year 1489. Although they constitute only a portion of the documents of cases treated by the city's court, they indicate that in practice, if not in theory, a presumption of decease had been admitted with respect to long-absent husbands. "In late medieval legal proceedings," Christina Deutsch comments, "a reversal in the burden of proof had occurred — to the detriment of the missing person." Wives were no longer required to demonstrate that their absent husbands were in fact deceased; instead, it was the hypothesis of the husband's continued life that stood in need of evidence. In the absence of contrary proof, the missing person now "counted almost as dead [*quasi als tot*]."[33]

In the tradition of Anglo-Saxon common law, the custom of presuming the death of missing persons can be traced to the early seventeenth century. Its origins are also tied to the casuistry of vanished spouses and the law of legitimate remarriage. The 1604 Act to restrain all Persons from Marriage until their former Wives and Former Husbands be Dead, better known as the Statute of Bigamy, exempts "any Person or Persons whose Husband or Wife shall be continually remaining beyond the Seas by the Space of seven Years together, or whose Husband or Wife shall absent him or herself the one from the other by the Space of seven years together, in any Parts within his Majesty's Dominions, the one of them not knowing the other to be living within that time."[34] To enable individuals to remarry following the disappearance of their spouses, this deed limits the rights of persons who "continually remain beyond the Seas" or "absent themselves" by other means. Absentees forfeit their rights to lasting conjugal relations. The missing person's marriage would be "classed with those that had been dissolved because of ecclesiastical divorce or nullity, or lack of consent."[35]

The duration of seven years again figures prominently in the 1666 Cestui Que Vie Act, which establishes the classical common law conditions for the presumption of death. "It hath often happened," the preamble to this act acknowledges, that persons "have gone beyond the Seas or soe absented themselves for many yeares that the Lessors and Reversioners cannot finde out whether such person or persons be alive or dead."[36] The act sets seven years as the period that must elapse before death may be presumed a legal fact:

> If such person or persons for whose life or lives such Estates have beene or shall be granted as aforesaid shall remaine beyond the Seas or elsewhere absent themselves in this Realme by the space of seaven yeares together, and noe sufficient and evident proofe be made of the lives of such person or persons respectively in any Action commenced for recovery of such Tenements by the Lessors or Reversioners in every such case the person or persons upon whose life or lives such Estate depended shall be accounted as naturally dead. And in every Action brought for the recovery of the said Tenements by the Lessors or Reversioners their Heires or Assignes, the Judges before whom such Action shall be brought shall direct the Jury to give their Verdict as if the person soe remaining beyond the Seas or otherwise absenting himselfe were dead.[37]

Presumptions of this kind became common statutes in the legislations of the United States. To select one case from many others, the State of New Jersey enacted its Death Act in 1797, relying on the rule of seven years absence to decide on the status of absentees:

> Any person who shall remain beyond sea, or absent himself or herself from this State, or conceal himself or herself in this State, for seven years successively, shall be presumed to be dead, in any case wherein his or her death shall come in question, unless proof be made that he or she were alive within that

> time; but an estate recovered in any such case, if in a subsequent action or suit the person so presumed to be dead shall be proved to be living, shall be restored to him or her who shall have been evicted; and he or she may also demand and recover the rents and profits of the estate, during such time as he or she shall have been deprived thereof, with costs of suit.[38]

In the last centuries, the words of this act have been modified more than once. Yet the crucial role assigned to the passage of seven years has remained unchanged. This statute decrees that for these years, an absentee is considered alive; in other words, proof is demanded for the allegation that he or she has died. After the elapsing of that interval, the legal situation is reversed: missing persons are considered as deceased, and evidence is required to demonstrate that they have yet to meet their end. Referring to an abstractly determined stretch of time, the law thus grants itself the power and the right to decide on the unknown.

Such resolutions concerning the life and death of missing persons are the rule in modern legislation, but there are also deviations and exceptions. The most important among them is that contained in the Napoleonic Code of 1804, which offers a treatment of the predicament that is in some sense unique. In contrast to Germanic and common law, this French legal system insists on the categorical difference between absence and death. As Planiol explains in his influential *Elementary Treatise of Civil Law*, whose first edition appeared from 1900 to 1901, "the idea that is the mother of all others in the French legal system is that *absence, however long it may last, never grants the certainty of death*."[39] The code itself leaves no doubt as to the validity of the category of legal absence. Its first article on missing persons states: "If there be necessity to provide for the administration of the whole or part of the effects left by a person presumed absent, or who has no accredited agent, a decree shall be therefore made by a court of the first instance, on the petition of the parties interested."[40] That article, however, is clear: in such cases, the object of the legal presumption is neither death nor life, but absence. Several articles on the jurisprudence of missing persons follow. They avoid any mention of a point at which the absentee counts as dead. This was a basic thesis of the code: "According to Tronchet's expression, and as extraordinary as it may seem, the absentee is 'neither dead nor alive' [*ni mort ni vivant*]; in this uncertainty, neither his death nor his life can be proven. It is, thus, doubt that ever prevails."[41]

The exponents of the Napoleonic Code explained that "veritable absentees" are to be distinguished from two varieties of deceptive doubles: "absentees in the vulgar sense of the word" and the "departed" (*disparus*). The first are those "about whose existence there is no doubt, although they are not at their residence." Such persons are unworthy of the name of "absent," being merely "nonpresent" (*non-présent*). Then there are "departed" persons, concerning whom death is an incontrovertible fact. Of a person who is known to be deceased, yet of whom a corpse cannot be recovered, the first consul himself is reputed to have declared, "very firmly": "One may say that he has *departed* [*qu'il a disparu*]; one may not say that he is *absent* or *missing* [*absent*]."[42] Yet within the single category of Napoleonic absence in the rigorous sense, various stages of vanishing nonetheless remain discernible. In the aftermath of a first "declaration of absence," the court appoints a notary or guardian to manage urgent matters and administer the estate of the vanished citizen.[43] Should the missing person be absent beyond four years, the presumed heirs may request a declaration of absence granting them "*provisional possession* of the [missing person's] goods."[44] That regime lasts two decades. "After the elapsing of thirty years from disappearance, or one of hundred years from birth, the heirs may request the *definitive possession* of the goods of the vanished person."[45]

While eschewing recourse to any presumption of death in the strict sense, such reasoning presupposes a tacit account of life expectancy. "With the passing of time, the probability of death may increase, and the law takes this fact into account," a commentator explains.

> During the first years, the law thus refuses to allow any interested parties to declare that the vanished person is in the state of absence [*en état d'absence*]; one must wait for the lack of news to have lasted for quite a while. Moreover, even as it authorizes the absentee's presumptive heirs provisionally to take possession of his goods, it grants them more extended powers when the state of declared absence has lasted over thirty years. The law thus makes steps in the direction of a presumption of death; but it never reaches it. The absentee is *never considered to be dead* and, for this reason, the present spouse is never allowed to remarry.[46]

These principles suddenly became obsolete in their country of origin when, in a major reform in 1977, France adopted legislation on missing persons that was similar to that admitted by the civil codes of Germany and Austria.[47] French law would henceforth distinguish no more than two states of absence: that following an official "presumption of absence," in which the missing person, being considered alive, may still acquire property, and that brought about by a definitive "declaration of absence," which establishes that the missing person is considered to be dead.[48] In 1977, "France thus abandoned the notion of doubt as the distinctive mark of its legal treatment, meeting up with the Germanic theory of certitude."[49] The Napoleonic Code's treatment of missing persons nonetheless survives in several legal systems in force today, such as those of Belgium, Luxembourg, Indonesia, and Uruguay.[50] In their provisions for absentees, these codes omit all reference to presumptions of life or death, referring solely to "the concept of absence, which obviously includes situations of vanishing that the law does not totally take into account."[51]

As Hernán Corral Talciani and María Sara Rodríguez Pinto have shown in detail, today, the world's other legal systems may be divided into two groups: those deriving from the Germanic tradition, first elaborated in the Prussian and Austrian civil codes of 1794 and 1811, respectively, and that of Anglo-Saxon common law. The Germanic treatments of missing persons are distinguished by being oriented toward the establishment of legal certainty. In these regimes, judicial processes aim to dispel the doubt surrounding the absentee's condition. A "declaration of absence" is equivalent to proof of death in systems modeled on the Germanic codes. By contrast, the common law systems "seem, with regard to the categories of civil law, to constitute a disorganized, fragmentary legislation, with a clear casuistic and procedural connotation. In these systems, the presumption of death appears, in reality, as a question of proof, even if one can detect in certain places the influence of legal categories dear to the civil law doctrine."[52] England and the United States are representatives of such systems. Yet there are also a number of civil codes, such as those of Louisiana, Scotland, Israel, and Quebec, that combine the two traditions.[53]

Certain questions recur throughout the treatments of legal absentees. That no one may remain an "absentee" forever, at least without changing status, is one point that all modern legislation seems to grant. Even the systems deriving from the Napoleonic Code, with its emphasis on the categorical difference between the "absent" and the "departed," recognize that a hundred years from birth, the personality of a missing citizen fades into that of the dead. To be sure, absence is never formally identifiable with decease, but thirty years from disappearance, or a hundred years from the birth of the missing person, the consequences of a "definitive" absence are difficult to distinguish from those of legal death. In the Germanic and common law systems, the continuance of absence beyond a certain number of years results in a declaration or a presumption of decease. Here, however, a question becomes difficult to avoid. A document of decease contains not only the registration of the fact of death. It also indicates a time, for no one dies without doing so at a certain moment. Yet when exactly does a missing person die?

Several solutions have been recorded by legislation and legal theory. Perhaps the simplest among them is to date the moment of decease to the end of the period for which a person gone missing may be presumed alive: the last day of the seventh year, for instance, where that period of absence is decisive. This is the practice proposed by the Scottish Presumption of Death Act and the State of Louisiana.[54] It has also been employed in other jurisdictions of the United States, from New York to Ohio and Wisconsin. As Frances T. Freeman Jalet remarks, the reasoning supporting it is "that the absentee must be presumed to have lived up to the last moment of the seven-year period because the presumption of the continuance of life prevails until that time."[55]

The arbitrariness of such a ruling is manifest. It treats the life of the missing person as simultaneous with the period of legal absence set by a code. In systems of Germanic civil law, "it was long customary to accord more attention to the determination of the probable date of death" as best could be conjectured. More recently, the Continental practice has drawn closer to that of common law, the current tendency being to date the missing person's death to the end of the period of absence.[56] Legal scholars have also proposed dating absentees' decease to the inception, rather than to the end, of the duration of their recorded disappearance. An absentee then dies for the law retroactively, long after having being declared missing while alive. D. Stone notes that the concern to identify the moment of decease with either the beginning or the end of such seven-year periods has, at times, "been carried to logical absurdity." In one British case, "R had last been heard of in 1873. The chief clerk presumed his death by 1880. The class of persons entitled if R was found to have died in 1873 differed from those entitled if R was found to have died in 1880." The court "refused to find in favour of either class. There was no evidence that death occurred on either date."[57]

What is certain is the demand that the period of "absence" ultimately end. There is to be some point—however probable or improbable, however documented or unknown—at which the missing recover some semblance of ordinary legal personhood, passing from their intermediary state to life or death. In the happy event of their return, they become persons in the ordinary sense, regaining the rights that were once theirs. If, after a lasting disappearance, they are instead declared deceased, any property they possessed will be irrevocably distributed; those bound to such persons will be freed from the contracts into which the absent one had entered. Estates will be transmitted to presumptive heirs; the spouses of the absent will be released from the responsibilities that tied them to those gone missing. The law knows how to set a point beyond absence and how to secure its effects. Having instituted the double of the human being that is the missing person — a being alive in one respect, yet dead in another, or alive for a certain time, or neither alive nor dead — legislation renders such a nonperson invalid. It annuls the absentee that it begot. The legal state of being missing is for this reason hardly absolute. Despite the pronouncements of those who distinguish it from its "vulgar" correlate in ordinary speech, civil absence, too, is relative. It lasts only for a while, being bound to some duration promulgated by the law. Time, measured by the acts and deeds admitted in civil codes, statutes, and precedents, proves the means for delimiting the vanishings of persons.

Outside the world of legal artifice and beyond the limits of its mechanisms, the varieties of absence are less easily ordered and disciplined. There are more ways to go missing than by not being present at a place or function or by vanishing according to the conditions of official disappearance. Absentees have been known to move in unrulier patterns and less representable rhythms. Often the circumstances of going missing, of course, are difficult to reconstruct with precision. Stretches of absence, by nature, are far from easy to conceive. Reconstruction by means of evidence and probability goes only so far.

Precisely for this reason, missing persons have always been exemplary subjects for investigation and invention in a field of writing beyond that of legal reasoning. Myth and literature have imagined what can be neither known nor decided. They contain archives of removals that are all their own. Listeners and readers know their powers well; those present at the event of recitation, narration, and reading have long found themselves in the difficult, if not indeed almost impossible position of accompanying the absented into their vanishings. For in fiction, missing persons accomplish what they cannot do in life and the law: they speak and speak for themselves. In relating their experiences, they testify to the disappearances that they have survived. In ways purely imaginable, if not imaginary, they also, therefore, recount the variously troubled conditions of their return.

CHAPTER THREE

Fictions of the Return

Before a person may be declared missing in the legal sense, certain events independent of any judicial proceedings must have come to pass: it is necessary for an unexplained absence to have been observed, reported, and accepted as a fact. Only once a mysterious disappearance has been granted may some civil authority declare persons to be absentees, treating their rights and claims according to the rules that hold for their special status. Questions pertaining to how exactly a vanishing occurred, what befell the absent person in the moment of going missing and in the time that followed it, are, for a declaration of legal absence, secondary. They may be temporarily or indefinitely unknown without perturbing the mechanisms of due process. Yet these circumstances have never been lost from sight. They constitute the crucial matter of which poetic and literary invention, in every age, has taken hold. Epic, fable, drama, and the novel have long appropriated what the law has been uninterested in ascertaining. The results are fictions of disappearance, in verse as well as in prose.

At times, such inventions have entered the field of legal reasoning. Juridical exposition then becomes the occasion for constructions of a literary kind. Interlacing the formulation of rules and precepts with the recounting of parables, allegories, and fables, the Talmud furnishes some striking examples. The Tractate Yebamoth, which bears on levirate marriage, contains several chapters concerning the conditions in which a woman who was once married may be joined to a new husband. An initial precept contained in the Mishnah appears to require that before any woman may enter into a second marriage, there be incontrovertible proof of her husband's decease: "Evidence [of the deceased's identity] may be legally tendered only on [proof afforded by] the full face with the nose, though there were also marks on a man's body or clothing."[1]

Yet the Rabbis also concede that there are conditions in which death may be legally presumed without any bodily evidence, as in the classic case of an accidental fall into a body of water. If the water "has [a visible] end," he will be considered to be dead, and his wife may remarry, but if he falls into "water that has no [visible] end," "his wife is forbidden [to marry again]," water with a visible end being defined as "[an area all the boundaries of which] a person standing [on the edge] is able to see in all directions."[2]

After such prescriptions, however, the tractate turns to elements of narrative. The exposition of halakhah, or legal rules, gives way to the domain of fables known as aggadah. A nameless rabbi relates how "it once happened" that, when casting nets in the Jordan, a man fell into a subterranean pond that had been built on its shore so as to retain the fish washed into it by the overflowing river. The fisherman seemed to vanish. "His companion, after waiting long enough for his soul to depart, returned and reported the accident to his household."[3] Having gone missing, the man was mourned as dead. No sooner did the sun rise the next day, however, than he found his way to the "entrance of the cave." The presumed deceased fisherman returned to his home. "'How great, exclaimed the Rabbi, 'are the words of the Sages!'" They establish that a fall into waters with a visible end may legitimately be presumed to cause death. Yet the parable of the Jordanian suggests that at times greater prudence is required. "In the case of water which has [a visible] end, the possibility of having remained in a subterranean fish pond should be taken into consideration! It is not unusual for a subterranean fish pond to be found with water which has [a visible] end."[4]

Rabbis Gamaliel and Akiva are reported to have witnessed cases no less remarkable. "I was once traveling on board a ship," Rabbi

Gamaliel recalls, "when I observed a shipwreck and was sorely grieved for [the apparent loss of] a scholar who had been traveling on board." When Rabbi Gamaliel reached the shore, however, the missing man appeared. "He came to me," the legal authority relates, "and sat down and discussed matters of halakhah." He was none other than Rabbi Akiva. "'My son,' I asked him, 'who rescued you?'—'The plank of a ship,' he answered me, 'came my way, and to every wave that approached me I bent my head.'" The Sages are now again lauded for holding fast to the distinction between waters of visible and invisible ends. The reader learns that Rabbi Akiva himself once observed a like experience. Seeing a ship "tossed in the sea," he grieved for a scholar, Rabbi Meir, who had been aboard it. Yet when he landed in the province of Cappadocia, he relates, the lost scholar

> came to me and sat down and discussed matters of halakhah. "My son," I said to him, "who rescued you?"—"One wave," he answered me, "tossed me to another, and the other to yet another until [the sea] cast me on the dry land." At that hour I exclaimed: How significant are the words of the Sages who ruled [that if a man fell into] water which has [a visible] end, [his wife] is permitted [to marry again; but if into] water which has no [visible] end, she is forbidden.[5]

The position of such fables with respect to the law of missing persons is more ambiguous than it may appear. Each time, an unexpected reappearance becomes the occasion for the confirmation of the Sages' wisdom; the Talmudic distinction between the types of waters is thus verified. Yet only one of the two outcomes foreseen by law finds parabolic illustration. Implicitly, the possibility of a disappearance without a narrative conclusion is excluded. Vanishing at sea may become the occasion of myth and parable only to the extent to which the water's edges are without any "visible end," for it is from their indefinite expanse alone that missing persons can be imagined to return to speak for themselves, explaining the conditions of their absence and the means of their return. From a disappearance in water that "has a visible end," there is, it seems, no exemplary lesson to be drawn—if not that, as in the case of the fallen fisherman, even such an aqueous expanse may in truth be unbounded, such that someone lost in its depths can find a way home.

Although the most illustrious narratives of the return derive from fields beyond the law, such fictions are rarely insensible to the consequences of juridical distinctions. The earliest example in Graeco-Roman culture, of course, is also the most influential. Odysseus, the man of many ways, is one of the first to go missing. While Agamemnon leaves for war and returns, meeting death at the hands of Clytemnestra, Odysseus lives out his ten years of adventures in prolonged absence from both Troy and Ithaca. When he finally washes ashore on his native island, his countrymen do not know whether he is alive or dead. Odysseus then passes from one variety of absence to another: after having been in unknown places, his life a matter of conjecture, Odysseus returns, but in concealment. Half the ancient epic concerns the period in which he hides himself at home, the better to set the scene of his unexpected reappearance. Throughout his voyages, Odysseus draws from his wanderings stories of wondrous deeds and occurrences. Yet there are signs that it is only at the conclusion of his travels, when he is at last reunited with his wife, that he offers a complete account of the circumstances of his long return. Only then, the narrator recounts, insisting on the totality of the telling, did shining Odysseus "recount all" (*pant'eleg'*): "the cares he inflicted / on other men" and "all that in his misery / he had toiled through." Penelope seems tacitly to grant that hers is the first finished *Odyssey*. She listens closely, refusing to sleep "until he had told her everything" (*paros katalexai hapanta*)."[6]

In the modern era, as Dieter Beyerle notes, "the situation is different."[7] The tidings of the voyage are often reduced to a minimum, even as the return increases in importance, its details complicated, sometimes beyond repair. Several sixteenth-century French chronicles recount the famously perplexing case of Martin Guerre, a man from the Basque lands on the French side of the Pyrenees.[8] At fifteen, he marries one Bertrande de Rols. Some ten years later, in 1548, he absents himself, following an apparent dispute concerning his patrimony. Seven or eight years later, Martin Guerre returns, regaining wife and home. In 1560, however, he stands accused; his presumed father-in-law and, after some hesitation, his apparent wife declare him not to be, in fact, the man who once went missing. As the trial unfolds in Toulouse, a most remarkable occurrence comes to pass: Martin Guerre returns again, denouncing the man who returned before him. Judgment is passed, and the false Guerre, having confessed the spuriousness of his pretensions, is hanged before the door of the home he called his own.

That such a decision struck some of its observers as less than certain can be gleaned from the terms with which Michel de Montaigne, in 1558, recalls his presence as a jurist at the trial:

> Being yong, I saw a law-case, which *Corras* a Counsellor of *Thoulouse* caused to be printed, of a strange accident of two men, who presented themselves one for another. I remember (and I remember nothing else so well) that me thought, he proved his imposture, whom he condemned as guilty, so wondrous strange and so far-exceeding both our knowledge and his owne, who was judge, that I found much boldnes in the sentence which had condemned him to be hanged.[9]

That "strange accident of two men" reaches completion solely through the event of an unexpected return. Only after his belated homecoming can the second Martin Guerre, ultimately revealed to have been the first, account for the conditions of his absence: after years in the military service of a cardinal, after battles fought in Spain and Flanders, the Basque lost a leg in battle and repaired to a monastery before making his way across the mountains to reach the trial of the one who had claimed his name.

Later recordings of the return of missing married men end far less conclusively. Perhaps the single most striking case in modern fiction is that of Honoré de Balzac's *Colonel Chabert*. First published in 1832 under the title *La Transaction* (The Negotiation), this "scene of private life" is set in the immediate aftermath of the Restoration.

The action opens with the repetition of an unsettling appearance: an outmoded overcoat, in 1816, hovers before the door of a Parisian legal office. The unidentified individual inside the garment has come to be known to the office clerks as "the old overcoat" (*le vieux carrick*).[10] Soon the narrative discloses more. Having succeeded in obtaining a private audience with the lawyer, the visitor removes his coat, revealing himself to resemble a figure just "dug up" from the earth. He recounts his tale, declaring himself to be none other than Hyacinthe Chabert, the once famous colonel generally believed to have been killed at the Battle of Eylau in East Prussia in 1807. "Unfortunately for me," the mutilated man observes, with remarkable perspicacity, "my decease is an historical fact."[11] He wishes to regain the rights he possessed while alive. Yet an obstacle now bars his path back toward legal personhood. His former possessions belong to the woman who had been his wife, who has joined herself to another. In his absence, she has remarried one Count Ferraud.

Chabert is the first to acknowledge the difficulty of his situation. "When I say these things to lawyers, to men of good sense," he avows to the sympathetic professional, Derville, to whom he entrusts his cause,

> when I, a beggar, propose to make my case against a count and a countess, when I, a dead man, stand up against a death certificate, a marriage certificate and several birth certificates, they show me out, either with the air of cold politeness — which you all know how to assume to rid yourself of a hapless wretch — or brutally, like men who think they are dealing with a swindler or a madman. It depends on their nature. I have been buried underneath the dead. But now I am buried underneath the living, under papers, under facts, under the whole of society, which wants to shove me underground again![12]

The lawyer suggests that a solution may be found, as long as the veteran assents to a condition. "You may be obliged," Derville advises Chabert, "to negotiate" (*il faudra peut-être transiger*). His interlocutor admits to being perplexed by that proposition: "'To negotiate' [*transiger*], Colonel Chabert repeated. 'Am I dead or am I alive?'"[13]

The novella constitutes an extended response to that question, setting out the conditions in which legal *transaction*, as both "negotiation" and "compromise," proves impossible.[14] At the beginning of the tale, Chabert is a "stranger" in every sense; he is a man from whom humanity seems to have receded. "If this is a man," one clerk asks another, pointing to the body of the insistently returning figure, "why do you call him the *old overcoat*"?[15] Once the legal experts accept the validity of the stranger's claims to his name, Chabert appears to regain a vestige of his former vitality, as if in preparation for entering the society from which he has been excluded. The language of the narrative, however, never ceases to mark the returning hero's particular legal and social position. The text refers to him as "the deceased" (*le défunt*) and "the dead" (*le mort*), lingering on his "cadaverous physiognomy" and waxlike immobility.[16]

A man of the Empire condemned to the society of the Restoration, Balzac's protagonist soon learns that he is no match for either the law or his former spouse. When Countess Ferraud is first told that "Chabert exists," she feigns disbelief, explaining to her lawyer that she has "already pushed away all the Chaberts" who in the years since his disappearance imposed themselves on her. When confronted with the undeniable fact of her first husband's survival, she arranges to meet Chabert without a legal proxy. In confidence, she contrives to persuade him to sign a document, assuring that, in exchange for part of her fortune, he will relinquish all claims to be the surviving Colonel Chabert.[17] She pleads her case: were Chabert to be restored to legal life, her second marriage would be judged invalid, and her children would be consequently declared illegitimate. Moved by her charms, Colonel Chabert resolves, at first, "to remain dead." Yet when he overhears his former spouse explaining to her lawyer that, should he refuse the terms of her "transaction," she will have him consigned to the Charenton asylum, the dead man makes a different choice. He confronts her, declares his contempt for her, and expresses thanks for the chance that has "disunited" them: "I will never reclaim the name that I may have decorated."

Chabert then "disappears."[18] At the end of the novella, the men of the law, having long lost his trace, come upon him in an infirmary for the aged, where he is living out his last days at the edges of society. Resembling "one of those grotesque carved figures we know from Germany," the erstwhile colonel now "takes enjoyment in drawing lines in the sand."[19] Chabert no longer responds to his own surname, except by denying it and replacing it with a figure: "Not Chabert! Not Chabert!" "My name is Hyacinthe," he exclaims, adding: "'I am no longer a man; I am number 164, Room 7.'"[20]

Obstinately returning husbands haunt the French literature of the nineteenth century. Five decades after Balzac, in 1884, Guy de Maupassant imagines another belated Odysseus in "The Return." In a Norman fishing village at a time impossible to identify with precision, an unknown man appears before the door of a modest house, where a woman sits inside, knitting in the company of her five children. Her husband is at sea. From the doorway, one of her daughters, peering into the street, calls out, in an insistent dialectal phrase: "*Le r'voilà*," "He's back."[21] The family does not know who he may be, although as the daughter has observed, he appears to know them well. The next morning, he returns, and the woman's husband, who is now at home, invites him in. The stranger reveals himself also to be the fisherwoman's husband: not the father of her three younger children, but the one who, having vanished at sea more than twelve years before, was long presumed dead. He explains the conditions of his return: how he and two shipmates saved themselves after the destruction of their boat, how they were "captured by savages," how his companions died, and how an English traveler brought him back to Normandy. It is too late for him to woo his former spouse, but he lays claim to his father's house, where he was born. In the last pages of the story, the two husbands resolve to pay a visit to the priest, to "put" themselves "in order" (*en règle*), although not without stopping, along the way, "for a drop" at the Café du Commerce. There the newcomer, identified as the one who had formerly "been lost," introduces himself by echoing the words with which the tale began: "*Mé v' là*," "I'm back."[22]

In the same years, Émile Zola conceives two of his variations on the return. In 1879, he publishes "The Death of Olivier Bécaille," a story whose first sentence sets on stage a first-person narrator bearing witness to his own past absenting: "It was on Saturday, at six o'clock in the morning, that I died, after three days of illness."[23] That day, Olivier Bécaille, a nervous and sickly husband, suffers a "syncope" of his "entire being"; left almost entirely immobile, he retains the faculty of hearing and some sight, his left eye perceiving "confusedly," his right eye having been "completely paralyzed."[24]

"My God! My God! He is dead!," he hears his wife exclaim. Like Edgar Allan Poe's Madeline Usher and Gustave Flaubert's Monsieur Ohmlin, Olivier Bécaille is entombed alive. Having regained control of his limbs inside his coffin, he succeeds, however, in freeing himself, climbing from the earth and, once below the sky, scaling the cemetery's walls. After a further loss of consciousness and a slow recovery in the home of a philanthropic physician, he revisits the street where he and his wife once lived. His former spouse is nowhere to be found. He enters a small restaurant in front of his old residence, where he observes a garrulous neighbor in conversation with a friend. She is explaining that his wife left Paris with a handsome young acquaintance, the same man who consoled her as Olivier Bécaille, paralyzed yet sentient, lay on his deathbed. "When she is no longer in mourning — isn't that so? — they'll do as they like."[25] "Listen!" the insistent neighbor concludes. "The other one did well to die. It's an opportunity."[26] Olivier Bécaille now sees all too keenly his own possibilities are few. "I was never her lover," he muses, pondering his devoted wife, "it is a brother that she has just grieved. Why would I change her life? A dead man is not jealous. . . . Well then! I was a good man for being dead, and I was certainly not about to commit as cruel an error as to resuscitate."[27]

In "Jacques Damour," published in 1883, Zola imagines a homecoming far closer in its setting to that related in *Colonel Chabert*.[28] After enduring the hardships of the War of 1871 and suffering the loss of his only son, Damour, one of the "last defenders of the Commune," is arrested and sentenced to "simple deportation" to New Caledonia. Before departing, he assures his wife: "I will return—wait for me."[29] The narrative follows him to Nouméa, where he seems patiently to expiate his crimes. His official pardon appears imminent "when, one day," the narrative relates, without explanation, Damour vanishes.[30] Five prisoners escape the penal colony, and Damour is one of their company. Three months later, the wrecked pieces of a boat are discovered on the shore; corpses of three French fugitives are found. One body is attributed to Jacques Damour. The truth, however, is that he is alive and well. Damour means to write immediately to his wife, but he happens on a newspaper containing "the account of his evasion and the news of his death." "From that moment onward, a letter seemed to him imprudent; someone might intercept and read it, discovering the truth. Would it not be better, for everyone, to remain dead?"[31]

Damour travels to America, England, and Brussels, having been granted a new freedom: "he was dead; he had no one in the world, nothing mattered any longer to him."[32] Ten years after his condemnation, however, he learns that in France, an amnesty has been decreed: "All the *communards* were returning. That woke him up."[33] Soon back in Paris, Jacques Damour succeeds in locating his wife, who has married a prosperous butcher in his absence. When he appears in her shop and reproaches her for the fact of her bigamy, she defends herself by showing him the now aged certificate of his death. She evokes a principle of good behavior: "When people are dead, they ought not to return."[34] Persuaded by her sincerity and the presence of her small children, Damour accepts her arguments. "I am finished, I am nothing," he tells her, "and you no longer love me."[35] Rescue of a kind comes through the solicitude of his daughter, who has become a wealthy courtesan. Father and daughter are reunited in the end: "He has only his daughter, who took pity on her old man. Moreover, he has refused to try to reestablish his civil status in any way. Why trouble government documents? . . . He is in his hole, lost, forgotten, no one."[36]

From these stories of return and thwarted resuscitation, Luigi

Pirandello drew the threads of his 1904 novel of multiple absences, *The Late Mattia Pascal.* The complexity of the plot defies summary, but its fundamental trajectory may be recalled. The eponymous character recounts how, after a series of acrimonious disputes with his wife and mother-in-law, he decides, one evening, to disappear without a trace. He flees his home in Liguria and makes his way to the casinos of Monte Carlo. Upon learning, from a distance, that a corpse found near his former residence has been identified as his own, Mattia Pascal embraces the unexpected situation in which he finds himself. He decides, as he later recalls, "to make of myself another man": "Now I was alone, and I could not have been more alone on earth, being suddenly loosened from every bond and every obligation, being free, new, and absolutely master of myself, without the weight of my past, and before the future, which I would be able to shape as I liked."[37]

He renames himself Adriano Meis and moves to Rome. Grasping, however, that, in the absence of any legal identity, he has the right neither to enter into contracts, such as marriage, nor to defend his remaining possessions from theft, he concludes that he is now "worse off than dead."[38] He contrives, therefore, to dispose of his second persona, constructing a scene that will suggest to his Roman circle of acquaintances that Adriano Meis has committed suicide. He returns to his former wife, who has married his best friend and become the mother of a small child. "I'll tell you everything," he tells the astonished couple, adding that he has learned that "playing dead is not a good profession." "I am making myself alive again," he promises; but, when faced with the prospect of regaining his former life, invalidating a new marriage, and rendering an infant illegitimate, he elects to live out his years in the absence of legal resurrection, tending to the shelves of a neglected library in a deconsecrated church.[39]

Like Olivier Bécaille, whose unbalanced eyesight he shares for a while, "the late Mattia Pascal" speaks for himself, his book being written solely in the first person.[40] Zola's character began his discourse with the mournful recollection of the day on which, as he writes, "I died." Pirandello's narrator announces himself in more complex terms that conjure up vertiginously plural and posthumous existences. In the first of the two prefaces to his novel of many lives, he stipulates that he is "bequeathing this manuscript of mine" to the library in which he works, on one condition: "No one is to open it until fifty years after my *third, last, and definitive* death."[41] "For I have died," he explains, "yes, twice; but the first time it was in error, and the second . . . you will hear."[42] As if in homage to "Jacques Damour," "the late Mattia Pascal" learns of his death from a distance and by reading a newspaper. Yet in Pirandello's novel, the documents of the protagonist's decease are abundant. Meaning to return by train from Monte Carlo, Mattia Pascal buys a paper and, perusing its pages, happens upon the report of a "corpse . . . later recognized as our librarian Mattia Pascal, who vanished many days ago."[43] Subsequently he procures for himself fifteen copies of the *Foglietto* that is his hometown's daily, which contains a lengthier article about the hitherto "inexplicable absence" of Mattia Pascal. The "late Mattia Pascal" who redacts the narrative of his lives includes this article in his book.[44] The narrative ends, moreover, with the scene of the visit that the self-surviving narrator pays to his own gravestone. The novel reproduces the epitaph in its entirety. As the posthumous narrator reads, like the future reader, of his death, the inscription fades into the text of which it is a part. The work becomes an extended epitaph, being at once proleptic and metaleptic, false and self-fulfilling.[45]

After the tales of Bécaille, Damour, and Chabert, the narrative of the "late Mattia Pascal" ends in impeded resuscitation. The book's author suggests that the last lesson to be drawn from his story of many lives is that there exists a survival beyond the law. To a friend's well-intentioned insistence that "outside the law and outside the particularities—be they happy or sad—on account of which we are ourselves, it is not possible to live," the keen-eyed autobiographer responds: "In no way have I entered again into the law, or into any of my own particularities. My wife is Pomino's wife, and I could hardly say that I exist at all [*non saprei proprio dire ch'io mi sia*]."[46] His newfound "life" thus reveals itself to be a literary afterlife. "The late Mattia Pascal" becomes the volume with whose title his proper name is homonymous. Both are creatures of the library.

In each of these narratives, the power of the return is unmistakable. Establishing the certainty of the departure in overtaking it at last, the homecoming surmounts, by different means, what would seem the most irreparable of occurrences. Absence, once recollected, gives way to a new presence. Nothing less than the statement "I died"—an utterance that is, in principle, inexpressible by any living subject—becomes a sentence not only written, but also spoken and repeated.[47] Vanishing, in short, is made relative. However distorted it may be, the circular trajectory of the ancient epic of homecoming is still distinctly perceptible in each of these narratives: from Balzac to Maupassant, Zola, and Pirandello, Odysseus and his story, concentrated into the narrative of a long return, remain the distant model. The end of the period of absence brings with it tidings of an unknown inception and unfolding, leading to a conclusion. Once a disappearance has been bounded in time, if not also in space, the condition of narrative is, in each case, fulfilled. Tales can then be told and retold.

Yet it could also be argued that such absences are only ever apparent. Each time, a narrative "negotiation," in Balzac's phrase, has been tacitly conducted. The line demarcating the state of being missing from that of being present has been redrawn, and the literary texts constitute nothing if not its retracing. A real state of being missing might possess a different structure. It could be that of an absence that persists without an end and, therefore, also without any clear beginning: an *Odyssey* not of return, but of constant vagary in which adventure follows adventure without any stable point of reference.

Within a decade of Pirandello's account of the variously posthumous Mattia Pascal, Kafka conceived of such a narrative of vanishing. It was his first novel, in which the seventeen-year-old Karl Rossmann is sent to wander across new lands, not despite being united with a woman at home, but rather as a consequence of this circumstance.

Rossmann, as the novel's first sentence states, has been dispatched "to America by his unfortunate parents because a servant girl seduced him and had a child by him."[48]

Kafka worked on his novel from 1912 to 1914, when he interrupted it. Introducing his project to Felice Bauer in a letter dated November 11, 1912, he insisted on its indefinite magnitude and its title: "The story that I am writing and that stretches out absolutely into the infinite is called — to give you a preliminary notion — *The Absentee* [*Der Verschollene*]."[49] When Max Brod published the manuscript in 1927, after Kafka's death, he renamed it *Amerika*, thereby effacing what was, in Kafka's letter as well in his diaries, the index of a technical legal notion that the author knew well: *Verschollenheit*, in other words, the "variety of absence" (*Art der Abwesenheit*), as Conrad Ernst Riesenfeld explained in a monograph that Kafka could have read, that combines the features of "a certain duration," the "unknown residence of the absentee," and a "lack of any reports as to the life or death of the same."[50]

Hawthorne, living in Massachusetts in the early nineteenth century, placed his missing man in "the great mass of London life." Kafka, writing in Prague in the early twentieth century, makes an inverse choice for his adolescent hero: the United States of America, with its "movement without end," its "restlessness, transmitted from the restless element to helpless human beings and their works," become the country of his youthful "absentee," the "one who disappeared," or, to choose another rendition of the German phrase, *der Verschollene*, "the one who was never heard from again."[51]

Critics have observed that it is far from obvious why Kafka called his youthful wayfarer "the absentee," in a phrase that pointedly omits any reference to the "person."[52] Several circumstances are noteworthy. There is first of all the question of Rossmann's age. He is seventeen when the novel opens; he therefore stands before the threshold of full legal personhood, his status being close to that of the "father of a minor age" (*minderjähriger Kindesvater*) that is said to have attracted Kafka's attention in his own legal studies.[53] One wonders whether Rossmann is missing as a legal minor or as an adult. It is conceivable that his "absenting" involves the transition between these two legal states. The most obvious question, however, concerns the setting of the young man's alleged "disappearance." When the reader first encounters him, Rossmann has already reached the continent to which his parents have remitted him; as Ulrike Vedder observes, he therefore seems "in no way an absentee."[54] From that moment onward, without becoming the subject of any mysterious disappearance, he errs across the expanse of a country at once historical and fantastic. Chabert, Bécaille, Damour, and Mattia Pascal all absent themselves, by chance or by choice; their odysseys are consequently subordinated to the variously interrupted homecomings that ensue. Rossmann, by contrast, wanders incessantly, without appearing to be the subject of a single vanishing.

Yet each of the incidents that compose Kafka's novel could also be read as the scene of a different deviation, presenting the circumstances in which Rossmann goes missing from the place where he may be meant to be: from the opening, in which the young man reaches New York and fails to disembark, to his sudden identification or misidentification as the nephew of a certain Senator "Jakob" with whom he does not expect to be united, from his escape or banishment from his transitory family home in America to his dismissal from the Hotel Occidental and his later admittance into the marvelous "Theater of Oklahoma," where it seems that "everything that he had done up until now would be forgotten, and no one would hold it against him."[55] Asked by the officials of the theater for the nickname by which he was known in his last position, Rossmann offers an answer that, in addition to being textually unmotivated, seems to render his own civil identity illegible: "'Negro.' 'Negro?' asked the boss, turning his head and pulling a face, as though Karl had now reached the height of preposterousness. The secretary too looked at Karl a while, but then he repeated 'Negro' and wrote it down."[56] Each time, Kafka's obscurely "missing person" confirms his place by being driven from it, if not by secretly renouncing it himself.

The uncertainties proper to Karl Rossmann's state of absence are the consequences of the work as its author left it. Since Kafka denied—or spared—this novel any conclusion, the reader cannot reconstruct exactly how or even if the "disappearance" began. In its plain and often disquietingly narratorless prose, Kafka's fiction thus implicitly rejects the legal axiom that for there to be a missing person, the circumstances of an absenting must be granted in advance. Yet in its concomitant refusal to concede even the suggestion of a return, it also defies a long-standing narrative presumption that is no less dogmatic: that a mysterious disappearance may become the subject of a finished tale alone. From the ship stoker's cabin to "Oklahama," from the "cozy room" in the attic of Hotel Occidental to the "little smoke-filled compartment" from which, in the novel's last fragments, he "begins to grasp the size of America," "guiltless Rossmann," as his author would later name him, journeys outside the wide compass of the *Odyssey*.[57] In error or in ignorance, "a little disappointed," if not disconsolate, he drifts through a new land that has no "visible end." For him, a father and a son too old to be a child and yet also too young to be a married man, there is neither departure nor return.

CHAPTER FOUR

The Transient Image

The disappearance of an individual can give rise to a number of new shapes, for in place of an absent human being, various substitutes may be set. The land of Kafka's obscurely "missing person" contains its own illustrations, at least one of which remains well known today. Starting in the second half of the nineteenth century, private detective companies and public law enforcement agencies in the United States began printing "wanted circulars" or "wanted posters" representing individuals sought by the police. Such documents rendered absentees present, by word and later by photograph, to facilitate their identification and arrest. Presumed criminals, however, are not the only missing persons to have been summoned by such means, and the printing of notices concerning those absent from their residences is not an invention of the New World. In England, an official registry system for missing persons was instituted in the Victorian period, following a disappearance recorded in 1894. Frederick Pople of the Salvation Army Factory Battersea had just visited a ward at Marylebone Workhouse with his wife Charlotte when she seemed to vanish. Concerned that his spouse, whom he considered "very weak-minded and childish," might have been "decoyed away for some evil purpose by the other female tramps," Mr. Pople sent a letter to the Local Government Board providing a summary of her distinctive traits: "Charlotte Pople, aged 24, 4 feet 10 inches high, rather stout, fair skin, brown hair and eyes, walks very badly as if crippled. Native of Bristol. She was wearing a black mantle trimmed with lace and beaded drab skirt, black stockings, laced boots, black straw hat. She has the marks of recent vaccination, about six weeks old, on left arm."[1]

Such descriptions began to appear in English newspapers as early as the first decades of the nineteenth century. They were often rich in detail. A notice published in the *Liverpool Mercury* in 1821 offers the following account of someone reported to have unexpectedly "strayed from his friends":

> A middle-aged man, of Irish extraction, about five feet eight inches high, a bald high forehead and pale complexion, with a sort of *theatrical* strut in his gait, and who may be further recognized by the following particulars:—he has a natural mark or mole on the forehead, the exact resemblance of a *rat*, which he is very careful to conceal with a richly embroidered cap, having a tassel and curiously wrought bells on the top. . . . Should he see a decent well-dressed female in the street insulted with abusive language by some sparks of fashion flushed with the juice of Bacchus, it is ten to one he presently mounts up on the top of a barrel, into a window, or some other elevated situation, and commences a speech, in which he assures a crowd of bye-standers that this lady has long been his most particular friend and acquaintance, for whom he entertains the greatest possible esteem, and that she is the most glorious, elegant, and accomplished creature in the universe.[2]

Edward Higgs writes that "in rural areas where the circulation of newspapers was limited," printed handbills served a function close to those of such announcements. Being longer than notices, handbills could specify many of the characteristic features of the disappeared. A seven-page pamphlet printed in Ireland in the mid-eighteenth century draws a portrait of a missing man actively sought by the police:

> DIONYSIUS, a brawny, strong-bodied jolly-looking Man, about Five Feet Nine inches and a half high; had on a Coat of Parsons Blue, lined with Black, Waistcoat and Breeches of the same, and a Grey Bob Wig; speaks loud and fast, is a notorious Lyar, a profane Swearer, and has much the Air of a Rogue, by a remarkable Squint or back Look, such as is observed in Horses that are vicious and apt to recalcitrate.[3]

No culture has lacked a means to record missing persons. Classical antiquity was familiar with a first example, which, in the traditional chronology of the war in Troy, precedes even Odysseus's long absence from Ithaca. Before any Achaean hero sets sail for Ilium, Helen, by force or by desire, goes missing. Alone in Argos, Menelaus subsequently confronts her absence in several forms. The first stasimon of Aeschylus's *Agamemnon* evokes this scene:

> She left among her people the star and clamor
> Of shields and of spearheads,
> The ships to sail and the armor.
> She took to Ilium her dowry, death.
> She stepped forth lightly between the gates
> Daring beyond all daring. And the prophets
> About the great house wept aloud and spoke:
> "Alas, alas for the house and for the champions,
> Alas for the bed signed with their love together.
> Here now is silence, scorned, unreproachful.
> The agony of her loss is clear before us.
> Longing for her who lies beyond the sea
> He shall see a phantom queen in his household.
> Her images in their beauty
> Are bitterness to her lord now
> Where in the emptiness of eyes
> All passion has faded."[4]

In the tragedy in which the chorus sings these lines, Agamemnon is returning to his wife, Clytemnestra, after his years away at the war in Troy. From her, he will soon learn, too late, that the house he ruled is no longer his. Yet first the chorus suggests that in the palace where Clytemnestra's sister Helen dwelt with Agamemnon's brother, the relations of man and wife are otherwise reversed. Deborah Steiner remarks that "it is Menelaus who assumes the pose of the wife, seated immobile inside doors, preserving the silence that is the customary portion of the woman."[5] The ruler's bodily position in the choral ode indicates that he is in mourning. Yet his wife, by all accounts, is not dead.[6]

While his spouse is far from him, Menelaus falls prey to the sentiment that the ancient Greeks called *pothos*: the variety of yearning, as Plato's Socrates explained, "that pertains not to that which is present, but to that which is elsewhere [*allothi pou*] or absent," which is called *himeros* "when its object is present," and known as *pothos* "when it is absent."[7] In that state of passion for a missing being, Menelaus perceives his wife in three new shapes. A "ghost" (*phasma*) or "phantom queen" appears (*doxei*) in his household with the suddenness, speed, and movement known to characterize Greek specters. Menelaus also discerns the "treads" or "traces" that his vanished spouse has left imprinted on some sensible surface; the chorus laments Helen's *stiboi philanores*, which signify either the traces of the steps she took as she fled the palace or the marks that her body left when last lying on the conjugal bed.[8] Finally, the chorus evokes some "statues" to which the ruler's eyes are drawn: "Images in their beauty" (*eumorphoi kolossoi*), "where in the emptiness of eyes / all passion has faded," or, to render the Greek text more literally, "the grace of the beautiful statues, which has become hateful to the man" once "in their eyeless gaze, all loveliness has departed."

The last objects are certainly the most monumental of this set of three. They may also be the most enigmatic. Recalling that "the difficulties of the stanza are legion," Steiner has noted that while Helen's "steps" or "treads" (*stiboi*) "pose textual problems that have never been resolved," "the conclusion of the strophe presents three fresh riddles: what is the nature of the *kolossoi*, what is their relevance to Menelaus and his bride, and how should the missing eyes be understood?"[9] Some critics are certain that the "images" evoked signify statues that represent the departed queen. Questions, in any case, remain. Pierre Chantraine admits that he can "hardly understand how, after Helen's departure, the statues (which represented Helen?) no longer have eyes and have lost their erotic charm (?)."[10] Others have claimed that the "images" are not depictions of a particular individual, but *korai*, that is, traditional representations of maidens of the kind that might have decorated a palace such as Menelaus's. Eduard Fraenkel comments that such typical statuary would have sufficed, in any case, to provoke the ruler's mourning, "every statue of a beautiful woman," as he writes, being "more than the deserted husband can bear."[11] Maurizio Bettini observes that however one reads the details of the scene, what might have been "a consoling image of the beloved (and, in this sense, an image 'of full eyes') turns into the hateful, painful image of empty eyes."[12] In "yearning" (*pothos*) for Helen, the hero finds himself surrounded by elements — a ghost, traces, or treads and, last, "*kolossoi* with no eyes" — that render her absence present. All become, for him, the objects of profound aversion.

The "images" evoked in the choral ode point to an artifact of which diverse and at times conflicting interpretations have been proposed. In 1930, Chantraine held that "the sense and history" of the noun *kolossos* are "well defined": "It always designates a 'colossal statue' and is attested above all in texts concerning Egyptian monuments."[13] Only the traditional etymology of the term seemed to him uncertain. He argued that no linguistic evidence supports the old derivation of the word from the term *kolekanos*, "large, thin man"; he claimed that with its ending in *-ossos*, *kolossos* most likely originated in an unknown "pre-Hellenic" and more exactly Aegean or "Asianic" language.[14]

Two years later, Émile Benveniste offered a different account of the word. Likening it to *Kolophōn*, "the name of a mountain in Asia minor and also one of the oldest and most famous cities in the Ionian federation of Lydia," Benveniste argued that *kolossos* evokes the idea of the "summit" or "apex": "*kolossos* rendered a notion of an 'erected thing, a raised image,' which immediately comes close to the Latin *statua*, postverbal of *statuō*, like *pugna* from *pugnō*."[15] Unlike *eikōn*, which signifies "any sculptured, graven, painted, drawn or even woven image," *kolossos* names a three-dimensional image placed in an upright position. Among the numerous Greek words for such representations (*bretas, xoanon, agalma, hedos*), *kolossos* has the further characteristic of being of an animate gender (masculine or feminine) for a reason: while the inanimate Greek nouns meaning "statue" point to "simple objects, which are venerable but lifeless," the *kolossos* is an image "gifted with an active force." Benveniste held it to be, more exactly, "the double of the dead."[16]

Herodotus appears to have employed the term for an image of this variety. Nowhere in his book on Egypt does he define the nature of the *kolossoi* that he observes, yet from his recurrent usage certain features may be deduced. When King Mycerinus's daughter died, he writes, her father gave his only child a burial "more sumptuous than ordinary," declaring that her body be placed in "a hollow cow's image of gilded wood." Herodotus himself saw it. Near that artifact, he reports, "in another chamber, there are the images [*eikones*] of Mycerinus's concubines, according to the priests of Saïs. There are, in fact, some twenty wooden *kolossoi* there, representing naked women."[17] Benveniste notes: "Nothing is specified concerning the dimension of these statues (the cow, which contained a human body, being simply 'of the size of a large living cow,' II, 131); what is more, the historian also designates them indifferently by *kolossoi* or *eikones*."[18] In the same way, Herodotus recalls that when the priests of the temple of Zeus at Thebes admitted him to their sanctuary, they drew his attention to standing figures: "They showed me wooden *kolossoi*, of the stated number; every high priest sets up a statue of himself [*ekona heautou*] there during his lifetime."[19] Again, *kolossos* and *eikōn*, "statue" and "image," are both employed; if these terms are distinct in sense, magnitude does not seem the differentiating trait.[20] Where the historian observes a large *kolossos*, he always specifies it by an additional indication.[21] Benveniste concludes that the received account of *kolossos* as "colossal statue" is to be corrected: no determinate size may be deduced from this ancient name. All that is to be inferred is that in each case, the statue stands in place of an absent individual.

Epigraphy as well as language and literature confirm this interpretation. In an inscription from Cyrene, Libya, concerning the arrival of unexpected guests in the home, an enigmatic allusion to *kolossoi* plays a major role. The first philologists to study this sacred text understood it to bear on suppliants. More recent scholars have instead argued that it involves not visitors, but "visitants": malevolent spirits, in other words, conjured up by spells.[22] The law in question stipulates that when a householder does not know the identity of the person who has sent such guests to his home, he is to address the sender according to a fixed form: "O human being [*ō anthrōpe*], whether you be a man or a woman. . . ." Then "male and female *kolossoi*" are to be fashioned from "either wood or earth." The host is to welcome such *kolossoi* at a meal, "setting beside them a portion of everything." The *kolossoi* are then to be "taken," with their portions, and "deposited in an uncultivated ground."[23]

Benveniste interpreted these acts as the replacements of funeral rites that had not been performed: "The presence of a departed one is prolonged, beyond the tomb, by the fiction of wood or clay. Some community with the living is continued with his image, even if death has deprived his flesh of it. Thus the deceased's ever insistent demands are met, and the maleficent forces freed by death are imprisoned in a symbol."[24] If one understands the "suppliants" of the inscription to be spirits, rather than human guests, one will judge the rite to be apotropaic; the elaborate treatment of the *kolossoi* distances the "visitants" precisely in welcoming them. "Appeasing and then removing" the images of the guests, Steiner comments, "the individual effectively drives the phantom from his home."[25] What is certain is that such "images" or "statues" need not be "colossal" in dimension. As Ulrich Wilamowitz-Möllendorf long ago suggested, they may be closer in size to "dolls" or "marionettes" (*Puppen*).[26]

A second inscription from Cyrene offers further evidence in support of this conclusion. It concerns an oath that was to guarantee the just relations between the island of Thera and its distant colony on the northern shores of Libya. A "curious ritual" would be performed.[27] *Kolossoi* were fashioned from wax and subsequently thrown into the fire while the following lines were declaimed: "May he who does not abide by this agreement, but transgresses it, melt away and dissolve like these images [*kolossoi*], himself, his seed, and his property."[28] Here the *kolossoi* clearly appear to be "figurines," rather than immense statues. Again, they function as doubles, but the position they occupy with respect to their makers differs from the one they possess in the first inscription. Commenting on the two appearances of the word in the laws of Cyrene, Jean-Pierre Vernant notes that "in both these rituals, the *kolossos* journeys between the world of the living and that of the dead. But the journey is made in one direction in the first case and in the other in the second. In one case, the dead are made present in the world of the living; in the other, the living are projected into death." After doubling for an unknown individual, the figure works in the second rite to represent a vanishing that no one would survive: "Through the *kolossoi* who represent them in the form of doubles, those swearing the oath cast themselves into the fire; this act anticipates their own life and social existence's liquefaction and disappearance into the invisible."[29]

That a standing image of a person can take the place of a being neither alive nor yet deceased is a possibility also evoked by the geographer Pausanias. In the ninth book of his description of Greece, he records the practices of the people of Orchomenus in Boeotia. Every year, they perform sacrifices to Actaeon, the hunter who, having once glimpsed Artemis bathing with her nymphs, was transformed by the goddess into a stag, before being torn apart by his own dogs. In the past, the Boeotians allege, a specter (*eidōlon*) ran throughout their countryside, ravaging it. The people turned for assistance to the oracle at Delphi. "The god bade them discover the remains of Actaeon and bury them in the earth," Pausanias relates, before continuing: "He also bade them make a bronze likeness of the ghost [*eidōlou khalkēn . . . eikona*], and fasten it to a rock with iron. I have myself seen this statue [*to agalma*] thus fastened."[30] In this case, one image acts as the double of another. Actaeon's ghost or "likeness" (*eidōlon*) is captured by the bronze image that the Boeotians place where his remains are buried. The hunter's mobile *psykhē* is thus arrested in being tethered to one place and shape. The term *kolossos* does not appear in the passage. Yet "the example," Vernant writes,

> shows clearly what the original purpose of the *kolossos* was. It served to attract and pin down a double that found itself in abnormal circumstances. It made it possible to re-establish correct relations between the world of the dead and the world of the living. The *kolossos* has this power to pin down because it is itself ritually embedded in the ground. It is not, therefore, merely a figurative symbol. Its function is both to translate the power of the dead man into a visible form and to enable it to be integrated into the ordered world of the living.[31]

In the Aeschylean choral ode, however, Menelaus wrestles with the power of not the dead, but the absent. Helen's "phantom," "treads" or "traces," and *kolossoi* belong to a person who is presumed alive, although she is not, in modern parlance, in her place of residence.

Hers are not the sole appearances of the absentee's *imago* in antiquity. If one believes Pliny the Elder, the art of "clay modeling" or *plastice* as a whole has its origins in the fixing of the shape of an absent lover. The famous example is to be found in the chapters of the *Natural History* devoted to the history of art. Pliny evokes "the question of the origin of the art of painting," recalls the Egyptians' "idle assertion" that painting was invented in their country, the contrary Greek views that it began either in the city of Sicyon or in Corinth, and writes: "All agree that it began with tracing an outline around a man's shadow and, therefore, that pictures were originally done in this way."[32] Paragraphs later, seeming to change subjects, Pliny returns to this beginning, offering a more detailed account of this invention:

> Enough and more than enough has now been said about painting. It may be suitable to append to these remarks something about clay modeling [*plasticen*]. It was through the service of that same earth that modeling portraits from clay was first invented by Boutades, a potter of Sicyon, at Corinth. He did this owing to his daughter, who was in love with a young man. When he was going abroad, she drew an outline on the wall of the shadow of his face thrown by the lamp. Her father pressed clay on this and made a relief, which he hardened by exposure to fire with the rest of his pottery. It is said that this likeness was preserved in the Shrine of the Nymphs, until Mummius overthrew Corinth.[33]

The invention may be of greater consequence than Pliny suggests. Although in this passage he specifies that he is discussing "clay modeling," Pliny elsewhere recalls that according to Pasiteles, "modeling" (*plasticen*) is more ancient than "sculpture," being the "mother of chasing, statuary, and sculpture."[34] The outlining of the lover's face would thus seem to constitute the point of inception for "*any* image possessing volume."[35] Yet one may go further. Bettini has drawn out the consequence that these details imply: "Boutades, as we know, was from Sicyon, and he made his first work precisely in Corinth; moreover, according to the mythic tale, the girl did exactly what, according to the concordant Greek views, gave rise to painting—that is, she drew the lines outlining a man's shadow. Were the potter and his daughter therefore tied, in some way, to the origin of *painting*?"[36] Were it so, the art of the planar image would share an origin with "chasing, statuary, and sculpture." The conclusion gives an unexpected sense to Pliny's remark that "the inception of the expression of likenesses" (*similitudines exprimendi . . . origo*) is to be sought in "modeling."

The "likeness" that Pliny evokes in the scene of making is complex. It has been noted that in the passage from the beloved body to the final work, there are two stages. Thanks to the projection assured by a lamp, a shadow is outlined; from that image, a relief is later made. A century after Pliny, Athenagoras recalls the process in slightly different terms: "The manufacture of dolls was inspired by a young woman. Very much enamored of a man, she drew his shadow on the wall as he slept; then her father, charmed by the extraordinary likeness—he worked with clay—sculpted the image by filling in the contours with earth."[37] Here, the first image is drawn not so much when a lamp was needed as when the beloved man slept. From that outline, the sculpting father then produces his image in clay. Similarity again appears to be crucial, but in both cases, it is contiguity that is key. "The beloved and his image do not so much resemble one another as exist in a relation of metonymy," as Steiner notes.[38] The outline of the face holds for the entire individual, and in Athenagoras as in Pliny, if the figure in relief has a body, it must conform to the molded head.[39]

In both versions of the tale, the contributions of daughter and father are therefore complementary. She traces an outline, reducing her lover to a pure appearance: the immobile shadow that she retains after his departure. Victor Stoichita comments: "The shadow is not 'the body.'" It is "the *other* of the body (like a 'spectre,' like a 'head'). . . . The father gives the specter a consistency. He places clay where there was nothing but the outline of a shadow; he gives the shape a relief (*typum fecit*) and then hardens the form in the fires of his kiln (*induratum igni*)."[40] The result is a double of the absentee.

It is difficult not to observe, moreover, that the making happens not only in two stages, but also at two times, which are separated by an indeterminate duration. The daughter's original action is one of anticipation: when her lover "was going abroad," but had not yet departed, she drew an outline on the wall. Her father's molding is much more difficult to date. It may, of course, be accomplished immediately after the tracing of the outline, but it may also occur long after the man's departure. Stoichita has argued in favor of the second possibility, claiming that the tale effectively proposes "the story of the surrogate image." Although Pliny does not say so explicitly, between the young man's departure and the finished relief, he infers, the daughter's lover has died. Boutades would then be the maker of "a semblance (*similitudo ex argilla*) whose function is to duplicate the one who has disappeared."[41] The reconstruction is plausible. Yet between the moment in which the young man has not yet left and the moment in which he has died, there is, in any case, an interval. The nameless potter's daughter seems uniquely sensitive to this period. It is the duration that she grasps, in a gesture that is preemptive or apotropaic, in her nocturnal tracing: the time in which the young man is no more and no less than absent. The outline of the sleeping head renders a body that will soon have been missing, even as it is suspended on the threshold of vanishing.

Ovid conceived of a case in which the elements of such a scene of amorous substitution are otherwise arranged. There, the woman does not draw, but write, and she declares herself to be in possession an image of her absent lover of whose production nothing is said. In the thirteenth *Heroida*, Laodamia sends a letter to the hero Protesilaus, who has departed, in the immediate aftermath of their wedding, for the war in Troy. She laments her solitude, wishes for his return, and evokes a dire prophecy: the first of the Achaeans to disembark in Ilium must die. The reader knows that Greek to be none other than Protesilaus; it was he, as the *Iliad* relates, who "leapt from his ship, by far the first of all the Achaeans," leaving behind him a "wife, cheeks torn to grief," and a "house half-completed."[42]

The Greek sources present multiple accounts of the aftermath of that scene. According to a version transmitted by Eustathius, the gods, moved by pity for the young husband's sudden death, grant Protesilaus the chance to return from the underworld to tell his wife of his fate. Soon thereafter, Laodamia dies, either from grief or by suicide. Hyginus maintains that it is the wife who, in effect, assures the return of her spouse, albeit in a new shape: after his death, she has a wax statue of him made. She adores it as if it were alive until a servant catches sight of an embrace taken to be adulterous, rather than memorial. Learning of the secret statue, Laodamia's father, now the sole master of the house, decides that it be burned. As it is melted down, the widow throws herself on the fire, consumed with the image of her beloved. Euripides, finally, appears to have presented yet a different version of the husband's return in a tragedy that has not survived. His Protesilaus comes to Laodamia by night as a double of a different kind: a figure in a dream.[43]

In the *Heroides*, Ovid imposes on the presentation of the myth constraints that are both formal and temporal. Since his Laodamia composes a letter to Protesilaus, she cannot consider him to be dead. A return from the underworld, consequently, is impossible. Protesilaus is missing when she writes; Laodamia conjectures that he may be in Aulis, but of this she is not certain.[44] She merely presumes that he is alive. At this point in the presentation of the material, the crucial elements of the narrative of the two lovers appear to be intractable. By modifying a single detail, however, Ovid compresses the tale into an instant, casting it in a new form. Concluding her letter, Laodamia confesses to her absent husband that prey to "persistent fear," she has been "compelled to imagine the worst / that could be as already having happened." She explains herself:

While you are away, a soldier in arms there,
I keep a wax figure of you here that brings
To my sight the dear lines of your face.
It hears the cherishing phrase, it hears the words
Of love that are rightfully yours and
It receives my longing embrace. Believe me
When I say, this figure is more than
It might seem. Add only a voice to the wax,
And it will be Protesilaus.
I gaze at it, I hold it to my bosom
In the place of my true lord and I
Reproach it for your long absence as if it
Might somehow make a reply to me.[45]

Ovid's innovation is unmistakable. "Contrary to all other versions, in which Laodamia creates the *imago* to console herself after his death," the heroine here takes pleasure in an artificial double of her spouse, even as she presumes him to be alive, albeit in some unknown location.[46] Hence the ambiguous structure of her apostrophe: while Laodamia addresses Protesilaus, she also has him in wax. The husband, in these lines, is at once a "you" and an "it." He is absent, while alive, and present, as an inanimate being crafted in the image of a person.

The "peculiarity" of the statue has hardly gone unnoticed. Laodamia's figure is, in Laurel Fulkerson's words, "both a funerary monument and a reminder of someone absent but expected home," a replacement and a mere placeholder for an absentee.[47] Her wax figure may be read as a *kolossos* that announces a dead husband, even as it forestalls his disappearance. In marked contrast to Menelaus, for whom the remains and reminders of Helen were a torment,

Laodamia finds in the double of her spouse the source of pleasure as well as consolation. "*Plus est, quam quod videatur, imago*": Ovid's Latin syntax is equivocal and suggests, as Bettini observes, two definitions of the beloved *imago* — that it is "more than it might seem" and also that it is "more than its capacity to be seen."[48] Whatever the nature of its excess with respect to vision, however, the wax statue, like the addressee, is obstinately mute. The "Protesilaus" of the third person of which Laodamia writes and the "Protesilaus" of the second person to whom she writes fade into a single voicelessness. They share an incapacity to respond.

The image of the absentee, however, need not be made in respect or love. It suffices to recall the possibility that the "guests" of the Cyrenean law are malevolent spirits to grant that a double may work otherwise than to bestow honor on a missing person. Some images have accomplished exactly the reverse. Perhaps the most striking example is that of the phenomenon known as *pittura infamante*: painting consisting of images of shame and, more exactly, infamy.[49] Here, *infamia* is to be taken in its classical legal sense, where it denotes the official privation of *fama*, defined, in the words of Callistratus in the *Digest*, the codification of Roman law begun under Justinian, as "the status of dignity without stain [*dignitatis illaesae status*], according to the established customs and laws, undiminished in any way."[50] To be sure, the word also possessed a nontechnical meaning in Rome: "To every reader of classical Latin literature, it is obvious that *infamia* is used of the ill repute which accompanies moral turpitude of almost every kind."[51] Yet following formal accusation and trial, several kinds of public and official "infamy" could be declared. Long ago, A. H. J. Greenidge enumerated the varieties of such disqualifications. Magistrates decreed one type of infamy, rendering candidates to civil "honors" (*honores*) incapable of receiving them. "Another *infamia* was pronounced by the praetor, with reference to a narrow object of his own, the control of his court." Roman criminal legislation and administrative law went so far as to establish "very many degrees of *infamia*," corresponding to the extent of the diminishment of rights.[52]

The medieval Italian city-states relied on the stigma of such public infamy. In Tuscany, as in Emilia, judgments of political crimes such as treachery, rebellion, banditry, and serious civil infractions of a financial kind such as bankruptcy and embezzlement resulted in formal condemnation to states of infamy. "Whoever was considered *infamous*," Gherardo Ortalli writes, referring in particular to the thirteenth century,

> would be excluded from office, functions, and honors. He could not "present his candidacy," bear witness, work as a tutor or a judge. He was open to the risk of punishments far more severe than those meted out to "upstanding" persons. His testimony was to be given under torture. Canon law, no less than civil law, constrains infamous persons; it forbids them access to the holy orders, rendering ecclesiastical dignities and functions as inaccessible to them as are worldly ones.[53]

Punitive measures against infamous persons, however, could always run up against a limit: the accused or condemned person might flee the city, eluding trial before punishment. Contumacy, or "contempt of court," was a danger to civil authority. "Such situations presented a double hazard to the often unpopular and distrusted communal constabulary," Samuel Y. Edgerton observes.

> Not only were the police expected to catch the culprit eventually, but they had to prove to the offended community from the moment the crime was reported that they were concerned, that they were doing everything from invoking heaven to scouring the earth to bring the guilty to justice. In other words, the very fabric of communal security depended on the visibility of police activity. For the authorities to appear impotent or indifferent in the face of outrageous crime would clearly undermine the whole system of law and order.[54]

The city could appropriate the belongings of a condemned absentee. It might also raze his house. "The arms and emblems of the person in contempt of court would be defiled in public — smeared with excrement, smashed, hung upside down, or even hung from the public gallows."[55]

There were many ways to assure that *infamia* outlasted the physical presence of the offender in the city. One involved the making of images that, once substituted for missing persons, could be humiliated in place of a missing body. The laws of Frignano thus stipulate that forgers are to be represented on the wall of the city hall in the act of writing a fraudulent document.[56] In 1315, the Council of Reggio nell'Emilia decreed a series of measures against the then powerful dalla Palude family. They were banished, stripped of rights and entitlements, and deprived of their possessions. But the city went further, demanding also that "said Lords Jacopino and Goffredo and their sons, both legitimate and natural, and the others banished on the occasion of the 'Bergenzoni et Corvarie' robbery be painted on the exterior wall of the old Palace of the Commune and their names and surnames be inscribed in large letters so that they could clearly be read and understood."[57] In 1377, the Florentines commissioned an "even more violent" representation of Rodolfo da Varano, once general of the papal forces, later a "captain of the people" in the Florentine Republic against the Papal States, before allying himself, again, with the pope. On the Palazzo of the Podestà and the Condotta, his figure was to be seen, hanging, head down, "over a pair of gallows, his hands, above, tied, his feet bound."[58]

Such "defaming painting" has been studied in detail. The practice becomes customary in Emilia and Tuscany in the early thirteenth century and reaches its "great age" in the mid-1200s to 1300s, before fading into disuse in the fifteenth century.[59] Thanks to the illuminating work of Edgerton and Ortalli, its distinctive features may readily be identified. *Pittura infamante* was "part of an organic penal-punitive system." For this reason, it was executed in ways officially stipulated by law, being "administratively subject to the formal decision of institutional bodies (judicial and political)" and entailing "serious legal consequences" for anyone sentenced to being depicted in such a form. In addition, "it was handed down as surrogatory (but certainly effective) punishment for offenders found guilty in their absence, and the images were displayed in appointed spots in particularly busy, central parts of cities, usually on the walls of government buildings in the main square."[60] The civil codes of the medieval cities contained statutes concerning this practice. The Florentine law books thus establish that any "merchant or person or other artisan" defaulting on a debt be pronounced infamous de jure and, within a month, be "painted and have his first and last name inscribed" on the Palazzo of the Podestà.[61] The familiar "Hanged Man" of tarot card decks has its origin in the iconography of such punishments. As David Freedberg notes, however, the medieval authorities disposed of several means to establish the infamy of the condemned in pictorial form. Frauds and traitors might be "represented as hanged," yet a "further step could also be taken: the images (both two- and three-dimensional) could be hanged.... Finally, the whole apparatus of execution could be employed upon images, not only in hanging, but also in pillorying, burning, quartering, and decapitating them."[62]

The singularity of this practice is worth establishing. As "a direct expression of public power (either political or juridical)," "images of infamy" are distinct from the humiliating representations contained in the "defamatory letters" (*Schmähbriefe*) that flourished in sixteenth-century Germany.[63] The law-bound medieval representations can also be distinguished from exceptional representations of enemies later commissioned by sovereigns, such as those that Louis XI had produced in 1447 to exhibit the treachery of the Prince of Orange.[64] "Defaming painting" constituted the execution of a civil sentence, which employed pictorial means to bring infamy upon the absent.

The artists who participated in such measures are far from unknown. Among their number, one may count Botticelli, Andrea del Sarto, and Andrea del Castagno, who came to be known, through his work, as "Andrea of the Hanged Men" (*Andrea degli Impiccati*). Today, the evidence of such infamous paintings, however, is almost exclusively indirect. The number of descriptions and mentions in medieval texts contrasts sharply with the scarcity of pictorial remains. A precious handful of "preparatory studies" have been identified, but "not a single one of these once numerous *pitture infamanti* from the Duecento and Trecento has survived anywhere in Italy."[65]

Scholars have adduced several reasons for this circumstance. The fact that the paintings were to be exhibited in public spaces facilitated their decay. Yet as testaments to the iniquity of citizens, the medieval "images of shame" also posed certain intrinsic problems that could render them not only troublesome to produce, but also difficult to preserve. That not all artists wished to participate in the making of such pictures seems certain. In Bologna, in particular, the artists who undertook such paintings constituted a suspect class. Between 1286 and 1289, the city authorities turned repeatedly to one Antonio di Rolando, known as Cicogna, for the depicting of the "infamous"; in those same years, Cicogna himself was implicated in a series of judicial processes. Of the approximately 112 figures of infamous persons produced in Bologna in the last years of the thirteenth century, "at least 59 were the work of painters accused of homicide."[66] The act of representing crime seems to have implied a special stigma. "When it came to painting the men who had attempted to rob the Cassa del Camera del Commune in Florence in 1292," Freedberg writes, "Fino di Tedaldo had to be forced to carry out the task; and Vasari records that half a century or so later, Giottino had to be similarly conscripted to paint the image of the banished duke of Athens."[67]

There was contagion in the tarnishing of *fama*, and it extended to the cities where the paintings were presented. In 1329, the Florentine Council formally restricted the persons who might be represented on the gates and walls of the city to Christ, the Virgin, the Roman Church, the king of France, and Charles d'Anjou. These measures safeguarded the purity of the subject matter of painting. As Helene Wieruszowski suggests, they also put an end to the "impairing and injuring" of individual citizens' reputations by figurative means.[68] By this point, a change in the perception of the paintings had occurred: "The images had come to be seen as a negative reflection on the people of the city and its government."[69] It is not inconceivable that the once ordinary "images of infamy" of the Duecento had also begun to incite a certain discomfort, if not shame, in the beholder. They would have obligated citizens to see their friends, their family, and their erstwhile neighbors defamed. Visitors to the city would discover in them evidence of a polity riven by discord, violence, and iniquity. Fragile in material, painful to produce, and disquieting to contemplate, *pittura infamante*, like legal absence itself, lasted only for a while.

Yet the punishing of absentees by imagistic means has had a long life. Its most extreme example involves the history of so-called "execution in effigy" (*executio in effigie*).[70] The principle of this procedure is in appearance simple: in place of some missing person, a "substitute body" or "pseudobody" (*Scheinleib*) is fashioned, tried, and finally destroyed, as if it coincided with the body of the person whom it represented. In 1329, Louis the Bavarian thus held a trial of Pope John XXII in Pisa. "In the presence and with the agreement of the king, a doll of wood and straw, 'decorated with the full papal ornaments,'" was to represent the second pope of Avignon, condemned for heresy. The image was burned.[71] The supreme pontiffs, for their part, adopted like procedures. In 1462, the Humanist Aenea Syblio de Piccolomini, better known as Pope Pius II, condemned two statues made by Paolo Romano to a "festive burning"; they were both figures of Sigismondo Pandolfo Malatesta, the "Wolf of Rimini," who was excommunicated in 1460.[72] Medieval cities also employed such procedures against persons who, having committed crimes, had eluded their control. When, in 1490, it became known that the steward or Meier of Rijmenam had intentionally allowed a thief to escape trial in the neighboring town of Mecheln, the official was required to erect a gallows at the border between the two cities. There, in the middle of the square, he was to arrange for a "counterfeit thief" (*geconterfeyte Dieb*) to be hanged.[73]

In a compendious study of "the image in the penal system," Wolfgang Brückner has argued that *executio in effigie* is in a strict sense a modern phenomenon. The civil code of the Romans, the laws of the Germanic peoples, and the jurists of the Middle Ages all lack any single term for such a practice, and "where the concept is lacking, so, too, the thing does not exist."[74] Only after the mid-sixteenth century does the expression "execution in effigy" become common in legal theory and judicial practice. Then the Italian jurist Prospero Farinacci explains in a chapter on "contumacy" that in cases where a person judged a heretic has absented himself, "his statue is to be burned." Should the condemned already be deceased, he writes, his bones are to be exhumed and cremated; "should he have no bones, his effigy is to be burned."[75] Similarly, Pierre Ayrault writes in 1575 that just as individuals may be "honored" by an effigy or by "the erection of a statue," so they may also "receive punishment and shame from it."[76] Under François I, execution *par figure* enters the vocabulary of military law. Such provisions in French penal law were lasting. Under Louis XIV, absentees sentenced to death are to be "executed by effigy."[77]

The visiting of death upon the image of the missing person is a practice that exceeds the legal history of any single state. It is a European phenomenon. In 1661, Kai Lykke is convicted of high treason in Copenhagen; since he is absent, a wax effigy is made in his likeness. "It was made to kneel in the sand, its necktie was removed, a blindfold placed over its eyes, and the hair tucked beneath it. Then the figure was decapitated, and the executioner's assistant held up the head by its hair. The parts of the body were dragged past the royal palace while heads and hands were nailed to the pillory in the marketplace."[78] Two years later, the crown of Denmark goes even further. Count Corfitz Uhlfeldt, erstwhile chancellor to Christian IV, is accused of treachery, tried, and sentenced to death while being himself in absentia. This time, the legal authorities succeed in "augmenting the gruesome effects," as Brückner notes, in what constitutes "the next theater of a perfected casting." The inside of the effigy is filled with animal intestines; the artificial head and hands are severed, the body is quartered, innards exposed, and "head and hand are nailed to the town hall wall, where they remain to be seen until the great fire in Copenhagen in 1728."[79] In Holland and the other United Provinces, similar procedures are enacted for crimes of treason. Johann Schulenberg was judged *in effigie* in 1662, and in 1673, the absent Jean Barton de Montbas, Hugo Grotius's French son-in-law, was tried and executed, represented by a "life-size painting" over which his name was written.[80] Such cases extend into the nineteenth century. In the aftermath of the uprising of 1849 in Budapest, the Austro-Hungarian authorities judged Gyula Andrássy and hanged him, in effigy, in 1852. In the meantime, he had escaped to Paris.[81]

The shadow of the archaic *kolossos*, placeholder of the missing body, looms over these artificial figures for reasons that are less historical than structural. From the "eyeless statues" that haunt Menelaus to the figurines to be made "of wood or earth" according to the sacred law of Cyrene, from the painted persons who, in the infamy of their crimes and punishments, were once exhibited in the centers of Bologna, Reggio, and Florence to the dolls of wood and straw that have served the judicial ends of modern law, a regular substitution may be observed: in place of the absentee, a double is produced and submitted to rites and established procedures. It is a temporary token, distinct in sense and function from the funerary artifact that it resembles and that it may one day become. That the two types of objects can be difficult to distinguish is certain: absence being of several kinds, its images are equivocal. The *kolossos* may well function as the replacement of the missing corpse, even as the beloved's artificial face and body, in Pliny and in Ovid, can be interpreted as the variously plastic figures of the deceased. Yet in all these shapes, a more unsettling figure also lies concealed. It is that of the absentee who, for some stretch of time, is presumed to be alive, albeit in some unknown location. In the interval in which such a likeness lasts, an insistent demand makes itself audible: that a person, in the trace or tread, doll or sculpture, remain present, if only for a while. To be adored or punished, to be welcomed, dreaded, or expelled, the image of the absentee is each time "wanted," after the manner of its wanting subject. The fragile semblance of a placeless body, it can be no monument.

PART TWO

Lessenings

CHAPTER FIVE

Decreases of the Head

The first and most familiar of the varieties of missing persons is the one declared in the aftermath of an unexplained disappearance. When someone has left a residence without notice and, despite summons, has not appeared again, or when someone known to have departed has failed to return as might have been expected, legal, social, ritual, and religious practice appeal to a common expedient. A double is fashioned and set in place of the absent individual. Such an artifact is a "person" (*persona*) in the sense familiar to the authors of ancient Rome. It is a mask through which a voice becomes audible: *per-sonat*, according to an etymology classical sources often evoke.[1] The representative of someone who is presumed, for a while, to be alive, albeit nowhere locatable, such a missing person functions as a placeholder, assuring that in the absence of a body, the rights of the individual are duly respected.

Whether legal or variously "plastic," judicial or ritual, secular or religious, a recurrent configuration is discernible in the constitution of such a transitory absentee. A mysterious removal becomes the occasion for the distinction of two entities that until that moment appeared to coexist, almost indiscernibly, in a single human being: the living organism and the subject of rights, the body and its representation, the physical individual and the legal person. This separation is the condition of the "missing person" familiar to modern legal practice, as well as the rites practiced in settings as diverse as archaic Greece, Renaissance Italy, and modern Europe and the United States.

It is worth pausing to recall the concept that arises through this distinction. One cannot state that the notion of such a represented missing person is simply synonymous with that of a human being, for if it is to serve the function for which it is crafted, the double of the absentee must stand in place of the one who is not there. This missing person is bodiless, while also the subject of civil rights of a certain kind. Yet it would be equally insufficient to conclude that such a missing person is no human being whatsoever, possessing a status akin to those granted such various beings as animals, plants, instruments, natural objects, and events. Substituting for someone who has vanished, the category of the absentee allows certain rights to be respected only if they may be applied to the artifact that is the missing person as if it were their proper subject. Defying any classical logic, the concept of the absentee thus demands that beyond the apparently exclusive opposition between being a person and not being a person, a third possibility be granted. It is the possibility of an intensely "personal" nonperson: that of someone — or something — nonhuman to which human beings alone, in absenting themselves, give rise.

There are also other nonpersons, which are no less deserving of investigation. The second of their order is in structure the inverse of the first. In the configuration that it supposes, a living body remains present, yet its right to representation diminishes. In the most extreme case, it is denied. Someone, assisted by something such as law, religion, or a social force, declares some human body to be unworthy of fully presenting itself or to be, for one of many reasons, unfit to claim proper personhood. From that decision a nonperson arises in a new irreducibility to being a person and to not being a person. Unlike the figure of the absentee in the strict legal sense, this nonperson is not an abstraction conceived to represent a non-present body; it does not sound a voice that would otherwise remain inaudible. The second variety of missing persons emerges, rather, through the formal judgment that a present person, while in appearance capable of language, may not lay claim to certain rights. This is a speaking body from which full personhood is missing: a nonperson conceived not by vanishing, but by lessening.

The Roman jurists, authors of the most systematic and influential of ancient legal systems, conceived of a practice by which missing persons of this kind could brought into existence. They gave it the name of *capitis* (or *kapitis*) *deminutio*: literally, "decrease of the head." The oddity of the expression is patent. Introducing the study of this institution that he published in 1877, Gaston Chabalet remarked that "it is practically impossible to translate" it adequately.[2] Its terms, however, may be defined. *Caput* (or *kaput*) denotes the "head," less as an anatomical part, for which the Romans possessed the word *testa*, than as a metonymic figure for the living body.[3] Its senses are at least three: "the individual as such," "the essential characteristic of every living thing," and in specifically legal parlance, "the juridical as well as social quality of the individual."[4] For the jurists, *caput* is therefore above all "a technical expression referring to the legal aptitude to be a subject of rights, that is, a legal personality."[5] For this reason, it has often been rendered into English by the indistinct plural term "rights" or the singular word "status."[6] *Deminutio* (or *diminutio*), for its part, has been variously interpreted. Yet it is certain that it points, like *minutio*, to some manner of reduction. Adolf von Scheurl and those who follow him argue that it is best rendered as "destruction, annihilation," such that "*deminutio* is equivalent to the extinction of personhood." Karl Friedrich von Savigny and those who concur with him hold, instead, that it points merely to "decrease," *capitis deminutio* being "an alteration, in different degrees, of personality."[7]

The oldest surviving example of a "decreased head" is that of a woman. Cicero explains in a passage of his *Topics* that in order for a woman to make a will bearing on goods bequeathed to her by her late husband, she must no longer be subject to her father's authority or *patria potestas*. The validity of her testament supposes that a condition has been fulfilled: in passing from her father's house to her husband's, the woman has undergone a change of status—more exactly, a *capitis deminutio*.[8] Later authors propose a typology of such "mutations" (*permutationes*). In the second century CE, Gaius devotes several articles of his *Institutes* to *capitis deminutio*, which he defines as "the alteration of a previous status" (*prioris status permutatio*). A decrease may come to pass, he explains, "in three ways [*modis*]." He presents them as three quantities: "maximal" (*maxima*), "intermediate" (*media*), and "minimal" (*minima*).[9]

These terms play a notable role in Justinian's *Digest*, which contains a chapter devoted to such alterations. The Roman jurist Julius Paulus explains in it that to each variety of decrease distinguished by Gaius there corresponds one of the "three things that we have": "liberty, citizenship, and family."[10] Each of those terms appears to be shorthand for a set of rights, the three together constituting the stratified order of the Roman citizen's prerogatives. When the head is decreased such that status within the family is lessened, while rights pertaining to liberty and citizenship remain intact, the *deminutio* is "least." When citizenship is suppressed, the decrease is "intermediate." When liberty, finally, is withdrawn, the reduction is most extreme: "maximal."[11]

Classical legal theory and practice afford ample illustrations of each of these types of change. A citizen, first, could lose his independence through adoption and submission to the authority of a new *patria potestas*; his "head," then, would undergo a minor decrease. A Roman might, second, be deprived of his citizenship, becoming *peregrinus*, a free provincial subject; alternately, to evoke a case adduced by Gaius, he might be "banished from home and hearth" and deprived of the right to fire and water (*aqua et igni interdictus*).[12] In both such cases, a *caput* undergoes an intermediate decrease. Finally, free Roman citizens could, by misdeed or by misfortune, be enslaved. They would then be submitted to *capitis deminutio maxima*, the loss of their "*entire* juristic personality."[13]

That such a decrease of the head involved a status distinct from death is certain. W. W. Buckland notes that "death caused a will to operate: no *capitis deminutio* did."[14] One must therefore conclude that for the jurists, maximally "diminished" individuals are so reduced as to be, for all legal purposes, less than dead. Yet what, one might wonder, would such a legal condition be? The truth is that today, much in the theory of the decreases of the head is obscure. The tripartition raises questions in itself. Was the Roman law familiar with three distinct *deminutiones*, or with one reduction that admitted of multiple degrees?[15] Did the most extreme form of decrease "apply originally only to enslavement and exile or also sale into civil bondage?"[16] Some scholars argue that no simple answer can be given to these questions, for the institution changed greatly in the long passage from the republic to the late empire. No matter how one interprets the statutes of *capitis deminutio* and their commentaries, however, it seems that in Roman civil law, a subject of rights could be diminished by degree, independent of any corresponding change to the individual body. In the most extreme case, the legal person could be loosened from the living body and completely nullified. What would remain, then, would be a former citizen alive and perhaps well, yet in the absence of any legal "head."

The euphemistic English rendition of *capitis deminutio* by "change of status"[17] betrays marked unease before the ancient doctrine of the decreases of the head. As has been noted, the discomfiting reality is that the "permutations of status" (*permutationes status*) that have been recorded are all "changes for the worse."[18] The terminology of the jurists is to this degree exact: the statutes foresaw a lessening, not an alteration. Through the operation that they effected, the laws succeeded in engendering a being of an intensely legal nature: an individual distinguished by the fact of being unfit for representation as a complete person.

Nothing would be more misleading than to conclude that the production of such a lesser being numbered among the unique accomplishments of ancient Roman law. The contrary supposition would be closer to the truth: those lacking in full personhood may be less the exception than the rule. Among the speaking beings who we are, diminishment is unceasing. When articulated in degrees, it is potentially numberless in its varieties. There is perhaps no human community that does not count persons of "decreased heads" among its members, precisely to discount them. Marginal or remarkable, neglected or remembered, if not still—and once again—intolerably contemporary, these nonpersons, in every case, demand our attention.

CHAPTER SIX

Rules of Diminution

Once it is granted that the personhood of human beings may be lessened, by nature or according to circumstance, the possibilities will be numerous. Forms of diminution will abound, differing in quality as well as quantity. At first glance, they may seem most visible beyond the limits of a single community. Mythography provides an example almost reassuring in the evidence of its unreality. In the medieval Latin treatise of uncertain date and authorship known to scholars today as *The Book of Monsters* (*Liber monstrorum*), the reader encounters a catalog of creatures that, while in shape and bearing human beings, fall short of deserving the name of man. They are, in each case, a "kind of people" of a deficient nature.[1]

"In India, next to the Ocean," the author relates, "we have learnt of a certain kind of people [*genus humanum*] hairy in their whole body, who are said to live on water and raw fish, covered in natural nakedness only by bristles like wild animals. And the Indians call them *Icthyophagi* ['fish-eaters'], and they are not only accustomed to the land, but dwell in streams and ponds." "*Cynocephali* are also said to be born in India, who have the heads of dogs, and spoil every word they say with mingled barks, and do not imitate humans but the beasts themselves in eating raw flesh."[2] Likewise, "they say there is a kind of people [*genus humanum*] whom the Greeks call *Sciapods* ['shade-feet'], because lying on their backs they protect themselves from the heat of the sun by the shade of their feet. They have only one leg each for their feet, and their knees harden in an inflexible joint."[3] "There are also people [*homines*] on an island in the river Brixontis who are born without heads, whom the Greeks call *Epifugi*. And they are eight feet tall and have all the functions of the head in their chests, except that they are said to have eyes in their shoulders."[4] And "there is a certain people of mixed nature [*gens aliqua conmixtae naturae*] on an island in the Red Sea, who are said to be able to speak the languages of all nations. In this way they astonish people who come from afar, by naming their acquaintances, in order to deceive them, and eat them raw."[5]

The image of "people" less than human, of course, need hardly be so fantastic. It can suffice for someone to be identified as a foreigner to be deemed lacking in humanity. Classical Greek and Roman historiography, geography, literature, and philosophy are all acquainted with the doctrine that alien nations are composed of human beings who are, in some crucial respect, deficient. In the first pages of the *Politics*, Aristotle recalls a pronouncement made by Iphigenia in Euripides's *Iphigenia in Aulis*. The philosopher takes it, rightly or wrongly, as expressing the position of "the poets": "It is right that Greeks rule barbarians, not barbarians / Greeks, for they are slaves, and we are free."[6]

In classical antiquity, foreigners are also regularly distinguished among themselves according to a graded scale of inferiority. Some "barbarians," as Iphigenia declares, are by nature slaves. Others have a different status, being enemies. That these two groups are closely related is a point the ancients often stress. Roman jurists are fond of stating that the Roman designation of the slave, *servus*, is derived from *servare*, "to save": slaves, according to their account, were once foes whose lives were "saved" or "spared."[7] Linguists contest that etymology.[8] Yet the proximity that it suggests between foreigners and slaves is undeniable. On its account, Henri Lévy-Bruhl long ago advanced a far-reaching claim. He argued that in classical Greece as in archaic Rome, "slavery is essentially an international institution." In the earliest period of Roman history, the slave is a foreigner; reciprocally, the foreigner is a slave.[9]

Alain Testart writes that "the first proposition may be true, but not the second." According to a well-known Roman legal precept, "every foreigner without protection *may* legitimately *be reduced* to slavery," without, however, being one by definition.[10] Benveniste argued that such a situation is also reflected in the Latin lexicon, where *servus* appears to be a non-Indo-European word, probably derived from the Etruscan: "Slavery being the condition of foreigners, the name of the slave could hardly be Roman."[11] Benveniste offered an analogous analysis of the ancient Greek word *doulos*, "slave," as an expression most likely borrowed from some language of Asia Minor: "One ought not to be surprised that Greek uses a foreign term to designate the slave, because—and this is often the case with this designation in Indo-European—the slave is necessarily a foreigner."[12]

Classical antiquity was also familiar with the idea that some alien groups are of such a kind as not to possess even the rank of enemies in war. Statesman and legal theorist, Cicero was to be the most eminent spokesman for this view. In his treatise *On Duties*, he states that "enemies" (*hostes*) ought always to be treated with good will: "There are laws of warfare and it often happens that fidelity to an oath given to an enemy must be kept. For if an oath has been sworn in such a way that the mind grasps that this ought to be done, it should be kept; if not, then there is no perjury if the thing is not done." He adds, however, that there are also cases in which that rule does not hold, for some strangers are unworthy of any promises:

> For instance, if an agreement is made with pirates in return for your life, and you do not pay the price, there is no deceit, not even if you swore to do so and did not. For a pirate is not included in the number of lawful enemies but is the common enemy of all [*Nam pirata non est ex perduellium numero definitus, sed communis hostis omnium*]. With him there ought not to be any pledged word nor any oath mutually binding.[13]

From this definition of the pirate as a less than rightful antagonist, Cicero draws a far-reaching consequence. It is the most perplexing of the seemingly moral rules stated in his book *On Duties*. As if anticipating the adage that one can do battle against a privateer only with "a privateer and a half," *à corsaire, corsaire et demi*, Cicero reasons that to subdue the enemies of all, one must fight exactly as they do: in the absence of good will, without oaths, and renouncing, therefore, the possibility of any truce.[14]

Yet it would be an error to surmise that for the ancient Greeks and Romans, individuals of a lesser civic status lie exclusively beyond the borders of the city, in barbarian empires, bands of thieves, and pirate communities. No city of antiquity failed to accord rights unequally to men and women. None was indifferent to the distinction between adults and those too young to bear their responsibilities. Yet a more extreme possibility of civic diminution cut across differences of age and gender. Classical law saw to it that inside the polity there were multitudes born into the condition that Orlando Patterson has called "natal alienation." In such a state, all ties of birth in "ascending and descending generations" are denied, "all formal, legally enforceable ties of 'blood'" are negated, and civic status is systematically annulled.[15]

In Greece, as in Rome, slaves, quite simply, were ubiquitous. Those who have written on ancient politics and society have not always fully measured the import of this circumstance, although there have been remarkable exceptions. M. I. Finley was one. To Fustel de Coulanges's claim that in the history of humanity, "slavery is a primordial fact, contemporary with the origin of society," its roots being "in an age of the human species when all inequalities had their *raison d'être*," Finley pointedly responded that the "Greeks and Romans, independently so far as we can see, transformed this 'primordial fact' into something new and wholly original in world history (and something rare throughout history), namely, an institutionalized system of large-scale employment of slave labour in both countryside and the cities."[16] Theirs were "slave societies" in the sense that "there was no action or belief or institution in Graeco-Roman antiquity that was not one way or another affected by the possibility that someone involved *might be* a slave."[17]

It is perhaps unsurprising that in seeking to account for the existence of such societies, ancient authors differ among themselves. In the first book of his *Politics*, Aristotle famously—or infamously—maintains that slavery cannot be reduced to mere convention or the contingencies of force; there exist, he argues, slaves "by nature."[18] The Roman legal tradition was familiar with a different position. The Latin jurists divide the varieties of right into three spheres of law: natural law, the law of peoples, and civil law. "Natural law" (*ius naturale*) holds for all living beings, the speaking and the mute. Insofar as they partake of this order, human beings are free, equal, and without differences of status, knowing nothing of the relations of property and exchange. Then there exists a second law, which follows it in chronology, yet not character.[19] Many sources suggest that natural law comes to an end with the outbreak of conflict. Groups are formed; battle leads to murder. Lives, however, are also spared; "prisoners" (*captivi*), in other words, are taken. Servitude may find its roots here. After the law of nature, the "law of peoples" (*ius gentium*) thus emerges, containing the principles of such various institutions as war, kingdoms, private domains, territorial limits, buildings, exchange, contracts, and obligations. With this law, the third legal order also arises: "civil law" (*ius civile*). It appears as a "particularization" of the law of peoples, civil law being, in Yan Thomas's words, "nothing but the internal projection of some universal law to which, in each city, certain rules are added, or subtracted."[20] Phrasing the ancient positions in modern terms, one might affirm, therefore, that for the Roman jurists, unlike Aristotle, slavery is not "by nature"; on the contrary, it defies the natural order, belonging exclusively to the law of peoples and the city.

There, however, slavery is fundamental. The Roman legal sources introduce the doctrine of the subjects of law with this partition: "The first division of human beings by the law of persons," as Gaius states, "is into those who are free and those who are slaves."[21] The code thus begins with the positing of a lessened status: that of people defined as lacking rights. Incapable of entering into contracts, possessing nothing of their own, being without any official name other than their masters', Roman slaves are less "persons" in the usual legal sense of the term than "things" (*res*) and, more exactly, chattel.[22] The Roman jurists define their status in various lapidary pronouncements that echo each other throughout their books while differing in accent and phraseology. "The slave has no head" (*servus . . . nullum caput habet*), the *Institutes* of Justinian establish.[23] Paulus maintains, rather, that "the servile head has no right" (*servile caput nullum ius habet*).[24] A characteristic of this status is that as W. W. Buckland notes, "over a wide range of law the slave was not only rightless, he was also dutiless."[25] "There is no obligation towards the person of the slave" (*in personam servilem nulla cadit obligatio*), the lawyers therefore decree.[26] When a judgment is declared against a *servus*, it is void of effects, binding neither the slave nor the master.[27] Some jurists resort to a starker formula, stating that "the slave is akin to the dead" (*servitus morti assimilatur*).[28] A *servus*, others reason, is more exactly *pro nullo*: "as no one."[29] He or she is a human being whose condition draws close to that of a nonhuman, yet one might also reason, on strictly terminological grounds, that this state is precisely that of a "human being"—and nothing more. *Homo*, in classical Latin, means not only "man" or "human being," but also "slave."

In addition to the variously lessened beings who are women, children, foreigners, enemies, pirates, and slaves, there are other diminished ancient people deserving of attention: those whose decreased status is not presupposed as the result of processes so old as to be immemorial, but rather established according to a judicial procedure. Where such processes come to pass, the difference between the undiminished and the diminished "head" emerges from the crossing of a border fixed by the conventions of civil law. The artifice of positing such entities as lesser speaking beings—rightless people, that is, who exist as legal "things," although they are humans, as dead, although they are alive, or as "no ones," although they are individuals—is then unmistakable. *Capitis deminutio maxima* is, in this sense, exemplary. By the power of this alteration, a civil subject passes from belonging to a family, a city, and its class of freemen to possessing the status of the slave, acquiring a "personality" in which rights are denied the living, speaking body that would be their material basis. Yet this "decrease" is but one of many cases, the codes of antiquity having also foreseen other means of civic degradation.

Aristotle relates that the "ancestral principles of the Athenians" reputed to have been written by Solon threatened any citizen who abetted a tyranny with *atimia*: "dishonor," a punishment that could imply a death sentence, but also the total or partial deprivation of rights by outlawry, banishment, or the reduction of civic status. "If any persons rise in insurrection in order to govern tyrannically," an archaic precept reads, "or if any person assists in establishing the tyranny, he himself and his progeny shall become *atimoi*."[30] Legislation of the fifth and fourth centuries BCE contains similar strictures for citizens judged guilty of subverting the democracy.[31] A law dated to 399 BCE stipulates that anyone undermining "the democracy at Athens, or holding any office when the democracy has been subverted," is to "be regarded as an enemy of the Athenians and may be killed with impunity"; "his property shall be confiscated and a tenth part of it devoted to the Goddess."[32] Similarly, a law from 337–336 BCE specifies that anyone who assists or belongs to the family of someone who assists in the overthrow of the *dēmos* and the establishment of a tyranny will be considered *atimos*; "his properties shall be confiscated, and a tenth given to the Goddess."[33] In the following centuries, *atimia* remained in force in Athens as a punishment in a narrower sense, constituting "a loss of civic rights, and served as a penalty for crimes other than high treason."[34] Other Greek cities took recourse to similar measures.[35]

Archaic Rome was also familiar with various means for the modification of civil status. Several institutions might deprive free Roman citizens of their customary rights and prerogatives, exposing them ineluctably to death. As a consequence of a crime such as murder or perjury, a citizen could be proclaimed *exsecratus*; without being put to death, he would be publicly cursed, excluded from the community, and remitted to the harshest of conditions.[36] Through the performance of the rite known as *sacratio*, a Roman citizen could also be declared a "sacred man" or *homo sacer*; he might then be killed by anyone without that act counting for the law as homicide or the execution of a sacrifice.[37] Such a "sacred man" might also be enslaved without acquiring the legal status of *servus*.[38] Individuals could also enact rites that would change their own status; in *devotio*, a citizen would thus vow to commit himself to the divinities of the underworld, giving up his life in combat. Roman tradition foresaw the possibility that he might nonetheless survive; in such cases, the *devotus* was to be excluded from public and private sacrifices.[39]

After these various practices of exclusion from the city, the jurists of the republican and imperial ages of Rome developed statutes of "lay sanction."[40] The first among them is the "forbidding of water and fire" *(aquae et ignis interdictio)*, a punishment imposed in various ways throughout Roman history. In the earlier period of the republic, it was issued in place of capital punishment when the accused was a Roman citizen; by the second century BCE, it became the standard punishment for all capital offenses. It entailed banishment, loss of property, and the withdrawal of citizenship.[41] Under the principate, its place was taken by the institution of *deportatio ad insulam*; decreed by the emperor or the *praefectus urbi*, this punishment remitted the condemned to an island, causing him to forfeit his rights and citizenship. The imperial age witnessed the institution of *servitus poenae*, by which a citizen was sentenced, for a variable duration, to forced-labor mining (*ad opus metalli*) or to hunting wild animals (*ad bestias*); in either case, his goods were confiscated, and he lost both freedom and civic rights.[42] It was established that those condemned to such "servitude" were diminished to the legal rank of slaves, although it remained a question whether they were best defined as belonging "to the emperor" (*servi Caesaris*) or as being "without master" (*sine domino*).[43]

From these various Roman institutions, the canon lawyers of the Middle Ages culled the elements of a new theory, which allowed them to sunder the legal *persona* from the individual body with unprecedented formal clarity. Brigitte Borgmann has shown how, on the basis of classical sources, the European jurists of the eleventh, twelfth, and thirteenth centuries progressively came to consider legal "death" (*mors*) as a genus admitting of two species.[44] The first among them is biological; in the medieval scholars' terms, it is "natural" (*naturalis*), being detectable by a study of the individual body. The second "death" is of another nature. As Pillius of Medicina explains toward the turn of the thirteenth century, this death constitutes a way of "ending a life otherwise" (*aliter vitam finire*). Marking the decease of the "person," rather than the body, it is a "civil death" (*mors civilis*). Pillius evokes two examples of such an event. He draws the first from the ancient institution of *deportatio*. The second involves a form of life absent from the Roman *Digest*: monastic existence. He reasons that men who join the brotherhood, like women who enter the nunnery, put an end to their civil status. To define the legal condition of the monk, the medieval jurists known today as "glossators" evoke a classical phrase employed for exiles, outlaws, and slaves: he is to be "viewed as dead" (*pro mortuo habetur*).[45]

Dissenting voices, however, soon made themselves heard. That the monk shares the status of the *servus* and *deportatus* was not always granted. One glossator remarks that with regard to a dowry or any pledge given upon signing a contract, entry into a monastery (*conversio*) is equivalent to civil death: it dissolves preexisting pacts and deeds, such that any pledges that may have been received must be returned to those who once gave them.[46] Another commentator raises the question of matrimony. The jurists accept that a *deportatus*, if married, retains his spouse, yet all hold that the monk does not. Conversely, the law stipulates that no *deportatus* may act as a witness, yet the monk may do so on condition that his superiors allow it.[47] Other questions arise. May the man who has entered a monastery certify a will? May he oversee the distribution of his erstwhile goods and properties? May he inherit or be disowned? What is certain is that although the *deportatus* and the monk each undergo a civil death, important legal differences between them must be granted. *Mors civilis* begins to ramify. Subspecies are soon identified. After an attentive study of the sources, Borgmann reaches a perplexing conclusion: "Deportation [*deportatio*] and monastic life [*vita monachalis*] can both be called 'civil death' [*mors civilis*], yet they share no special legal consequences."[48] Having distinguished legal from biological decease, the jurists have no choice but to take a further step: they concede that the kinds of civil death are many.

Later canon lawyers confront the complex problems that arise from the plurality of diminished legal subjects. There is the question of the *bannitus*, or "banished person," as defined by the civic authorities of the Middle Ages. Bartolus argues that despite apparent resemblances to classical *deportatio ad insulam*, the institution of *bannitio* possesses features of its own that make the "death" of the deported distinct from that of the exile.[49] There is also the problem of excommunication. Some treat this ecclesiastical institution as similar in effect to that of the ancient "forbidding of water and fire." Others define it as a kind of *bannitio* with respect to the community of the faithful.[50] With the emergence of mendicant orders, further difficulties arise. Francis bids his brethren to abandon all property, including that held in common; through adherence to his "rule of life," they are to dwell in "highest poverty."[51] That resolution raises new questions concerning the legal status of such monks. Bartolus proposes treating friars, legally speaking, as "disabled persons" (*incapaces*) while admitting that upon joining the order, they retain the ability to bequeath their possessions. He reasons that entry into the order has the effect of both "civil death" and "natural death," such that property is immediately transferred. Baldus, for his part, presents these deaths as the first goal of the pious life: in joining the brotherhood, the monk renounces not only worldly goods, but also the "person" that lays claim to rights. His is, in short, a voluntary incapacity: a self-induced legal diminishment.[52]

The institutions of civil death were to be widespread and long lasting. In England, according to a legal rule thought to have been incorporated into Saxon law at the time of the Norman Conquest, a man convicted of a capital crime and subject to a judgment of outlawry or death would be in the extraordinary condition known as "attainder." Blackstone explains: "He is then called attaint, *attinctus*, stained or blackened. He is no longer of any credit or reputation; he cannot be a witness in any court: neither is he capable of performing the functions of another man: for, by an anticipation of his punishment, he is already dead in law."[53] Two consequences follow from this declaration: forfeiture and corruption of blood. By virtue of the first of these penalties, all lands, tenements of inheritance, and chattel interests claimed by the "stained" subject of the law are transferred to the king, including any dowry that the accused may have received upon being married. By virtue of the second implication, an attained person can "neither inherit lands or other hereditaments from his ancestors, nor retain those he is already in possession of, nor transmit them by descent to any heir." All "escheat" to his lord, "subject to the king's superior right of forfeiture."[54]

In France, "diminishments of the head," infamy, and civil death remained stable points of orientation for the jurists and monarchs of the early modern age. Henry II thus justified the banishment of criminals to Corsica in an edict of 1556 in terms of *deportatio* and exile familiar to the Roman legal tradition, declaring that he had condemned "many malefactors and delinquent persons," some to "civil death, confined in a region of our realm," others to perpetual banishment from it.[55] Entry into the monastery and the taking of monastic vows, moreover, continued to be conceived as causes of "civil death."[56] In the seventeenth century, as Franz Weithase has shown, civil death becomes a full-fledged legal "state." "*Civil death*," Jean Domat explains in his *Civil Laws* of 1694, "is the name for the state of those whose goods are confiscated. For this reason, this state has been compared to natural death, for it severs those whom it befalls from society and civil life, rendering them as slaves to the punishment that is imposed on them."[57] Introducing the notion of *societas*, the jurist restates his perspective: "Civil death possesses the same effect with respect to society as natural death. For in being outside the state of acting, with his goods confiscated, a person is, with respect to society, as if he were dead."[58] Eighteenth-century scholars of criminal law echo these formulations while lingering on their consequences for citizenship. According to Pierre-François Muyart de Vouglans, "civil death is the absolute severing from society and from all the rights that are attached to the quality of citizen."[59] For Daniel Jousse, it is the variety of decease "that, without removing natural life, causes the loss of all the rights connected to the quality of citizen."[60]

In 1755, French jurist François Richir, signing as "Lawyer of the Parliament," publishes a compendious *Treatise of Civil Death, Both That Which Results from Condemnation on Account of Crime, and That Which Results from Vows in Religion.*[61] He introduces his work as treating one of "the most important subjects of our jurisprudence." "It is a matter of the respective links of society with its members," he explains, "and of its members with society."[62] He recalls that as "everyone admits," "man is born to live in society." He supposes that a distinction must be made between the law of peoples (*droit des gens*) and civil law (*droit civil*). Each is the source of a set of rights and therefore a particular variety of "life." Leaving one's homeland, a man takes on the status of a foreigner; he forsakes the civil rights from which foreigners are excluded, yet he retains his civil life. "However, when a man has committed some crime that causes society to cut him from its breast, the condemnation deprives him not only of his civil rights [*droits de cité*] but of his civil life [*vie civile*]." Such a man is "civilly dead, because he no longer participates in the rights of the French any more than if he were truly dead. Society regards those who are in this state as no longer being among the living: as those to whom it owes no succor, no assistance, and from whom it expects none whatsoever."[63]

Richir insists upon the artificiality of such a state. "Civil death is a fiction by which one regards someone who has undergone it as naturally dead, relative to civil law," when he is in fact alive. Recalling that all fiction strives to "imitate truth and take on its appearance, so that the fiction disappears," Richir argues that to be true to its nature, civil death must be irreversible: just as no one can be dead only for a while, those who are civilly dead ought to be so forever.[64]

Yet as in Rome, extreme legal diminishment seems to imply a position somehow greater than death, for the consequences of civil death as he defines them exceed those of natural decease. "A civilly dead man's goods are confiscated; his marriage is dissolved; his legitimate children are treated as bastards; he loses his aristocratic titles; he can have no heir, nor receive any inheritance. Infamous, he is deprived not only of the exercise, but even the enjoyment of the set of his civic and civil rights."[65] This follows from the extended definition that Richir proposes for this condition of legal inexistence:

> It is the absolute proscription of a citizen; it is his severance from civil society; it is a member ripped away from it; it is the state of a man on whose forehead a public infamy has been printed; it is the state of a citizen with whom all commerce, all pledges, all promises are forbidden; it is the state of a man who has been cut from the catalog of the living; finally, it is the state of a man that society has acknowledged never to know as such, viewing him as already belonging among the class of the dead, and who has been reduced to having neither fatherland nor family.[66]

The thinkers of the Enlightenment did not all grant the validity of such rules. Evoking the penal practice of banishment and confiscation in his 1764 treatise *On Crimes and Punishments*, Cesare Beccaria observed that such judgments sever "all the ties between society and a malefactor" without, however, exacting the loss of the malefactor's natural life: "In such a case, the citizen dies and the man remains, and as far as the body politic is concerned, this should have the same effect as natural death." Beccaria forcefully contested the justice of such measures, not because of their juridical "subtlety," as he specified, but because of their gratuitousness, as well as the toll they exacted on the families of the condemned: "What more afflicting sight could there be than that of a family which is brought into disgrace [*infamia*] and destitution by the crimes of its head, when their legally decreed submission to him prevented them from averting his crimes, even if there had been a way of doing so!"[67]

It might be assumed that with the 1789 Declaration of the Rights of Man and of the Citizen, whose first article declares men to be born and to remain "free and equal in rights," such a legal condition would no longer have been admissible in France. The Penal Code of September 1791 did, in fact, remove civil death from French law.[68] Within a few years, however, the institution was reinstated. The Terror had begun, and in March 1793, the Convention passed a decree declaring all émigrés "forever banished and *civilly dead*," their possessions belonging henceforth to the French Republic. Any infraction of the rule of banishment would now be punishable by physical death. "Reintroducing into revolutionary law the most terrible legal fiction of the Old Regime . . . which had hitherto never been applied on such a scale and with such rigor," Anne Simonin writes, "the Terror produces a variety of dead men that the overattention to the death penalty and the guillotine has shrouded in darkness."[69] The novelty of this revolutionary death was not lost on those who lived to suffer it. One émigré, Trophime Gérard de Lally-Tollendal, noted in 1797 that the decree "makes us dead while we are alive, to take our possessions, and it makes us live after our death, to take the possessions of our relatives."[70] Such a new afterlife could also uncannily double the old. The Marquis de Sade, who was imprisoned for almost a year between 1793 and 1794 and who did not leave Paris during the Revolution, learned in 1797 that his name was on a list of "émigrés from the Vaucluse." Despite his best efforts to disprove the accusation, he was therefore judged civilly dead. Some twenty years earlier, in 1777–1778, the Old Regime had already declared him so. By 1814, the year of his physical decease, he had been twice dead to the law.[71]

From the medieval institution of civil death, modern French law drew the elements for a series of new diminishments of the person. Under the Old Regime, civil death functioned as an "auxiliary punishment to permanent banishment from the realm."[72] Under the Terror, it became a crucial instrument in the disenfranchisement of various political opponents, being applied to émigré aristocrats, officers, soldiers, and deported priests.[73] The Civil Code of 1804 proposed a new distribution of punishments. Traitors were stripped of their rights through the loss of nationality, while civil death would be reserved for those who lost their rights through criminal convictions. The force of the legal institution only grew. "As an affirmation of what law could withhold," Miranda Spieler writes,

> civil death at the turn of the nineteenth century dissolved more than it ever had. The new form of civil death nullified the marriage bond and the bond between children and a civilly dead parent. In the final version of the Civil Code, civil death rendered the wife of a civilly dead man a type of widow; children born before civil death took effect were orphans, while those born afterward were bastards. In contrast, during the Old Regime, marriage was a sacred bond recognized by the state that the state's laws could not cancel.[74]

In the course of the nineteenth century, French jurists would further develop categories for such diminishment. The Criminal Code of 1810 established a temporary state of "legal interdiction" (*interdiction légale*) for those sentenced to punishment by forced labor, as well as a permanent "civic degradation" (*dégradation civique*), which applied to felons, barring them from public employment or functions, forbidding them from sitting on juries, testifying, or acting as guardians or trustees, including when the wards were their own children.[75] By 1832, Anne Simonin argues, "civic degradation" constituted a new sanction: "civic death."[76]

That the permanent reduction of the person was a possibility at odds with the principles of modern legal theory was a point not lost on the jurists of the nineteenth century. In his 1824 *Reflections on the Penal Law of France and England*, Alphonse-Honoré Taillandier dubbed civil death "a barbaric fiction" entailing "the most deplorable" of consequences.[77] In 1831, he became the advocate for its abolition. Many shared his position, and in June 1854, his cause prevailed: civil death in France was declared "abolished."[78] The conditions and effects of this event, however, were less univocal than might appear. Some critics of the institution were in fact opponents solely of its most recent form. Antoine-Marie Demante argued for the removal of the legal fiction from the code of law because it entailed the nullification of past marriage bonds, "whose indissolubility is an article of faith for the Christian conscience."[79] In other words, he would have been "content with civil death in its Old Regime form."[80] Historians have shown that the abolition of 1854 was also followed by the qualification of a civil status so close in effects to civil death as to raise the question of what had been withdrawn from the code. "Legal interdiction" took on many of the properties of "civil death,"[81] while judgments of "civic degradation" became increasingly widespread. "With the abolition of civil death in 1854," Simonin observes, "the number of 'civic deaths' rises, with the addition of all those condemned to perpetual afflictive punishments, civic degradation, and legal interdiction taking the place of civil death. For 1855 alone, 2500 supplementary *civic deaths* can thus be recorded."[82]

The jurisprudence of civil death was never restricted to Europe. In the United States, it also played a role in law, with consequences still discernible today. After the War of Independence from England, the founders were explicit in their rejection of much of the inherited legal tradition. English "attainder" was an institution that they expressly set aside. "The Congress shall have Power to declare the Punishment of Treason," the Constitution stipulates, "but no Attainder of Treason shall work Corruption of Blood or Forfeiture except during the Life of the Person attainted."[83] Civil death, however, was not formally prohibited, and numerous states passed special civil death statutes. As late as 1939, eighteen states contained such provisions.[84] The laws of civil death in the United States justified neither seizing the property of the condemned nor blocking the transmission of his possessions, yet they allowed a living convict's properties to be passed to his heirs, according to the old fiction, as if he were dead, while he was in fact alive. In the United States, Kim Scheppele writes, "the convict was held to be dead for *only some purposes* in the law, and so civil death did not bring with it all the consequences of natural death."[85] A civilly dead offender could not vote, hold office, serve on juries, bear arms, or inherit. Yet his legal person was far from inexistent. Although he did not possess the right to bring an action, he might be sued; although he could not collect a debt, his own possessions might be seized by creditors.[86] While unable to enjoy the full rights of citizens, the civilly dead of the United States were, in each case, subjects of the law. In classical legal terminology, they remained persons of "decreased heads."

By the end of the nineteenth century, the institution of civil death had become the object of acute criticism, and within half a century, many civil death statutes in the United States were either "repealed or wholly or partially voided."[87] Yet legal scholars have argued that in the United States, a number of the penal consequences that followed from civil death have nonetheless persisted. Today, conviction for a crime or a misdemeanor may still reduce the legal person. In many jurisdictions, "when an offender is sent to prison for the commission of a crime," as Howard Itzkowitz and Lauren Oldak write, "his punishment does not end with his release," for "the ex-convict who has completed his prison term is subject to a variety of civil disabilities that remain in force for the rest of his life."[88] The most striking among such "civil disabilities" concerns what is often viewed as the democratic right par excellence: suffrage. It was estimated in 2004 that as many as four million adult citizens of the United States had been indefinitely barred from voting because of a criminal conviction, regardless of whether they had been or were still incarcerated.[89] United States law also lessens its subjects' rights in further ways. Following conviction, a noncitizen may be deported; criminal registration and community notification may be obligatory; an individual may be judged ineligible to work, reside, or be present in a certain location; and such a person may be subject to occupational debarment or deemed ineligible to initiate or hold family relations.[90] "Collateral consequences" of conviction involve "the actual or potential loss of civil rights, parental rights, public benefits, and employment opportunities." In Gabriel L. Chin's terms, such deprivations constitute "a new civil death."[91]

It would be rash to suppose that this novelty will be the last. As long as it is granted that civil status constitutes a quantity susceptible to diminution, further reductions may still be invented. They will remain the declinations of a single case: that by which the law, in its theory and its practice, fashions nonpersons. Here, too, nonpersons are not the contraries of legal persons, if by "contrary" one means a being opposed to another in such a manner that when one affirms one of these two beings, the other must be absolutely denied, and conversely. From the Roman slave to the types of civilly dead in the Middle Ages, from the condemned traitor of common law to the convicted offender in the United States who never regains the full rights of citizenship, even after a punishment has been executed, legal nonpersons remain persons; they never cease to be the subjects of the legal code that degrades them. The "non" of "nonperson," for this reason, denotes no "exception," if one takes that word in its etymological sense, as pointing to an item "taken out" of some field of reference. Just as ancient slaves constituted a crucial part of the cities in which they were stripped of any right to family, belongings, and citizenship, civilly diminished persons are the inhabitants of modern states. They are the diverse, yet recurrent witnesses of the possibility that speaking beings may judge themselves—and therefore others—to be unworthy of the uncertain names they give themselves. Conceived as being of decreased heads or as headless, as things, as dead, or as somehow dead and alive at once, the monstrous "kinds of people" imagined and identified in the city illustrate the principle of its constant governance. They wear the masks of an infinitely variable lessness.

CHAPTER SEVEN

Of Ignominies

When Captain Lemuel Gulliver awakens on the morning of one November 6, he is far from his native England. Summer is beginning. The day before, his ship, the *Antelope*, was wrecked upon a rock. His companions were killed or scattered, and he was left to drift on the open waters, "pushed forward by Wind and Tide," as he informs the reader, until, letting his "Legs drop," he could "feel Bottom." He walked a great stretch toward dry land. Advancing farther, "near half a Mile," he failed to discover "any Sign of Houses or Inhabitants."[1] "Extremely tired" and "much inclined to sleep," he lay down "on the Grass, which was very short and soft."[2] Daylight brought with it the experience of an unexpected immobility: "I attempted to rise," he recalls, "but was not able to stir: For as I happened to lie on my Back, I found my Arms and Legs were strongly fastened on each Side to the Ground; and my Hair, which was long and thick, tied down in the same Manner."[3] Soon his senses, active while disjoined from each other, give him some idea of his situation. Perceiving a "confused Noise," without being able to see anything "except the Sky," Gulliver feels "something alive moving on my Leg, which advancing gently forward over my Breast, came almost up to my Chin."[4] It is "a human Creature not six Inches high, with a Bow and Arrow in his Hands, and a Quiver at his Back": the first of the great number of inhabitants of the Empire of Lilliput, where Gulliver will remain captive for some time. To these "human Creatures," the voyager is not so much a foreigner as a marvel of nature, an individual at the edges of conceivable humanity, to be denoted not by any ordinary person's name, but rather as *Quinbus Flestrin*: "the *Great Man Mountain*."[5]

In the next part of his 1726 *Voyages into Several Remote Nations of the World*, the intrepid traveler finds himself in a landscape no less remarkable. After the destruction of the *Adventure*, he washes up on the shores of an unknown land in the vicinity of North America. He will learn that it is Brobdingnag. Glimpsing an "Inhabitant" who "appeared as Tall as an ordinary Spire-steeple; and took about ten Yards at every Stride," Gulliver is "struck with the utmost Fear and Astonishment." He runs to conceal himself "in the Corn, from whence," he writes,

> I saw him at the Top of the Stile, looking back into the next Field on the right Hand; and heard him call in a Voice many Degrees louder than a speaking Trumpet; but the Noise was so High in the Air, that at first I thought it was Thunder. Whereupon seven Monsters like himself came towards him with Reaping-Hooks in their Hands, each Hook about the largeness of six Scythes.[6]

Scale is again askew. "Undoubtedly," the narrator sagely comments, "Philosophers are in the Right when they tell us, that nothing is great or little otherwise than by Comparison."[7] Protagoras, in particular, might have offered the educated traveler a principle by which to measure the constancy of his discoveries: in Lilliput, as in Brobdingnag, "man is the measure of all things." Yet Gulliver and his reader must confront a difficulty that the Greek thinker seems not to have had a need to pose: Which is the man and which the nonman, which the "the human Creature" and which the "Monster"—the traveler or the extraordinary "Inhabitant" he encounters? As Hugh Kenner writes, "Swift's great irony amounts to this, that whereas Gulliver fancies himself the accidental emissary of the human race to parts unknown, and hence the perpetual observer and recorder, it is Gulliver himself for the most part who is constantly under observation."[8] And to the reasonable people he encounters, the upstanding Englishman seems to be, voyage after voyage, undeniably inhuman. In his subjection to the emperor of Lilliput, to his inimical counterpart in Blefuscu, and to the king of Brobdingnag, the man from Nottinghamshire continues to suffer, as he himself recalls, "the Ignominy of being carried about for a Monster."[9]

Each of the narrator's words is well weighed. As several critics have observed, "monster" is to be understood in the etymological senses of the Latin *monstrum*: from land to land, Gulliver appears as a "Sight," a "marvel," as well as "freak," who must "act a Part" for the delight of a curious and fascinated public.[10] The term "ignominy" is less often considered in itself, but it is at least as telling. Today, the expression seems largely synonymous with "disgrace," "indignity," and "infamy." An author of the eighteenth century would have also been familiar with the more restricted sense that it possessed in the language from which it derives. According to its construction, which consists of a privative prefix *in-* (or *ig-*) attached to the noun *nomen*, Latin *ignominia* suggests, more precisely, the condition of being deprived of a proper name—or being denied any name not undiminished by some formal process of degradation.[11]

The technical use of the term in this sense dates to the Roman republican age. During the ceremony known as the "census," the names of all citizens would be recorded on tablets, arranged so as to display the property, "moral character, age, *familia*, and physical characteristics" of free persons.[12] When a censor judged a particular individual to be of reprehensible habits and behavior, he would set a "mark of reprobation" beside his name: a "note" or sign of censure (*nota censoria*). This annotation was the original brand and instrument of *ignominia*. Hence the definition of the word that Nonius Marcellus, a late antique grammarian, proposes of it: "*Ignominy* is the note of the name" (*ignominia est nominis nota*).[13] "To understand what could be meant by a punishment bearing on an individual's name," Georges Pieri explains, "one must keep in mind the religious and magical importance of the *nomen* among the Ancients, for whom it represented the personality of its bearer." In Rome, naming played a crucial role in public rituals. As evidence, one may evoke *devotio publica*, in which those judged guilty of inexpiable crimes would be named before suffering a "consecration of the head" (*consecratio capitis*), and *sacratio*, in which *mala nominare*, "naming badly," referred to the official act by which a man was declared killable without being capable of being sacrificed.[14] Just as "infamy" (*infamia*), in Rome, was a "bad fame" (*mala fama*), "ignominy" was, in short, a "bad name" (*malum nomen*). While the first was an oral sanction, the second was written, being both official and administrative in kind.[15]

Ancient society was hardly the only one in which the public status of a human being could be lessened by the marking—if not the staining—of a proper name. An early classic of the literature of the United States draws its central and enigmatic matter from the institution of what seems, without doubt, a Puritan "censor's note": Hawthorne's 1850 novel, *The Scarlet Letter.* Hester Prynne, a woman of Salem, New England, is introduced to the reader as the wife of a man who, having long gone missing, is unknown to the people of her adoptive town. Giving birth to an infant whose father she will not name, Hester is sentenced to an "ordeal": day after day, she must stand on "a sort of scaffold at the western extremity of the market-place," meeting the opprobrium of "the public gaze."[16] "The very ideal of ignominy was embodied and made manifest in this contrivance of wood and iron," the narrator comments. "There can be no outrage, methinks, against our common nature,—whatever be the delinquencies of the individual,—no outrage more flagrant than to forbid the culprit to hide his face for shame; as it was the essence of this punishment to do."[17] Yet Hester Prynne must do more than appear, with her child, on the scaffold. She must also exhibit a *nota censoria* that spells out her guilt. It is an "ignominious letter,"[18] the first of the alphabet: "The letter A, in scarlet, fantastically embroidered with gold thread, upon her bosom."[19]

In Hawthorne's novel, a woman's textile thus takes the place of the Roman republican tablets. The function of writing, however, is unchanged. The letter shames. Evoking the punishment that the city authorities have imposed on Hester Prynne, the narrator calls to mind the classical Roman sanction of the name repeatedly, almost obsessively, insisting on its classical public function. The embroidered *A* is a "red ignominy,"[20] "an open ignominy,"[21] or "public ignominy,"[22] an "ignominious brand."[23] The letter makes of its bearer a living "statue of ignominy,"[24] condemned to suffer "the terrible ordeal of her ignominy":[25] an "ignominious exposure"[26] in the "magic circle of ignominy"[27] to "the world's ignominious stare."[28]

Hawthorne's characters appear to share the narrator's fascination with the diminishment of her good name. "Thus will she be a living sermon against sin," a stranger comments, observing the woman, "until the ignominious letter be engraved upon her tombstone."[29] Hester Prynne's own reputation is of course the first object of the note's power. But the embroidered sign does more than "brand" her identity. It also disguises another: that of Arthur Dimmesdale, Puritan minister and Hester Prynne's erstwhile lover, who declares himself, in the novel's final act, to be marked by a censorious note of his own, "his own red stigma," as he avows, which is "no more than the type" of the writing that has seared his "inmost heart."[30] Dimmesdale makes his final confession on the scaffold, "to die," as he exclaims in expiring, "this death of triumphant ignominy before the people."[31]

In the "Conclusion" that serves as an epilogue to the action of the novel, Hawthorne's narrator turns to the scene of a different writing. After inscriptions made on fabric and on flesh, a lapidary epitaph retains his attention. It is the writing borne on the monumental tombstone that the "two sleepers" share in death:

> On this simple slab of slate — as the curious investigator may still discern, and perplex himself with the purport — there appeared the semblance of an engraved escutcheon. It bore a device, a herald's wording of which might serve for a motto's brief description of our now concluded legend; so sombre is it, and relieved only by one ever-glowing point of light gloomier than the shadow: — "*On a field, sable, the letter A, gules.*"[32]

Here the American novel takes a step beyond the old sanctions of ignominy. The Roman censor's measures held solely for living persons judged to have trespassed against "good morals" (*boni mores*).[33]

In antiquity, strictures of a different nature might be applied to the dead, whom later authorities might view as having acted—by weakness, vice, or treachery—to harm the common good. "Memory sanctions" against past officials and sovereigns could dictate that certain names be partially or completely removed from monuments and public inscriptions. A "condemnation of memory" (*damnatio memoriae*), to use the familiar, if anachronistic term, would then be enacted.[34] In the conclusion to Hawthorne's novel, however, life and death partake of a single stain. Confounding the distinction between the sanctions against the present and the departed, the "herald's wording" testifies to a past breach in *mores*, even as it conserves the note of its censure. A present sign of a past infraction, it is at once memorial and likeness, the recollection and the reconstitution of dishonor.

The twentieth century discovered and invented still more disquieting ignominies. A first case may bring into focus a new development in the treatment of personhood. In George Orwell's 1949 novel *Nineteen Eighty-Four*, Winston Smith is a clerk in the Ministry of Truth whose profession is to rewrite published articles in accordance with the dictates of a dystopian regime. Among the directives he receives from Big Brother are missives concerning persons branded by a variety of infamy that, more clearly than any other, renders the old distinction between life and death irrelevant. In the jargon of Newspeak, persons stained by this status become "*unpersons*." When the word first appears in the novel, it is glossed in "Oldspeak (or standard English)" as "non-existent persons."[35] The translation runs the risk of attenuating the sense of the expression, for the nonbeing of such persons is neither natural nor given; the "non-existent" personhood in this case is instituted, pertaining to individuals known to have been real. Sometimes such persons even are—or were—of considerable acclaim. "A certain Comrade Withers, a prominent member of the Inner Party, had been singled out for special mention and awarded a decoration, the Order of Conspicuous Merit, Second Class," the reader learns, before being "disgraced" for reasons not made known. In unrolling one of the official messages sent to him from the pneumatic tube, Winston learns that Withers has been branded an "unperson." Immediately, he deduces that Withers must be dead. Yet he also infers more. Withers must have been "abolished." Winston concludes: "He did not exist: he had never existed."[36] Notaries will proceed to rewrite historical records accordingly. In the world of this novel, the opposition between "being a person" and "not being a person" is therefore far from exhaustive. There also exists a third condition for the person. It is the state of an infamous existence (or inexistence) in which a variety of "personality" persists while being ruined, to become the object of a constant, censorious suppression.

The ignominy proper to such political "unpersons" is doubtless a rare phenomenon, even in the conditions of Orwell's fiction of a once future society. Practices that bring about a deprivation of the name, however, can be both real and quotidian. Orwell studied them, as well. In his 1946 essay "How the Poor Die," he recalls the weeks that he spent in a Paris hospital in 1921. He was suffering from pneumonia. His clothes having been taken from him upon entering the hospital, he was given a linen nightshirt and a flannel dressing gown and led to "a long, rather low, ill-lit room, full of murmuring voices and with three rows of beds surprisingly close together." "As I lay down," he recalls,

> I saw on a bed nearly opposite me a small, round-shouldered, sandy-haired man sitting half naked while a doctor and a student performed some strange operation on him. First the doctor produced from his black bag a dozen small glasses like wine glasses, then the student burned a match inside each glass to exhaust the air, then glass was popped on to the man's back or chest and the vacuum drew up a huge yellow blister. Only after some moments did I realise what they were doing to him. It was something called cupping, a treatment which you can read about in old medical text-books but which till then I had vaguely thought of as one of those things they do to horses.[37]

Before he had finished pondering the "barbarous remedy," Orwell found himself its subsequent beneficiary: "The next moment, however, the doctor and the student came across to my bed, hoisted me upright and without a word began applying the same set of glasses, which had not been sterilised in any way. A few feeble protests that I uttered got no more response than if I had been an animal."[38]

It was a charity hospital, and as Orwell explains, "as a non-paying patient, in the uniform nightshirt, you were primarily *a specimen*."[39] Numbers, rather than names, were the terms employed to denote patients.

> About a dozen beds away from me was *numéro 57*—I think that was his number—a cirrhosis of the liver. Everyone knew him by sight because he was sometimes the subject of a medical lecture. On two afternoons a week, the tall, grave doctor would lecture in the ward to a party of students, and on more than one occasion old *numéro 57* was wheeled in on a sort of trolley into the middle of the ward, where the doctor would roll back his nightshirt, dilate with his fingers a huge flabby protuberance on the man's belly—the diseased liver, I suppose—and explain solemnly that this was a disease attributable to alcoholism, commoner in the wine-drinking countries. As usual he neither spoke to his patient nor gave him a smile, a nod or any kind of recognition. While he talked, very grave and upright, he would hold the wasted body beneath his two hands, sometimes giving it a gentle roll to and fro, in just the attitude of a woman handling a rolling-pin. Not that *numéro 57* minded this kind of thing. Obviously he was an old hospital inmate, a regular exhibit at lectures, his liver long since marked down for a bottle in some pathological museum. Utterly uninterested in what was said about him, he would lie with his colorless eyes gazing at nothing, while the doctor showed him off like a piece of antique china.[40]

To be "shown off" in such a manner is to become the object of a peculiar treatment whose exercise is far from restricted to medical establishments. In many circumstances, present persons are treated as if they had no name or as if they were, like "animals," "specimens," or "antique china," unworthy of being directly addressed. Erving Goffman was perhaps the first scholar to discuss and define these comportments, drawing evidence from both literature—including George Orwell's essays and fiction—and his own observations.[41] In his 1953 doctoral dissertation, "Communication Conduct in an Island Community," Goffman proposed a "study of conversational interaction" based on fieldwork that he conducted between 1949 and 1951 on the Isle of Unst in the Shetlands.[42] "Kinds of exclusion from participation" play a major role in this early work.

Goffman bases this work on the principle that social interaction always occurs within a certain enclosure whose boundaries may be established in several ways. Two people may "stop to talk to each other on an otherwise deserted road or in an otherwise deserted empty room," in which case the enclosure will be "physically closed." When persons are more numerous, as in a large hall or pub, they can "separate off into more than one cluster or grouping, with each cluster maintaining a separate and distinct interplay."[43] Where social enclosures cannot be so tidily delimited, behavior can establish those who partake of an interplay, being, in Goffman's terms, "accredited as participants," and those who, by contrast, remain external to it while being nonetheless in its vicinity.[44] In seating arrangements in cafeterias, those who "involuntarily find themselves in range of an interplay convey (by appropriate undirected cues) that they are paying no attention to the message which they are in a position to overhear." "Accredited participants," in turn, "sometimes return the courtesy by censoring their own messages for words that might provide too much temptation for the outsider or that might cause him offense should he happen to fail to keep his attention withdrawn." In Goffman's terminology, enclosure is in such cases not physical, but "effective." With such modest symbolic means as a rope, a blackboard, the edge of a table or a stage, or without any material means at all, enclosures will still be respected. Although it may be "very difficult to arrange and maintain when the accredited participants enclose among them, ecologically speaking, a person who is not an accredited participant," effective closure may still allow the accredited participants of an interplay to "act as if they were not being overheard" while in the presence of strangers who can perceive their discourse.[45]

After evoking the physical and effective boundaries beyond which a person can be barred from participating in a social interplay, Goffman enjoins his reader to consider a third possibility of exclusion. A person can be treated, in his words, "as a non-person": "That is, as someone for whom no consideration need be taken."[46] Goffman draws his first illustration of this state from Orwell's "How the Poor Die."[47] Yet he acknowledges that examples may be culled from many social settings. Sometimes such behavior "constitutes an extremely brutal sanction," as in "the silent treatment," in which "a person is excluded from consideration as a means by which others present can consciously and concertedly convey their dislike of him."[48] Sometimes, however, a person may be more simply excluded from consideration "in an automatic, unthinking way because of his low ceremonial status."[49]

> Domestic servants and waitresses, in certain circumstances, are treated as not present and act, ritually speaking, as if they were not present. The young and, increasingly, the very old may be discussed "to their faces" in the tone we would ordinarily use for a person only if he were not present. Mental patients are often given similar non-person treatment. Finally, there is an increasing number of technical personnel who are given this status (and take the non-person alignment) at formally organized interplays. Here we refer to stenographers, cameramen, reporters, plainclothes guards, and technicians of all kinds.[50]

Nonpersons are far from being an exception in society, and after introducing them in his dissertation, Goffman detected their shadows in many situations. In his 1956 monograph *The Presentation of Self in Everyday Life*, he sets out to analyze social practices in dramaturgical terms, considering the ways in which "the individual in ordinary work situations presents himself and his activity to others, the ways in which he guides and controls the impression they form of him, and the kinds of things he may and may not do while sustaining his performance before them."[51] After a treatment of "performances," "teams," and "regions and region behavior," he turns to "discrepant roles," by which someone participates in "the actual interaction between the performer and audience" without belonging fully to either "team." Examples include the informer, the shill, the spotter, and the go-between.[52] Nonpersons also belong to this set. "Those who play this role are present during the interaction but do not, in a sense, take note either of performer or of audience, nor do they (as do informers, shills, and spotters) pretend to be what they are not."[53] Goffman evokes the servant as the "classic type of non-person in our society," adding: "This person is expected to be present in the front region while the host is presenting a performance of hospitality to the guests of the establishment."[54] Yet he also notes that "the very young, the very old, and the sick" are "common examples" of this "role." As if by a principle of nonpersonal contagion, those who interact with such people may also be treated as if they were not there:

> Thus, on the island studied by the writer, when the British Public School doctor attended patients in the homes of poor crofters, the residents sometimes handled the difficulty of relating themselves to the doctor by treating him, as best they could, as if he were not present. . . . In such situations, the important show is to show the outcast that he is being ignored, and the activity that is carried on in order to demonstrate this may itself be of secondary importance.[55]

In his 1963 book *Behavior in Public Places: Notes on the Social Organization of Gatherings*, Goffman places the nonperson role in a different theoretical frame. He divides the study of "situational proprieties" into "two analytical parts": "Unfocused interaction, concerned with what can be communicated between persons merely by virtue of their presence together in the same social situation," and "focused interaction, concerned with clusters of individuals who extend one another a special communication license and sustain a special type of mutual activity that can exclude others who are present in the situation."[56] In situations in which two persons are "mutually present" without being "involved together in conversation or other focused interaction," one of them may transgress the rules of ordinary civil interaction by staring, "gleaning what he can . . . while frankly expressing on his face his response to what he sees." Goffman gives the example of "the 'hate stare' that a Southern white sometimes gratuitously gives to Negroes walking past him."[57] Yet it is also possible for someone to show every sign that despite the presence of another person, he considers himself alone: "It is possible by his staring or his 'not seeing,' to alter his own appearance hardly at all in consequence of the others. Here we have the 'nonperson' treatment; it may be seen in our society in the way we sometimes treat children, servants, Negroes, and mental patients."[58]

Goffman contrasts such negatively qualified comportments with the behavior that he calls "civil inattention," which defines social relations in ordinary situations. In polite interaction, "what seems to be involved is that one gives another enough visual notice to demonstrate that one appreciates that the other is present (and that one admits openly to having seen him), while at the next moment withdrawing one's attention from him so as to express that he does not constitute a target of special curiosity or design."[59] One person's gaze of another will be considered "civil," in this sense, if it is not a stare, a studied "not seeing," or a full recognition. Properly polite nonconsideration requires no less. When the courtesy is "performed between two persons passing on the street, civil inattention may take the special form of eying the other up to approximately eight feet, during which time sides of the street are apportioned by gesture, and then casting the eyes down as the other passes—a kind of dimming of lights." It is "perhaps the slightest of impersonal rituals, yet one that constantly regulates the social intercourse of persons in our society."[60]

That most minimal of "impersonal rituals" merits attention, if only because of the discomfiting resemblances that it bears to the treatment that it is to oppose. Goffman himself contrasts the respect shown in "civil inattention" with the "brutal sanction" effected by "the 'non-person' treatment." Yet as Andrew Travers has argued, the two behaviors are difficult—if not impossible—to distinguish.[61] Goffman's own account of the two attitudes raises the problem of their distinction. To offer "hardly" any recognition to other persons, as the rules of propriety demand, one must do more than to omit all acknowledgment; one must positively demonstrate, by means of a discernible gesture, that one is not looking at them. Yet this show of nonrelation is precisely what defines the "'non-person' treatment." Moreover, in characterizing the ordinary attitude taken toward certain persons, one might in many cases evoke either behavior: the cultivated indifference commonly shown professional assistants, cameramen, and technicians could be understood as expressing a relation to nonpersons, as Goffman suggests, or as a courtesy to strangers with whom conversation has not begun. The least one may conclude is that the typology of the forms of "focused interaction" may stand in need of revision. More troubling is the possibility that a virtual relation to the nonperson lies concealed in civility itself. For if propriety demands a variety of inattention that is indistinguishable from the attitude shown to the outcast, then even in the most courteous of relations, the threat of a censorious social branding may not be far removed. A slight modification in behavior could suffice for someone to be excluded from polite relations — or, inversely, for a presumed outcast to be given the treatment accorded to respected others.

Without further developing the concept of the nonperson in his later writings, Goffman continued to explore the ways in which "participants" in social interactions could be qualified as accredited and discredited.[62] In his last works, he proposed a far-reaching analysis of what he calls "forms of talk," which reflect the various roles that persons adopt in differently framed social situations. Responding to the influential theory of "speech acts" advanced by J. L. Austin, Goffman argued that the notions of "speaker" and "hearer" familiar to the philosophy of language are too crude to account with precision for "how to do things with words" and too "gross" to allow for a comprehensive analysis of the "conversational encounter."[63] As James D. McCawley noted, building on Goffman's studies, the notions of "speaker" and "hearer" "conflate several quite different roles that are in most cases played by the same person but which can be dissociated from one another quite easily."[64] Depending on the circumstance, the "speaker" of a given speech may be its author, the one who delivers it, or the one committed by its words. Similarly, a "hearer" can be someone to whom discourse is exclusively addressed, someone whose possible perception has been taken into account, or someone whom the "speaker" did not mean to address or even meant pointedly not to address. Nothing would be more misleading than to suppose that by a law of its form, language passes from persons speaking in their own names to persons whom they address or that, inversely, those who understand what has been uttered must also be the "ratified recipients" and intended addressees of direct discourse. Speech also follows other circuits, relayed by persons as diverse as copyists, imposters, and eavesdroppers and in such uncertain forms as indirect questions and commands, insults, exclamations and "response cries," jokes, and innuendo.[65] Just as some persons express themselves without being "accredited" as speakers, others glean what has been uttered without having been addressed by name.

Captain Gulliver knew this all too well, not from theory, but from experience. The last message that he received — and the most painful — reached him in a "form of talk" reserved for those to whom ratified participants would not stoop to speak. He himself was again the nonperson, a lesser someone in an unusual social interplay. After traveling to the empire of the Lilliputians and making, as he recalls, "a great Progress in Learning their Language,"[66] after discovering the land of Brobdingnag and acquiring the rudiments of its tongue from the nine-year-old daughter of his host, a "School-Mistress," "very good natured, and not above forty Foot high, being little for her Age,"[67] and after his subsequent instruction in the various idioms of Laputa, Balnibarbi, Luggnagg, Glubbdubdrib, and Japan, Gulliver, once more alone and utterly forsaken, reaches unknown shores after the wreck of a second *Adventure.* He discovers a terrain divided "by long Rows of Trees, not regularly planted, but naturally growing," with "great Plenty of Grass, and several Fields of Oats."[68] Gulliver arrives in the country of the Houyhnhnms.

It is the least familiar of the territories described at length in his *Voyages*, being, without a doubt, also the most unsettling. Upon arriving, Gulliver beholds "several Animals in a Field, and one or two of the same Kind sitting in Trees." "Their Shape was very singular, and deformed, which a little decomposed me," he recounts,

> so that I lay down behind a Thicket to observe them better. Some of them coming forward near the Place where I lay, gave me an Opportunity of distinctly marking their Form. Their Heads and Breasts were covered with a thick Hair, some frizzled and others lank; they had Beards like Goats, and a Long Ridge of Hair down their Backs, and the fore Parts of their Legs and Feet; but the rest of their Bodies were bare, so that I might see their Skins, which were of a brown Buff Colour. They had no Tails, nor any Hair at all on their Buttocks, except about the *Anus*; which, I presume Nature had placed there to defend them as they sat on the Ground; for this Posture they used, as well as lying down, and often stood on their hind Feet.[69]

Gulliver will learn that they are known, in the language of this country, as "Yahoos." "Upon the whole," he remarks, "I never beheld in all my Travels so disagreeable an Animal, or against which I naturally conceived so strong an Antipathy."[70] Lest the point be lost on his reader, he repeats himself: "I never saw any sensitive Being so detestable on all accounts; and the more I came near them, the more hateful they grew, while I stayed in that Country.[71] Yet in time, Gulliver comes to grant a truth more intolerable even than the ugliness of these "Monsters": they are, by any morphological criteria, indistinguishable from himself.[72] In the properties of "this abominable Animal," he will, to his horror, discover "a perfect human Figure."[73]

Enlightenment comes to Gulliver through the teaching of intelligent equines: "Houyhnhnms," as they name themselves, employing the noun that, in their language, "signifies a *Horse*; and in its Etymology, *the Perfection of Nature*."[74] They are the rational animals of this country and the only ones of such a kind that either they or the impressionable and all too educable voyager will recognize.[75] "Endowed by Nature with a general Disposition to all Virtues," free of any "Conceptions or

Ideas of what is evil in a rational Creature," the Houyhnhnms live by a single "grand Maxim": "To cultivate *Reason*, and be wholly governed by it."[76] Gulliver quickly takes to them. He considers himself blessed to have been accorded a modest place in the household belonging to the horse whom he calls "my Master." "I had not been a Year in this Country," he writes, "before I contracted such a Love and Veneration for the Inhabitants, that I entered on a firm Resolution never to return to human Kind, but to pass the rest of my Life among these admirable *Houyhnhnms* in the Contemplation and Practice of every Virtue; where I could have no Example or Incitement to Vice."[77] Dwelling in a room "made after their Manner, about six Yards from the House," its "Sides and Floors" plastered with clay, and covered with mats made from hemp, Gulliver takes delight in admiring the "Manners and Virtues of this excellent People" while enjoying "perfect Health of Body, and Tranquillity of Mind," living in serenity without "the Treachery and Inconstancy of a Friend, or the Injuries of a secret or open Enemy."[78]

Day after day, he devotes himself by studied means to mastering the Houyhnhnm tongue: "I pointed to everything and enquired the Name of it, which I wrote down in my *Journal Book* when I was alone, and corrected my bad Accent, by desiring those of the Family to pronounce it often."[79] The Houyhnhnms' is a language similar in certain respects to those that Gulliver has learned, but it also possesses distinctions of its own. It lacks any lexical means "to express Lying or Falsehood," if not by such a cumbersome periphrasis as "*the Thing which is not*."[80] It is without any word

> to express any thing that is *evil*, except what they borrow from the Deformities or ill Qualities of the *Yahoos*. Thus they denote the Folly of a Servant, an Omission of a Child, a Stone that cuts their Feet, a Continuance of foul or unseasonable Weather, and the like, by adding to each the Epithet of *Yahoo*. For Instance, *Hhnm Yahoo, Whnaholm Yahoo, Ynlmndwihlma Yahoo*, and an ill contrived House *Ynholmhnmrohlnw Yahoo*.[81]

In terms of articulation, the Houyhnhnm tongue is "pronounced," Gulliver takes pains to note, solely "through the Nose and Throat," in a manner "most nearly" approaching "the *High Dutch* or *German*," while being "much more graceful and significant."[82]

Gulliver himself is a marvel in Houyhnhnmland on account of his unlikely faculties. Not without a certain pride, he informs the reader that "Several Horses and Mares of Quality in the Neighbourhood came often to our House, upon the Report spread of a wonderful *Yahoo*, that could speak like a *Houyhnhnm*, and seemed in his Words and Actions to discover some Glimmerings of Reason."[83] Yet these "Glimmerings" are ultimately the cause of Gulliver's exile from his newfound home. He recalls this scene: "In the Midst of all this Happiness, when I looked upon my self to be fully settled for Life, my Master sent for me one Morning a little earlier than his usual Hour. I observed by his Countenance that he was in some Perplexity, and at a Loss how to begin what he had to speak."[84] At last Gulliver surmises what his master hesitates to recount. At the recent Houyhnhnm "general Assembly," "the Representatives had taken Offence at his keeping of a *Yahoo* (meaning my self) in his Family more like a *Houyhnhnm* than a Brute Animal," not only because of the unnatural quality of such a practice, but also because it is feared that, having "some Rudiments of Reason, added to the natural Pravity of those animals," Gulliver might draw creatures like himself "into the woody and mountainous Parts of the Country, and bring them in Troops by Night to destroy the *Houyhnhnms* Cattle, as being naturally of the ravenous Kind, and averse from Labour."[85] A decision has therefore been reached: Gulliver must henceforth be "employed" as a common Yahoo, dominated as a beast of the field, or "swim back," in his words, "to the Place from whence I came."[86]

The equine counselors have not imparted this judgment directly to him. The highest Houyhnhnms will not address him by name — for several reasons. It would seem, first, that they do not know it, being unfamiliar with proper names.[87] Yet by any accepted equine standard of civility, Gulliver is also unfit to be accorded the privilege of address. At the very best, he is "a wonderful *Yahoo*, that could speak like a *Houyhnhnm*," without, of course, being one himself.

Upon learning that he is to be cast forth from his adoptive horse-land, Gulliver suffers a momentary loss of his rational capacities: "I was struck with the utmost Grief and Despair at my Master's Discourse," he recalls, "and being unable to support the Agonies I was under, I fell into a Swoon at his Feet."[88] Regaining his senses, he concedes the "solid Reasons" on which "all the Determinations of the wise *Houyhnhnms* were founded," adding that his hosts were in any case hardly of such a kind as "to be shaken by Arguments of mine, a miserable *Yahoo*."[89] Given two months to build a boat with the help of some of his master's servants, Gulliver constructs "a sort of *Indian* Canoo, but much larger," which he covers, as he writes, "with the Skins of *Yahoos*, well stitched together, with hempen Threads of my own making."[90] Taking leave of his master, he is shown a treatment he dared not expect: "As I was going to prostrate myself to kiss his Hoof, he did me the Honour to raise it gently to my Mouth." Here Gulliver pauses and offers this commentary to his reader:

> I am not ignorant how much I have been censured for mentioning this last Particular. Detractors are pleased to think it improbable, that so illustrious a Person should descend to give so great a Mark of Distinction to a Creature so inferior as I. Neither have I forgot, how apt some Travellers are to boast of extraordinary Favours they have received. But if these Censurers were better acquainted with the noble and courteous Disposition of the *Houyhnhnms*, they would soon change their opinion.[91]

Only the humblest member of the household, the Sorrel Nag, "servant" and "valet" of the master, erstwhile mentor of the surprisingly loquacious "Creature," deigns to bid him farewell. As he leaves the shore, Gulliver hears this mournful call: "*Hnuy illa nyha maiah Yahoo*, Take Care of thy self, gentle *Yahoo*."[92]

The subsequent and final pages of these *Travels* are the most terrible of all. His "Canoo" having been retrieved by amiable Portuguese seamen, Gulliver is brought to Lisbon; from there he sails to England. Long missing, he returns to his "House at *Redriff*." "My Wife and Family received me with great Surprize and Joy," he recounts, "because they concluded me certainly dead; but I must freely confess, the Sight of them filled me only with Hatred, Disgust, and Contempt; all the more, by reflecting on the near Alliance I had with them."[93] He is an Odysseus revolted by forced repatriation in Ithaca who will take back neither Penelope nor Telemachus. Without ever mentioning the proper names of his spouse or progeny, he remarks: "When I began to consider, that by copulating with one of the *Yahoo*-Species, I had become a Parent of more; it struck me with the utmost Shame, Confusion and Horror."[94] Having survived his life as a "wonderful *Yahoo*," at best a nobody in a country of talking horses and monstrous hominids, Gulliver's own ignominy is past. Another, however, now begins:

> At the Time I am writing, it is five Years since my last Return to *England*: During the first Year I could not endure my Wife or Children in my Presence, the very Smell of them was intolerable; much less could I suffer them to eat in the same Room. To this Hour they dare not presume to touch my Bread, or drink out of the same Cup; neither was I ever able to let one of them take me by the Hand.[95]

To the once reasonable English voyager, every human being is henceforth untouchable. Civility and kinship alike are stained. Beside the common name of man, a mark has been inscribed, and it is indelible. For the mature Captain Gulliver, humanity is "*Yahoo*-Kind," to which he will not be "reconciled."[96]

CHAPTER EIGHT

Fictions of Persistence

In archaic Greece, as in ancient India, glory is the work of poets. They sing the words and deeds of heroes, granting them an "imperishable fame": *kleos aphthiton, śrávas ákṣitam.*[1] It is a glory that sounds in proper names, for without them, even the noblest of great actions is forgotten. Some names, however, survive those who bear them in ingloriousness, rather than in glory. From the Homeric poems, one might evoke as examples Thersites, the most ignoble of the Achaeans, and Elpenor, remembered mainly for having fallen to death, after drinking, from the roof of Circe's dwelling.[2] Beyond the sphere of the epic alone, one might also cite such variously infamous individuals as Medea, Clytemnestra, Sextus Tarquinius, and Nero, who commit and suffer ignoble violence. They have a share in infamy and fame. The legendary persons of the vernacular poetry of the Middle Ages testify to a persistent ignominy in a different sense. Although they are far from being villains, the valor to which they lay claim is profoundly troubled. The poets who record their adventures linger on the gravity of their failures no less than on their remarkable accomplishments.

Chrétien de Troyes, in the twelfth century, is in this respect an innovator. In bequeathing the names of Arthur's knights to the European tradition, he founds a line of heroes remembered for their poor judgment, foolishness, and misfortune. When Perceval, a boy reared in ignorance of all things, not least his name, unexpectedly finds himself in the presence of the grail, he misunderstands a lesson he believes himself to have to learned, missing his chance to save the Fisher King. Belatedly, he realizes his error and at the same time discovers his own name: he is "Perceval the Wretched" (*Percevax li cheitis*).[3] Lancelot gains a different infamy. Searching to retrieve his abducted queen, he demeans himself, madly hoping that his self-abasement will bring him closer to his beloved Guinevere: thus he enters a "cart" reserved for the most heinous of offenders, exchanging his hitherto illustrious name and reputation for the title of "the Knight of the Cart." Omniscient and exacting, the queen will later reproach him not for having humiliated himself by stepping into the conveyance of criminals, but for having hesitated "for two steps."[4] *Yvain* presents a case of failure that is in a certain sense more extreme. Here, the all too amiable "Knight of the Lion" promises to return to his beloved lady by a certain date, only to miss it. The romance gives no reason for his mistake. When the knight grasps that he has forgotten the crucial day, he goes mad, removing himself from all human company. He is perhaps the first major figure of European letters to live "as an insane and savage man" in the woods, mute and unclothed.[5]

Each of these cases is unique, yet all involve individuals whose names, in poetry, persist in evoking a nobility in ignominy. There are also others. From the twelfth century to the fifteenth, authors evoked the adventures of a knight and poet who lived out the long aftermath of a terrible mistake. During the voyage back from Ireland to Britain, Tristan and Yseut, King Mark's future bride, unwittingly drink a love potion brewed for the royal pair. What follows is an illicit passion that defies family and feudal structure, binding the queen to her husband's nephew and vassal. Compelled to betray his king, Tristan becomes a master of deception. He is observed, accused, and outlawed. Some versions of the narrative material present scenes in which, after banishment from the court, Tristan lives in the wilderness, alone with his lady or in solitude. Others present him as a fool or a madman returning to court, disguised or transformed, to draw close to the queen.[6] Occasionally, medieval poets observed that however diverse his extraordinary adventures may appear, they are in each case the consequences of a destiny sealed in his name. It was explained that if Tristan's tale is one of misery, it is because, as the Latin adage held, *nomen omen*. The hero's name contains with it the French word "sad" (*triste*). Recounting the conditions of Tristan's baptism at the start of his adaptation, Gottfried of Strasbourg's narrator remarks: "The name accorded with the life" (*der name / dem lebene was gehellesame*).[7]

In the same period, the authors of Old Norse literature craft a body of prose that recalls the fates of people remarkable for the exclusion they endure. The so-called "outlaw sagas" imagine the lives of the condemned, banished, and persecuted, showing how evil can become the condition of a fame won in infamy. The ancient legal code of Iceland foresees that as punishment for crimes, individuals may be deprived of their rights and denied participation in ordinary relations. "Heads," in Roman terms, can in such circumstances be legitimately "decreased."

In Iceland, as in antiquity, the reduction of persons is scalar, admitting of degrees. The social and legal institution known as "outlawry" (*útlegð*) is of several kinds.[8] *Grágás*, a twelfth-century legal code, thus distinguishes "lesser outlawry" (*fjörbaugsgarðr*), a sanction entailing exile for three years, from "full outlawry" or "going into the forest" (*skóggangr*): permanent banishment from the country. Once submitted to such a judgment, a man is considered "outside the bounds of society," or, in one modern scholar's terms, "a nonperson."[9] Such a human being is called by the Old Norse legal term *vargr*, which is cognate with Latin *wargus*, German *warg*, and Old English *wearg*, and which carries the combined meanings of "wolf," "criminal," and "thief." In the Germanic codes, such an outcast would be known as a "man without peace" (*Friedloser*). The law demanded that he be pursued by all, "driven from society and hanged."[10]

Icelandic literature draws some of its most memorable inventions from these institutions of exclusion. The *Saga of Gisli*, most likely composed in the first half of the thirteenth century, follows Gisli Sursson from the unhappy consequences of his unthinking defense of family honor to the time when, in hiding from his foes and absent from the assembly, he is outlawed. A life of constant movement follows. Without the right to a residence, Gisli must disguise himself by ever-changing ruses until his enemies find him and kill him with impunity. The *Saga of Hord*, most likely from the beginning of the fifteenth century, leads from Hord's birth to his passage to Norway, his return to Iceland, his outlawing, and the circumstances of his violent death. The fourteenth-century *Saga of Grettir the Strong*, perhaps the most fully conceived of the "outlaw sagas," tracks one man through the various stages of civil diminution, which it projects over the variegated territory of medieval Iceland. Grettir Asmundson is born, reaches maturity, and distinguishes himself by great strength and poor judgment. He fails to respond wisely to misfortune and is condemned to lesser outlawry before being declared a full outlaw and beginning his long flight. Excluded from any regular community, he survives by plundering farms in the West Fjords, settling temporarily in central Iceland, taking up residence in a cave, and joining the company of a giant and his three daughters in a glacier. In the end, he reaches the island of Drangey, beyond Iceland's northern shores. There he lives out his days before meeting an unnatural end.[11]

Despite their obvious diversity, these medieval European evocations of outcasts partake of a single literary structure. They are for the most part narratives recounted in the third person in which an outlaw appears in the discourse of another author. Classical Arabic letters, by contrast, is familiar with a means to summon the lives of the excluded in a way at once starker and more direct: in the oldest stratum of Arabic poetry, the ignominious speak for themselves. They are the "bandit poets" or "robber poets" (*ṣaʿālīk*) of the pre-Islamic age. Al-Shanfarā, Ta'abbaṭṭa Sharran, ʿUrwa ibn al-Ward: these names were to be renowned in the Arabic tradition long after it was forgotten exactly why their bearers had once been outlawed. Like their illustrious contemporaries, the authors of the seven famous "Hanging Poems" (*Muʿallaqāt*) said to have been suspended on the Ka'aba in Mecca, the Arabic bandit poets are known above all as makers of "odes" in the extended and rhymed meters of ancient Arabia. That these poets were poor is suggested by the term *ṣaʿālīk*, an expression employed to denote men so indigent as to be able to survive solely by raiding the livestock of neighboring tribes. The sources suggest that the *ṣaʿālīk* may have violated the accepted conventions for plunder. It was tacitly granted that when poverty demanded it, nomads might make incursions into the encampments of others, seizing goods and livestock. Yet such attacks were perilous: a lack of skill or bad luck could result in inadvertent acts of violence, such as the killing of a herdsman.[12] This would entail dire consequences. For such a deed, a man could be disowned by his tribe and forced to live alone, subject to an outlawing and banishment (*khalʿ*) without end.

The odes of the bandit poets are monuments to their ignominious exclusion. Since the Middle Ages, the classical Arabic ode (*qaṣīda*) has been analyzed as being regularly composed of three parts: a *naṣīb*, evoking the poet's beloved; a *rahīl*, summoning the hardships of the poet's desert journeys; and a *fakhr*, lauding the author and his tribe. The outcast authors defy this classical pattern in many ways. Renouncing the praise of the tribe with which the classical odes often conclude, the *ṣaʿālīk* focus instead on their forced solitude and the means by which they sustain it. They praise their own speed, determination, and self-sufficiency. In the most famous of the bandit odes, al-Shanfarā's so-called *Lamiyya*, or "Poem Rhyming in L," the outcast "sings of his sovereign isolation from all others."[13] A nonman among men, he casts himself as a "lean grey wolf," his movements perceptible only to the watchdogs guarding the encampments by which he passes.[14] His true "people," he avows, are desert beasts: the "swift wolf," "the smooth-coated leopard," "the long-haired jackal."[15] "With them, entrusted secrets are not told; / Thieves are not shunned, whatever they may dare."[16] He has nothing to share with other human beings. According to the rhetoric of these lines, those who hear the poet's words are therefore implicitly removed, with him, from any human community. They listen to a wanderer who speaks to no one.

In its structure, the address that sustains the bandit's ode is not merely archaic. It is also modern. Long after the medieval period, individuals of diminished civil personhood would again demand complicity from their imagined readers. The appeals to special forms of communication between excluded authors and those to whom they write would be too numerous to enumerate. Yet none may be as radical in its form and as vertiginous in its consequences as that claimed by a uniquely unfortunate character who long haunted European and American letters. The glory of this man, such as it was, lay in his lack of luck and good judgment — a lack reflected, so to speak, in the aspect of ordinary personhood that he was missing. In *The Marvellous History of Peter Schlemihl*, which he first published in German in 1814, the Franco-German author Adelbert von Chamisso introduced his readership to a narrator excluded from human society for the most extraordinary of reasons. His "Peter Schlemihl" had lost his shadow — or rather, he sold it, for reasons for which he himself was in part to blame.

Chamisso has his character recount the circumstances of his deprivation in his own voice. Yet his Peter Schlemihl insistently addresses himself to one reader: Adelbert von Chamisso, who was thus himself drawn into the tale of loss to which he attached his name. Before the beginning of Schlemihl's recollections, Chamisso sends a letter of his own, dated September 27, 1813, to one Julius Eduard Hitzig. Here, Chamisso introduces Schlemihl as an individual with whom he and his correspondent were once personally acquainted: "You, who forget no one, must surely remember one Peter Schlemihl, whom you used to meet occasionally at my house — a long-legged youth, who was considered stupid and lazy, on account of his awkward and careless air. I was sincerely attached to him. You cannot have forgotten him, Eduard."[17] Chamisso goes on to explain to Hitzig that he is writing to transmit "pages" that are not of his own drafting, recently delivered to him by an unidentified person: an "extraordinary-looking man, with a long grey beard, wearing an old black frockcoat, with a botanical case hanging at his side, and slippers over his boots."[18] Amid those sheets, Chamisso has found the *History* that he divulges.

By a conceit dear to Romantic writers, the apparent author thus presents himself as an editor, the work itself having been ostensibly composed by its hapless narrator, Peter Schlemihl. "After a felicitous, but to me very wearisome, voyage," the *History* soon begins, "we came at last into port. Immediately on landing I got together my few effects; and, squeezing myself through the crowd, went into the nearest and humblest inn that first met my gaze."[19] The discourse of the novella remains in this first person's voice. That the narrative is destined for one reader is soon apparent. At the start of his second chapter, Schlemihl breaks off his tale to offer commentary. An address interrupts the action: "Imagine, my friend, what I then began to do? O my dear Chamisso! Even to you I blush to mention what follows."[20] Yet Chamisso is not only addressed in the "pages" he claims to have received; he also appears in them as a figure imagined by the man of his own invention. Only a few lines after the apostrophe to "my dear Chamisso," Schlemihl makes a confession to his author:

> I dreamed of you. It seemed to me that I was standing behind the glass door of your little room, and saw you seated at your table, between a skeleton and a bunch of dried plants. Before you lay open the works of Haller, Humboldt, and Linnaeus; on your sofa lay a volume of Goethe, and *The Enchanted Ring*. I stood a long time contemplating you and everything in your apartment. Then, turning my gaze upon you, I perceived that you were motionless. You did not breathe. You were dead.[21]

Chamisso appears in his book through the lens of a "double duplication," the authorial image being discernible in the image of the man that is the corpse.[22]

When the "marvels" of Peter Schlemihl's adventures begin, the unlucky man is, as his first lines suggest, only arriving. The reader never learns whence he came. All that is certain is that from the start, he is an outsider.[23] Schlemihl carries a letter of recommendation to one Mr. Thomas John, to whose elegant party he hastens. His affluent host, largely indifferent to the contents of the letter, receives him, in Schlemihl's recollection, "very well—just as a rich man welcomes a poor devil."[24] In such company, Schlemihl keeps to himself, striving not to show that he does not belong. He soon steals away, only to be overtaken by the most mysterious member of Mr. John's gathering: a "Grey Man," who makes him an unusual proposition. "'During the short time in which I have had the pleasure to be in your company," the Grey Man begins, "I have—permit me, sir, to say—beheld with unspeakable admiration your most beautiful shadow, and remarked the air of noble indifference with which you, at the same time, turn from the glorious picture at your feet, as if disdaining to vouchsafe a glance at it. Excuse the boldness of my proposal, but perhaps you would have no objection to sell me your shadow?'"[25]

From this point, the plot of the novella moves swiftly. After a moment's hesitation, Schlemihl agrees to exchange his shadow for "Fortunatus's purse," which the Grey Man offers him: a pouch from which infinite amounts of gold can be drawn. Remitting the magic object to Schlemihl's hands, the Grey Man kneels down on the ground. Schlemihl recalls this scene: "I beheld him, with extraordinary dexterity, gently loosen my shadow from the grass, lift it up, fold it together, and at last put it in his pocket. He then rose, bowed once more to me, and directed his steps towards the rose-bushes."[26] Schlemihl is now rich. Excitedly, he hastens to his room and, extracting a heap of gold pieces from his new purse, falls asleep. He promptly dreams of Chamisso, dead at his desk. That vision announces a future decidedly less bright than the one that Schlemihl had foreseen. He learns that he must, as best he can, avoid venturing out by daylight. At such times, his characteristic lack is too clearly discernible.

When strangers do not confront him directly, informing him, in astonishment, that he seems to have no shadow, they comment on the fact among themselves, treating him as an outsider, although they remain, in effect, within his range of hearing: "I heard a couple of women exclaiming, 'Jesu Maria!'" Schlemihl recalls, "'The poor man has no shadow.'"[27] Now he has the means to court a young lady whom he saw from afar at Mr. John's lavish party, but he knows he must take precautions. At an evening gathering of his own arrangement, he proposes that "the lovely Fanny" join him on a walk, only to suffer the most deplorable of surprises. When the moon suddenly emerges from behind a cloud, his companion perceives "only her own shadow": "She started, looked at me with terror, and then again on the ground in search of my shadow."[28] "I should have burst into a loud fit of laughter," Peter recalls, "had I not suddenly felt my blood run cold within me." Fanny falls from his arm in a fainting fit, and Schlemihl, acutely aware of the misfortune of his situation, rushes off "with the rapidity of an arrow," leaving the stricken maiden among the "astonished guests."

He flees, crosses "frontiers and mountains," and reaches a new town, where he catches sight of a second maiden, as virtuous as she is beautiful. He falls in love. Mistaking his extraordinary wealth for the certain sign of nobility, the townspeople believe Schlemihl to be the king of Prussia. When corrected, they still refuse to concede that he is an ordinary man. Grudgingly, the foreigner admits to being recognized as "Count Peter." He courts his beloved maiden, Minna, proposing marriage. She reveals her devotion to him. Schlemihl is moved and confesses himself to her:

> I declared to her that I was not what I seemed — that I was a rich man, but an unspeakably miserable one — that a curse was on me, which must remain a secret, although the only one between us — yet that I was not without a hope of its being removed — that this poisoned every hour of my life — that I should plunge her with me into the abyss — she, the light and joy, the very soul of my existence.[29]

Before long, Schlemihl is exposed again. He has been careful not to leave his palace during daytime and, after his unhappy evening stroll, he has studiously avoided moonlight. Eventually, however, rumors overtake his house. A servant confronts him: "Count Peter," one, named Rascal, asks him, "may I beg most respectfully that you will favour me with a sight of your shadow? The sun is now shining brightly in the court below."[30] Distraught, Schlemihl tries to quell his servant's doubts by giving him more gold. Rascal, unperturbed, insults him: "'From a shadowless man,' he said, 'I will accept nothing'" (*von einem Schattenlosen, nehm ich nichts an*).[31] He denounces his lacunar master. In the presence of a weeping Minna, the would-be father-in-law calls off the betrothal. "The world," Schlemihl concludes, "seemed shut out to me forever."[32]

That the absence of a shadow makes Schlemihl an outcast is all too evident. What exactly Chamisso's poor "rich man" is missing, however, is another matter. In an influential essay published in 1911, Thomas Mann wrote that "the shadow has become in *Peter Schlemihl* the symbol of all bourgeois solidity and human belonging."[33] The missing shade has also been interpreted otherwise: "As a symbol representing outward honour, the fatherland, national identity, the social persona, the world of appearances, the integrity of the personality, solidarity with the human community."[34] Searching to assign a meaning to Schlemiehl's condition, scholars have turned to folklore, in which shadows have been known to shrink and vanish and the motif of the absent double of the man signals a range of troubling consequences, from incipient social contamination to imminent and real stigma, illness, and death.[35] Yet any account of the shadow as a "symbol," by its structure, runs a critical risk: that of covering over the blankness of which Schlemihl has agreed to be deprived. As has also at times been observed, the shadow in the *Marvellous History* is unreadable: a "deferred signifier,"[36] an "empty site"[37] in the construction of the narrative, a "placeholder for the absence of another sign."[38] It resists interpretation, even as it seems to demand it.

Chamisso himself provides a gloss on the missing shadow that is both scientific and ludic. In the preface that he adds to the 1837 French edition of his novella, he recalls how, his book having fallen "into the hands of thoughtful people, accustomed to read solely for their own instruction," he was repeatedly asked "what the shadow was." Chamisso admits that the question made him "blush with ignorance." He therefore undertook some "learned research," of which he imparts the fruits. He sets before the reader two extracts from the Abbé Haüy's *Elementary Treatise of Physics*:

> An opaque body can only ever be lit in part by a luminous body; and the area that is deprived of light, which is situated on the unlit part, is what we call the shadow. Strictly speaking, the shadow thus represents a solid, whose form depends at once on the forms of the luminous body, the opaque body, and the position of the latter with regard to the former.
>
> Seen on a surface, behind the opaque body that produces it, the shadow is nothing but a section of the surface in the solid that represents the shadow.[39]

Chamisso does not linger on these theses, which are far from pellucid in themselves. As Michael Lommel notes, they are "not only pedantic but also tautological," in that they explain one shadow by another, deriving the shadow figure on a surface from the shadow area between two bodies.[40] A further uncertainty in the two propositions concerns the question of what is a "body" and what a "representation": while the first thesis holds that "strictly speaking, the shadow . . . represents a solid," the second refers to the "the solid that represents the shadow."

In the French preface, Chamisso himself draws a lapidary conclusion from this primer in modern physics: "What is in question in *The Marvellous History of Peter Schlemihl* is therefore this solid." He explains: "The art of finance teaches us enough about the importance of money; that of the shadow is less generally recognized. My imprudent friend coveted money, whose price he knew; he did not think of the solid." Hence the "lesson" that Schlemihl so "dearly paid," from which Chamisso enjoins his readers to reap profit: "Think of the solid! (*Songez au solide!*)"[41] Yet the truth is that "the solid" evoked in this passage is equivocal, as readers since Hitzig have observed. "The solid" may be understood in strictly physical terms, as a "bodily space" (*ein körperlicher Raum*) or, instead, as "something real" (*etwas Wirkliches*) in a spiritual sense.[42] Few natural phenomena illustrate this ambiguity more distinctly than the shadow. Schlemihl's error, in this sense, is both subtler and more serious than it might seem.

Omitting to "think of the solid," he fails to grasp that the meaning of "solidity" itself is anything but firm.

In his gravely "imprudent" eloquence, Peter Schlemihl remained long audible, and he and his mobile shadow reappeared beyond the limits of Chamisso's *History*. In E.T.A. Hoffmann's 1815 "A New Year's Eve Adventure," the reader meets one Erasmus Spikher, who suffers the almost unprecedented misfortune of being deprived of his own reflection:

> Erasmus, trembling, looked into the mirror, completely dejected. It remained blank and clear; no other Erasmus Spikher looked back at him. "It is just as well that the mirror does not reflect you," said his wife, "for you look very foolish, Erasmus. You must recognize that if you do not have a reflection, you will be laughed at, and you cannot be a proper father for a family; your wife and children cannot respect you."[43]

Cast out from his home at the end of this "Tale of the Lost Reflection," Spikher has no choice but to go "into the wide world." There he briefly believes himself to have found a companion. "He struck up with a certain Peter Schlemihl, who had sold his shadow; they planned to travel together, so that Erasmus Spikher could provide the necessary shadow and Peter Schlemihl could reflect properly in a mirror. But nothing came of it."[44]

After the literary survival of Schlemihl, the ruined human being with no shadow, there came the posthumous movements of his bodiless shadow, which was itself no human being. The narrator of Hawthorne's "A Virtuoso Collection," published in 1842, relates how upon entering a "new museum" on the "sunny sidewalk of our principal thoroughfare," he came to see the most extraordinary of legendary objects: the skin of the wolf that devoured Little Red Riding Hood, beside that of the far more clement beast that nursed Romulus and Remus; the white dove that brought "the message of peace and hope to the tempest-beaten passengers of the ark," now stuffed; Aladdin's lamp; "the original fire which Prometheus stole from Heaven"; the philosopher's stone. All appear to be the property of the Virtuoso, who exhibits them in his "Collection." Having "completed the circuit of the spacious hall," "feeling somewhat wearied with the survey of so many novelties and antiquities," the narrator sits down to rest. Against the opposite wall, he catches sight of a mobile figure: "the shadow of a man, flickering unsteadily across the wainscot, and looking as if it were stirred by some breath of air that found its way through the door or windows. No substantial figure was visible, from which this shadow might be thrown; nor, had there been such, was there any sunshine that would have caused it to darken upon the wall."[45] After having been put away in the Grey Man's pocket, the shadow has somehow reached a museum on a Massachusetts thoroughfare. "'It is Peter Schlemihl's Shadow,' observed the Virtuoso, 'and one of the most valuable articles in my collection.'"[46]

There was also a third possibility. After Chamisso's *History*, the shadow, separated from the body to which it once belonged, was heard to speak for itself. Nietzsche developed this possibility in a dialog at the end of *Human, All Too Human*, where the Wanderer finds himself solicited by a being too intimate to identify:

> *The Shadow*: As it is so long since I heard your voice, I would like to give you an opportunity of speaking.
>
> *The Wanderer*: Someone said something:—Where? And who? It almost seems as though it were I myself speaking, though in an even weaker voice than mine.[47]

In Pirandello's *Mattia Pascal*, the twice dead yet living man receives a less satisfying response from the surface against which he directs his ire. It remains mute. Mattia recounts how, viewing himself as "forever shut out from life, without the possibility of going back into it," he fears "falling into the bonds of life." He feels "alone, alone, absolutely alone, diffident, and shadowy."[48] On a solitary walk, he looks out on the street. "My eyes settled on the shadow of my body, and I remained staring at it for a while. Finally, I angrily put a foot on it. But I couldn't do it; I couldn't step on it, not on my shadow!"

He is no longer certain of the difference between the two bodies. He has lost, in Chamisso's terms, a proper sense for "the solid." "Which of the two of us was more a shadow? It or I? Two shadows! There, on the ground — anyone could walk over it. Crush my head, crush my heart — and I would stay silent. The shadow would stay silent."[49]

The most original aspects of *The Marvellous History of Peter Schlemihl* were more seldom echoed, being less easily perceptible. The plot of the novella has often been treated as a "variant" of Goethe's *Faust*, which was published six years before it.[50] Peter Schlemihl, however, is no ambitious doctor, and the nameless "Grey Man" hardly Mephistopheles. The distance between the works is perhaps clearest in the aftermath of Schlemiehl's fateful transaction with the Grey Man. A year after relinquishing his shadow to his obsequious acquaintance, Schlemihl again meets the Grey Man and begs him to release him from the contract. The Grey Man refuses. Instead, he proposes a second transaction: Schlemihl may have his shadow back if he agrees to sign a deed forswearing his soul. To persuade Schlemihl of the care with which he preserves the objects of his purchases, the Grey Man displays his earlier acquisition. "He drew my shadow out of his pocket," the narrator relates, "and shaking it cleverly out of its folds, he stretched it out at his feet in the sun — so that he stood between obedient shadows, his own and mine, which was compelled to follow and comply with his every movement."[51] Schlemihl recalls his despair: "On again beholding my poor shadow after so long a separation, and seeing it degraded to so vile a bondage at the very time that I was so unspeakably in want of it, my heart was ready to burst, and I wept bitterly."[52] Yet he does not negotiate. When, later in the narrative, the Grey Man again offers him the chance to sign away his soul, Schlemihl does more than merely to decline. Throwing the "jingling purse into the abyss," he conjures the perfidious salesman, "in the name of God," never again to appear before his eyes.[53]

It is the beginning of the most wondrous chapters in the *Marvellous History*. Lacking a shadow, Schlemihl remains an outcast. Without his magic pouch, he is also penniless. He is, in short, unredeemed, yet he has also refused to condemn himself. Avoiding the opposition between salvation and damnation, Schlemihl can only err, like a forgetful medieval knight or young Rossmann in the land of missing persons. Chamisso lends an unexpected shape to the wanderings of his "imprudent friend." Soon barefoot after wearing out his old shoes, Schlemihl visits a market fair, where he acquires a second-hand pair of boots. They seem to him "pretty good and strong," yet his first steps in them are intensely disorientating: they bring him in quick succession to a forest, a frozen landscape, rice fields, steppes, deserts, and China.[54] Schlemihl quickly grasps that there is but one explanation to be drawn: "I had now no doubt that I had seven-league boots on my feet."[55] "Shut out from all human society," the shadowless man thus comes to find a new calling. "The earth was granted me as a rich garden; and the knowledge of her operations was to be the study of and object of my life." Schlemihl becomes a natural philosopher. Like Chamisso himself, who spent years as an itinerant botanist and whose name would, in time, be tied in Latin to several species of Amaranthoideae, the unlucky adventurer devotes himself to the study of the earth.[56] The solution to his life of solitude is science as a vocation.

Yet even after his wondrous acquisition at the market fair, Schlemihl remains ill-fated, and his *History* continues to be that of his insistently recurrent accidents. To avoid moving at excessive speeds when he wishes to advance slowly and with caution, the botanist adopts an ingenious, albeit indecorous expedient: over his boots, he pulls a pair of slippers, which he calls his "restraining shoes" (*Hemmschuhen*). They are the same coverings that a bewildered Chamisso observed on the "extraordinary-looking man, with a long grey beard, wearing an old black frockcoat, with a botanical case hanging at his side," who brought him his strange "pages." The subtleties of such footwear, however, prove too much for Schlemihl. "One day, as I was gathering lichens and algae on the northern coast," he recalls, "a bear suddenly made his appearance, and was stealing towards me round the corner of a rock." Schlemihl quickly conceives a plan: he must remove his slippers and "step across to an island, by means of a rock, projecting from the waves in the intermediate space, that served as a stepping stone." But he bungles the act. With "one foot," he remarks, "I reached the rock safely but instantly fell into the sea with the other, one of my slippers having inadvertently remained on."[57] Schlemihl almost freezes to death, yet he reaches the shore and hastens to "the Libyan sands," where he rests in the sun. From there, he hurries "from east to west, and from west to east," before suffering fever, delirium, and a further mishap: an accidental treading, as he dimly recalls, on "someone's foot." He receives an angry blow and loses consciousness.

Schlemihl comes to in a place both fantastic and all too real: "I found myself lying comfortably in a good bed, which, with many other beds, stood in a spacious and handsome apartment. Someone was sitting next to me; people seemed to be walking from one bed to another; they came beside me and spoke of me as *Number Twelve*."[58] He has passed from one type of nonpersonhood, in Goffmanian terms, to another. Long an outcast, he has become a "specimen," to employ Orwell's word. More simply and in more modern parlance, Peter is now a patient. Yet this is no ordinary hospital. On a black marble plaque set on the wall at the foot of his bed, he reads two familiar words, which are inscribed in gold letters: "PETER SCHLEMIHL." He has found his way to the "Schlemihlium": an establishment run by his faithful former servant, Bendel, and his former fiancée, Minna, now dedicated to the memory of the man who was not to be her husband. Every day, the two philanthropists exhort the ailing lesser persons to whom they tend "to pray for Peter Schlemihl, as the founder and benefactor of this institution."[59] "Number Twelve," in the meantime, remains unidentified, even as he regains his health. The hero is so far from being noticed for who he is that in a final twist of the plot, he is taken to be an outsider of a kind hitherto unmentioned in this *History*. In perplexity, the narrator remarks in passing upon these circumstances: "From my long beard, I was supposed a Jew, but was not the less carefully nursed on that account. No one seemed to perceive that I was destitute of a shadow."[60]

The narrator's erstwhile name, in all its ingloriousness, has now been scattered. Everyone treated in this place of numbered persons is by antonomasia "a schlemihl." Yet as the teller of the tale well knows, the logical uses of such a predicate and the homophonous proper name are scarcely compatible; where each person is one member of the species, there can be no place for Peter Schlemihl himself, the one and only individual. When his name virtually becomes a common noun, the hapless hero thus suffers an ulterior lessening, his "head" diminished by a further degree. Long shadowless, he becomes nameless.

The two developments may well be linked, although the nature of their relation is far from evident. Is the name the double of the shadow? Or might the shadow, rather, be the echo of the proper name? Pierre Péju has remarked that if the Grey Man no longer appears in the final chapters of the novella, it is because "the rapid movement 'over the five continents' has made of Peter a kind of inoffensive equivalent of the Evil One, according to a tendency that had always been present in him." At this point, Schlemihl traverses the planet almost imperceptibly, and "the problem of the shadow cannot be posed when one has become transparent."[61] Now Schlemihl has no reason to reacquire the shadow he once sold. Being himself effectively a shade, he no longer lacks one.

Perhaps it is for this reason that by the end of the novella, this most distinguishedly undistinguished of modern literary men begins to retreat from view. Only his aged dog, Figaro, distant relative of Odysseus's Argos, still recognizes him. In the closing pages of his *History*, Schlemihl is almost no one. Alive, but undetected, not yet damned, but nonetheless unsaved, the shadowless scholar tends in solitude to his papers and his coming research trips. He hopefully announces the imminent completion of a Latin *History of the World's Stems and Plants*, an "extensive fragment" of his *Universal Flora of the Earth* and a substantial part of his future *System of Nature*. "I am now working industriously on my fauna," he declares, not without a note of pride. Lest his findings be lost to posterity, he promises to take care, "before dying," to deposit his remaining manuscripts at the University of Berlin.[62] No news of them, however, was to be heard.

It was his ignominy that outlived him. Some three decades after Chamisso's *History*, Heine recalled the fate of its hero's proper name in one of the "Hebrew Melodies" of his 1851 *Romanzero*. "What the word *Schlemihl* denotes," Heine wrote, "is / known to us."

> Long since,
> Chamisso saw to it that it got German
> civic rights — I mean the word did.

> Was das Wort Schlemihl bedeutet,
> Wissen wir. Hat doch Chamisso
> Ihm das Bürgerrecht in Deutschland
> Längst verschafft, dem Worte nämlich.[63]

Heine went on to draw his readers' attention to a fact of language that Chamisso had scrupulously avoided mentioning in his famous book. The name "Schlemihl," which appears in the *Marvellous History* as a proper designation like any other, long precedes the Franco-German author's novella of the luckless botanist. That Chamisso was aware of the traditional meaning of the term can be gleaned from a letter he sent his brother on March 17, 1821, explaining: "Schlemiehl or Schlemiel is a Hebrew name and means 'beloved of God' [*Gottlieb*], Théophile or *aimé de Dieu*. This is in the customary language of the Jews the designation of clumsy or unlucky people, for whom nothing in the world works out. A Schlemihl breaks off his finger in his waistcoat pocket; he falls on his back and breaks his nose bone. He always comes at the wrong moment."[64] Chamisso conceived his work in awareness of this legacy of his hero's name, even if the sole passage in which he would allude to it is the incidental scene in which Peter is — inexplicably and even absurdly, as it seems to him — "supposed a Jew."[65] Chamisso chose to replace the proverbial figure of the "clumsy or unlucky" person, who by nature lacked any proper places and dates, with a man in possession of a modern *History*.

There, the old figure of Jewish tradition all but vanished. His name alone remained.

It was an enigmatic residue, for however clear "what the word *Schlemihl* denotes" may be, the nature and genealogy of the proper name itself is obscure. The designation would appear to derive from a little-known passage of the Hebrew Bible at the start of Numbers that relates the circumstances in which the children of Israel dwelt in the wilderness of Sinai. In the second year after their liberation from bondage in Egypt, the Lord commands Moses to assemble an army.[66] The prophet draws one man from each of the twelve tribes. From the line of Simeon, he selects an Israelite called "Shelumiel, the son of Zurishaddai."[67] This "Shelumiel" is an individual hitherto unmentioned in scripture who appears solely in four other verses of Numbers. They present him as "captain" and "prince" of the children of Simeon, as well as "host" of their tribe.[68] Like the other leaders of the divisions of Israel, Shelumiel performs one sacrifice.[69] Without initiating other actions, without playing any additional role in sacred history or being distinguished by any remarkable traits, he seems a figure destined to be forgotten.

The Rabbis of the Talmud argued otherwise. They pointed to a later passage in the Bible as a sign of the tacit persistence in sacred history of a Shelumiel. Many chapters after the explicit mention of "Shelumiel, the son of Zurishaddai" in Numbers, the biblical narrative turns to events unrelated to the deeds committed by the twelve princes. Moses and his people have departed from Sinai. The Israelites have rebelled against the Lord and been punished for their impudence. They have sent spies to the land of the Canaanites, been discovered, and endured an attack. Balaam and his ass have made their famous pronouncements. Now "Israel abode in Shittim, and the people began to commit whoredom with the daughters of Moab."[70] When an Israelite man lies with a Midianite woman in violation of a divine command, Phinehas, son of Eleazar, son of Aaron, metes out a punishment: "He rose up from among the congregation, and took a javelin in his hand; and he went after the man of Israel into the tent, and thrust both of them through, the man of Israel, and the woman through her belly."[71] The biblical text identifies the two ignoble parties: "Now the name of the Israelite that was slain, *even* that was slain with the Midianitish woman, *was* Zimri, the son of Salu, a prince of a chief house among the Simeonites. And the name of the Midianitish woman that was slain *was* Cozbi, the daughter of Zur; he *was* head over a people, *and* of a chief house in Midian."[72]

This most inglorious of mentions is the first and the last that the Hebrew Bible accords Zimri, son of Salu, and his Midianitish companion, Cozbi, daughter of Zur. The Babylonian Talmud, however, says more, linking the perfidious Israelite to a person named earlier in Numbers. In the Tractate Sanhedrin, Rabbi Yoḥanan asserts that the Zimri whom Phinehas kills *in flagrante* possessed, in truth, no fewer than five appellations, of which the two explicitly mentioned in the Book of Numbers are but the first. The reader learns that this man was known as "Zimri" and "son of Salu," but he was also called "Saul, the son of the Canaanite woman, and Shelumiel, son of Zuri Shaddai." The Sage explains these many titles: "*Zimri*, because he became like an addled [*hamuzereth*] egg [as a result of engaging in multiple acts of intercourse]; *son of Salu*, because he evoked [*shehishisli*] the sins of his family; *Saul* [*Shaul*], because he lent himself [*hish'il*] to sin; *the son of the Canaanitish woman*, because he performed an act of Canaan [that is, in depravity]. Yet his [real] name," the Rabbi concludes, "was *Shelumiel, son of Zuri Shaddai*."[73]

The commentator offers no explanation for the last of these five designations, perhaps because, being the perpetrator's "real" or "given name" (*shem*), it is an index and no more: a sign without any meaning but its referent. If one believes Rabbi Yoḥanan, the name "Shelumiel, son of Zuri Shaddai" has been omitted, in clemency or in scorn, from the biblical narrative of the infraction of the holy law and its consequences. Only the Talmudic gloss preserves a trace of the identification of the "son of Salu" with the prince of the tribe of Simeon named earlier. Despite its brevity, however, the Rabbinic gloss sufficed to bring infamy upon the memory of the man. For

"Shelumiel" is simply the Hebraic form of the proper name that would one day be known in Germanic pronunciations of the holy tongue as "Schlemihl," "Shlemiel," or "Shlemil." In Hebrew, the designation literally means "my peace is God," or, as Chamisso would patiently explain, availing himself of German and French, "'beloved of God' [*Gottlieb*], *Théophile* or *aimé de Dieu*." With time, that enviable signification was to fade away—and be subjected to the cruelest of semantic ironies: "Beloved of God" became a euphemism for an unlucky or hapless person, a bumbler or a fool, always in the wrong place at the worst time.[74]

One may suppose that Heine knew these few facts in the history of the unhappy name. Yet in evoking Chamisso and Schlemihl in his *Romanzero*, Heine proposes a different account of the origins of the Hebrew-Yiddish appellation. He attributes it to the same Julius Eduard Hitzig to whom Chamisso addressed the opening letter of his *History*. According to the explanation that Heine claims to have received from Hitzig, the associations of the word "Schlemiel" derive from a bungled act in the history of the Jews: an event unmentioned in both the Bible and the Talmud, yet nonetheless preserved, through strictly oral transmission, in collective memory. Recalling the events narrated in Numbers, Heine reminds his reader how Phinehas, the priest, once set out to smite the lascivious Israelite, Zimri son of Zurishaddai. The poet then supplies a crucial detail missing from the written representations of the event: the priest,

> blind by fury,
> Unawares struck not the sinner
> But an innocent bystander [*ein ganz Unschuld'gen*],
> One Schlemihl ben Zuri-shaddai.

Heine thus admits the basic narrative presupposition of the Talmudic commentary. He accepts that despite going unnamed, Shelumiel (or Shlemihl) was present at the divinely sanctioned execution of the lovers. Yet Heine suggests that the role of the man named "Schlemihl" was considerably more modest—and more pathetic—than the Talmudic Sage maintained. Rabbi Yoḥanan charged Shelumiel with having committed an act to which capital punishment alone was adequate. Heine takes him, rather, to have been a guiltless party present at the scene of a crime. Somehow, he managed to be in the wrong tent at the wrong time, and for this reason and this reason alone, he was the victim of a most unfortunate mistake. Yet Heine also casts "Schlemihl ben Zuri Shaddai" as the initiator of a long line whose members bear, with him, the force of his inglorious appellation. To this most misfortunate of ancient Israelites, the poet accords a quasi-aristocratic title: "Schlemihl the First," "Forebear of the race and lineage / Of Schlemihls" (*Anherr des Geschlechtes / Derer von Schlemihl*).[75]

This "race and lineage," for Heine, is that of poets. They sustain the ignominy that their progenitor first illustrated. Forging a new word for an ancient condition, Heine dubs it "Schlemihldom" (*Schlemihltum*).[76] "We are descended / From Schlemihl ben Zurishaddai" (*Wir stammen / von Schlemihl ben Zuri Schaddai*), he writes, before adding:

> To be sure, we have no mention
> of heroic deeds by this one;
> We know only what his name was,
> and that he was a Schlemihl.
>
> Freilich keine Heldentaten
> Meldet man von ihm, wir kennen
> Nur den Namen, und wir wissen
> Daß er ein Schlemihl gewesen.[77]

Both name and glory here acquire a new sense. The proper name is no longer that by which great words and deeds persist. It is, rather, what remains of ignominy. In this insistent trace, *designans* and *designatum* can hardly be told apart: all that the poet knows of his solitary ancestor is that he was called "Schlemihl" and that, with perfect circularity, he deserved his title, being its exemplar. Dismissed from the minor part he might have played in ancient history as "Zimri, the son of Salu, a prince of a chief house among the Simeonites," deprived of the shadow he was long known to have renounced, shorn of his ungainly slippers and his magic boots, distanced even from his modest claims to the advancement of scientific knowledge, this Schlemihl is little more than a name.

> We have no mention
> of heroic deeds by this one;
> We know only what his name was,
> and that he was a Schlemihl.

Like a Tristan reduced to being *triste*, he is *schlimm* and little more: a literary person "grave," if not serious, undeniably misfortunate, though perhaps of no particular consequence. If he lays claim to any glory, it is that lost in recurrent accidents. His is a life inextricable from errancy and mishap that persists solely in diminishment.

PART THREE

Survivals

CHAPTER NINE

Returning to Riva

Between 1916 and 1917, a most unusual person makes a small number of fleeting appearances in Kafka's unpublished papers. One is in a diary entry dated April 6, 1917:

> Today, in a little harbour, which apart from fishing boats is normally used only by the two passenger steamers that ply the lake, there lay a strange bark. A clumsy old craft, relatively low and very broad, as filthy as if it had been swamped with bilge water, which still seemed to be dripping down the yellowish sides; the masts incomprehensibly tall, the upper third of the mainmast snapped; wrinkled, coarse, yellowish-brown sails stretched in confusion between the yards; patch-work, too weak for the slightest gust.
>
> I gazed in amazement at it for a time, waited for someone to show himself on deck. No one appeared. A workman sat down beside me on the harbour wall. "Whose ship is that?" I asked. "This is the first time I have seen it." "It puts in every two or three years," said the man, "and belongs to the hunter Gracchus."[1]

No introduction or commentary accompanies these sentences, which Kafka most likely wrote while in his Prague apartment. They evoke a set of events and conversations that he had begun to record in his notebooks four months earlier.

A longer sequence in the so-called *Oktavhefte*, dated to December 1916, sets out a similar scene of arrival in fuller detail:

> Two boys were sitting on the harbour wall playing dice. On the steps of a monument a man was reading a newspaper in the shadow of the sword-wielding

> hero. A girl was filling her tub at the fountain. A fruit-seller was lying beside his wares, looking out across the lake. Through the empty window and door openings of a tavern two men could be seen drinking their wine in the depths. Out in front the proprietor was sitting at a table dozing. A bark glided silently into the little harbour, as if borne on water. A man in a blue overall climbed ashore and drew the ropes through the wings. Two other men, wearing dark coats with silver buttons, carried out past the boatman a bier draped with a great tasselled cloth of flower-patterned silk, beneath which there evidently lay a human being. No one on the quay troubled about the newcomers; even when they lowered the bier to wait for the boatman, who was still busy with the ropes, no one approached, no one asked them a question, no one gave them a closer look.[2]

This passage identifies the place of these occurrences. It is the town of Riva, on the northern shores of Lake Garda, where Kafka spent holidays in 1909 and 1913. It is striking that in both the diary entry and this sequence from the notebook, certain human beings are awaited and yet missing from the scene. The author of the text in the diary recalls expecting "someone to show himself on deck" before specifying this general absence: "no one appeared." In the longer rendition in the notebook, the desertion is developed into a series of sentences about "no one." In both texts, however, the observation of absence gives way to the introduction of a name and title belonging to one person. Each time, the reader learns that the hunter Gracchus has arrived—or rather that he has returned in his customary fashion. Men in "dark coats and silver buttons," in the notebook, proceed to convey the hunter's bier to a "yellowish two-storied house that rose abruptly on the left close to the water." Next, they carry it "through the low but gracefully pillared doorway" into a "cool, spacious room at the rear side of the building, from which no other house, but only a bare grey-black wall of rock was to be seen." The "carriers" light candles at the head of the bier, but it seems that only a play of shades is perceptible. The candles "gave no light to the room; it was just as if shadows had been merely startled from their rest and sent flickering over the walls."[3]

At this point in this longer sequence from the *Oktavhefte*, the "human being" aboard the barge is described. "The cloth covering the bier had been thrown back. Lying there was a man with wildly matted hair and beard, his skin sunburned, rather like a hunter in appearance. He lay there with his eyes closed, motionless and apparently without breathing, yet only the surroundings indicated that perhaps this man was dead."[4] The seemingly incidental word "perhaps" (*vielleicht*) soon shows itself to be crucial. A "gentleman" of considerable importance, "an old man with a top-hat and a mourning band," enters the house, proceeds to the room, and steps up to the bier, laying "his hand on the brow of the recumbent figure." He kneels down to pray, indicating to the "carriers" as well as the solitary boatman that he is to be left alone with the body of the unknown "human being." "At once" the man lying on the bier opens his eyes, turns "his face towards the gentleman with a painful smile," addressing him: "Who are you?" That question is easily answered; the distinguished gentleman is Salvatore, burgomaster of Riva. Far less certain are the terms with which the reclining hunter himself responds to his interlocutor's queries: "'Are you dead?' 'Yes,' said the hunter, 'as you see. Many years ago, indeed it must be an uncommonly long time ago, I fell from a rock in the Black Forest — that is in Germany — when I was hunting a chamois. Since then I have been dead.' 'But you are alive, too,' said the burgomaster. 'To some extent,' said the hunter, 'to some extent I am alive too.'"[5]

Undoubtedly deceased and yet also "to some extent" (*gewissermaßen*) alive, the hunter Gracchus has been forced to become a traveler. "My death boat went off course," he avows. "A wrong turn of the wheel, a moment's absence of mind on the part of the helmsman, the distraction of my lovely native country, I cannot tell what it was; I only know this, that I remained on earth and that ever since my boat has been sailing."[6] Gracchus is, in his words, "forever on the great stairway" to the other world. "On that infinitely wide and open stairway I clamber about, sometimes up, sometimes down, sometimes on the right, sometimes on the left, always in motion. But when I soar up with a supreme effort and can already see the gate shining above me, I wake up on my old boat, still forlornly stranded in some earthly sea."[7] To the burgomaster's pointed and far from uninterested question as to whether the hunter now means to take up residence in his lakeside city, Gracchus, making light of such a possibility, offers few assurances. "'Now have you a mind to stay here in Riva with us?' 'I have no mind,' said the hunter with a smile, and to excuse the jest he laid his hand on the burgomaster's knee. 'I am here, more than that I do not know, more than that I cannot do. My boat has no rudder; it is driven by the wind that blows in the nethermost regions of death.'"[8]

The hunter Gracchus is a diminished human being in a sense that is new in this investigation into variously missing persons. It would be imprecise and insufficient to consider him an "absentee" according to any traditional definition of that term, even if by his own account his whereabouts have been unknown for an unusually long time: "Fifteen hundred years," as he wistfully recalls in one of Kafka's other accounts of him.[9] Unlike a missing person in the legal sense, he cannot be presumed to be alive; in his every appearance, he insists that he has died. It would be at least as dissatisfying, however, to infer that he is a nonperson after the manner of those who suffer a "decrease of the head." Although it is likely that Gracchus may not lay claim to the rights and prerogatives of any ordinary subject of the law, it is certain that the death that he claims to have suffered is not exclusively civil. His case, in short, is neither that of the legal person crafted in the absence of a body nor that of the living body that persists in the diminution or nullification of the legal person.

Nonetheless, like the representation fashioned in the aftermath of the missing body and the peculiar status of the human being diminished by some formal legal or social procedure, the hunter Gracchus is, in a precise sense, a nonperson. For he is a being about whom — or which — it is impossible to maintain either of these contradictory propositions: that "he is a person" or that he "is not a person." In his return to Riva, as in his intermittent appearances in Kafka's papers, he raises a disquieting, yet intractable question: the question of what, in a human being, outlasts death, being "to some extent" alive.

Any consideration of Kafka's accounts of Gracchus must begin with the observation that they are unpublished and unauthorized; in principle, all were to be destroyed according to the author's wishes. None of the surviving texts can be considered complete in any simple sense, and the variations, commonalities, and breaks among the extant "versions" of the material have been variously interpreted. It remains uncertain how many Gracchus texts there are. Some scholars argue for the existence of three versions of the material, others for five.[10] Malcolm Pasley, the editor of the German critical edition, suggests, on the basis of a convincing study of Kafka's papers, that there are four "Gracchus fragments."[11]

The surest point of entry into the universe of this multiple, yet insistently loquacious dead man may lie in the formal architecture of Kafka's four narrations. They rely on a single set of grammatical possibilities: those afforded by personal pronouns. Each time, it is by means of an *I*, a *you*, or a *he* that Gracchus is announced.

The "fragments" can be ordered by means of the role these persons play. The diary entry consists first of sentences belonging to some third person's perspective and then of an exchange in direct discourse, involving an *I* and a *you*. This sequence first relates the events that occurred "today, in the little harbour," in an impersonal voice; then it introduces the view of a narrator, who appears as a witness to the arrival of the "clumsy old craft." He recalls striking up a conversation, in perplexity, with a workman near the water: "I gazed at it in astonishment for some time, waited for someone to show himself on deck. No one appeared. A workman sat down beside me on the harbour wall. 'Whose ship is that?' I asked." The passage ends with an answer, in direct discourse, which concerns neither the speaker nor the addressee, but the unseen owner of the bark: "'It puts in every two or three years,' said the man, 'and belongs to the hunter Gracchus.'"

By contrast, the longest of the Gracchus narratives in the notebooks lacks any reference to a narrator. This sequence begins resolutely in the third person, with sentences that seem to admit of no subjective perspective, according to the Flaubertian model of impersonality that Kafka admired and made his own.[12] The scene at Riva is laid out absolutely, without any indication of time with respect to storytelling, such as "today," and without any indication of perspective with respect to the origin of the discourse, such as "I" or "you." No one recounts these few details: "Two boys were sitting on the harbour playing dice. On the steps of a monument a man was reading a newspaper." It is only once the burgomaster and Gracchus are alone in the dark room that the discourse shifts. Diegesis gives way to mimesis. The first words are those of the man on the bier: "Who are you?" The two men begin to converse. Each addresses the other as a second person; each uses the first person for himself. This text ends with the words of the hunter, which do not explicitly evoke anyone: "My boat has no rudder; it is driven by the wind that blows in the nethermost regions of death."

The notebooks contain a further account of Gracchus that possesses a different grammatical and literary form. This sequence begins and proceeds without any narration, consisting solely of the exchange of direct discourse in conversation. Everything occurs within one cabin on the "old boat." The inception is a question that is addressed to the hunter and that refers to speech omitted from the text: "'What is it you say, hunter Gracchus, you have been sailing for hundreds of years now in this old boat?' 'For fifteen hundred years.' 'And always in this ship?' 'Always in this bark. Bark, I believe, is the correct expression. You aren't familiar with nautical matters?'"[13] Here there are only two persons, and both are speakers. Over a bottle of wine, Gracchus answers his interlocutor's questions about his vessel, its recently deceased master, and his own origins, death, and survival—until he learns of his conversation partner's ignorance. Belatedly, it occurs to the pensive hunter to pose a question whose answer proves the occasion for the end of the discussion:

> "I say, do you know the Black Forest?" "No." "You really don't know anything. The little child of the helmsman knows more, truly far more, than you do. Who wafted you in here anyway? It's a calamity. Your initial modesty was only too well justified. You're a mere nothing I am filling up with wine. So now you don't even know the Black Forest. And I was born there. Until I was twenty-five I hunted there. If only the chamois hadn't led me on — well, now you know it — I'd have had a long and happy hunter's life, but I was lured by the chamois! I fell and was killed on the rocks below. Don't ask any more. Here I am, dead, dead, dead. Don't know why I'm here."[14]

This rapid summary of the syntax of three Gracchus texts suffices to define their permutations of grammatical and narrative form. There are, in short, two sequences that begin in a third person before passing into dialog and introducing speakers: the diary entry and the extended narrative from the notebooks. There is, moreover, one sequence that consists wholly of dialog: the conversation in the cabin. The fourth "fragment," however, is of another form. It knows neither the third person nor the second; in it, narration and dialog remain equally absent. There, a first person writes alone. He reflects on his condition: "As I write this I am lying on a wooden board; I wear — it is no pleasure to look at me — a filthy winding-sheet; my legs are covered by a large woman's shawl of flower-patterned silk with long fringes."[15] He recalls the origins of his state:

> I have been lying here ever since the time when I, still the live hunter Gracchus at home in the Black Forest, was hunting a chamois and fell. Everything happened in good order. I gave chase, I fell, I bled to death in a ravine, I was dead, and this bark was supposed to convey me to the next world. I can still remember how cheerfully I stretched myself out on this board for the first time; never had the mountains heard such song from me as was heard then by these four still shadowy walls. I had been glad to live and was glad to die; before stepping aboard I joyfully flung down my miserable accoutrements, rifle, knapsack, hunting coat, that I had always worn with pride, and I slipped into my winding sheet like a girl into her wedding-dress. I lay there and waited.[16]

The fourth version might seem to complete a circuit of narrative possibilities drawn out in the other three "fragments." After texts of narration in the third person and texts of dialog in which each speaker addresses a second person, the reader encounters a statement in the first person. But the truth is that this fourth rendition stands apart. The others contain elements suggesting the possibility of a transition, in storytelling, between speaking subjects. From a third person, they move to a first person and to a second person; from a first person, they pass to a second person and conversely leave open the eventuality of a transition to a third. Yet the sequence in which Gracchus writes on his wooden board refuses the perspective of any third person; this recounting excludes any viewpoint but that of the solitary writer. For this reason, it precludes the possibility of an interlocutor, forbidding dialog as such. Alone, the writer draws out this consequence:

> No one will read what I write here. No one will come to help me. Even if there were a commandment to help me, all the doors of all the houses would remain closed; all the windows would stay closed; all the people would lie in their beds with the blankets drawn over their heads; the whole earth one great nocturnal lodging. And there is sense in that, for no one knows of me; and if anyone knew of me, he would not know where I could be found; and if anyone knew where I could be found, he would not know how to help me. The idea of wanting to help me is a sickness, and it has to be cured in bed.[17]

It has often been noted that by its structure, writing in general anticipates the vanishing of its author, being language crafted to survive the cessation of speech. This text renders that disappearance brightly visible. In the notebook, this passage appears to follow the statement, "I am the hunter Gracchus; my home is in the Black Forest in Germany." But after those words of self-identification, Kafka draws a line. Only then does he write "No one will read what I write here."[18] As Roland Reuß has noted, the consequence is that it is not immediately evident to whom this statement belongs; only in the next folio is it referred to the hunter Gracchus.[19] The most striking

A page from the manuscript of Kafka's "Hunter Gracchus" fragments

From *Franz Kafka–Ausgabe. Historisch-kritische Ausgabe*, eds. Roland Reuß and Peter Staengle. Oxforder Oktavhefte 2, 9 verso. Mss. facsimiles.

feature of this passage, however, concerns not the effacement of the writer, but the programmatic denial of the possibility of a reader. "No one will read what I write here" seems to be the statement of an uncompromising exclusion. The truth is that it is equivocal. In a first sense, it establishes a simple inexistence: there will be no reader for what is written. In a second sense, the statement has a different meaning: according to the paradoxically affirmative syntax of its form, it suggests that there is a reader — one who is, however, "No One."

This would be Kafka's Roman hunter's variation on Odysseus's ancient ruse. Gracchus guarantees that even — or especially — where his words are heard, they will be perceived by someone utterly lacking in identity or individuality, or both. They are for No One. To the obvious question of who might this No One be? Gracchus suggests an answer: it is a person such as himself, the solitary writer. Reader and writer share in a single impossibility. Each is no one, either on account of being of no consequence, "a mere nothing being filled up with wine," according to the dialogic sequence of the material, which casts the hunter's conversation partner as an amiable Polyphemus, or on account of being so untimely as to be unknowable. Yet there is also a further sense in which the writer, like the reader he denies, is no one, and it is still more disquieting. Being someone or something that is "to a certain extent" alive past death, Gracchus eludes the very idea of a human being. He is not *a* person, but rather the indeterminate and indeterminable remains of one.

What is certain is that Gracchus writes, and he does so solely for himself, whoever or whatever he may be. Without troubling himself to add an indication of time or place, he composes a diary of a kind, if only on a single page, without preface or continuation. In this sense, he is not entirely unlike the writer called "Kafka," which in Czech means "jackdaw" or, in the language of the Romans, *gracchus.*[20] An imagined No One or the real and only author, a first person, a second person, or a third, the hunter Gracchus can in any case be only an absentee. Nonetheless — and for this very reason — he and the questions he raises make appearances and reappearances, visits and visitations, in Kafka's own books and diaries and beyond them: in the variegated fields of law, mythology, ritual, and theology. From time to time, Gracchus returns to Riva, place and also "shore" (*riva*), living on, defying the power to name and to represent.

CHAPTER TEN

The Semblant Body

The bodies of the dead pose a challenge, even when, outside the domain of fiction, they do not speak for themselves. The first difficulty is one of substance. What, quite simply, is the nature of a living human body's remains ? That a corpse is no human being seems obvious, yet it is equally certain that it is no ordinary thing. Once again, the apparently exclusive opposition between being a human being and not being a human being fails to account for a possibility that is all too real. A human cadaver is neither a person nor *not* a person. It is a nonperson in a special sense, which requires commentary and elucidation.

That the corpse demands a treatment different from that accorded any other thing or person seems a constant among otherwise variable human communities. Among all peoples, it is a principle that, as the ancient Roman jurist Papinian once observed, "there is a public interest that corpses not lie about unburied" (*propter publicam utilitatem, ne insepulta cadavera iacerent*).[1] Mortuary practices are among the most ancient attested human activities, stretching back into prehistory.[2] They are also among those most strictly respected of traditions, as Herodotus, inventor of ancient Greek anthropology and history, remarked, almost in passing, in the fifth century BCE. "If it were proposed to all nations to choose which seemed best of all customs," he wrote in his book on Persia, "each, after examination, would place its own first; so well is each convinced that its own are by far the best." For this general principle, Herodotus adduced a single "proof":

> When Darius was king, he summoned the Greeks who were with him and asked them for what price they would eat their dead fathers' bodies. They answered that there was no price for which they would do it. Then Darius summoned those Indians who are called "Callatiae," who eat their parents, and asked them (the Greeks being present and understanding through interpreters what was said) what would make them willing to burn their fathers at death. The Indians cried aloud, that he should not speak of so horrid an act. So firmly rooted are these beliefs; and it is, I think, rightly said in Pindar's poem that law [*nomos*] is king of all.[3]

Herodotus was most interested in the diversity of the dictates of this sovereign "law," but there are also commonalities among even varying conceptions of the dead. In this respect, languages furnish a precious archive, for in the history of words, certain recurrent traits may be discerned. A first characteristic involves the representation of the deceased human being as being a body and no more. The English expression "corpse" illustrates this fact, originating in the Latin word *corpus*, which means "body." Until the seventeenth century, "corpse," in English, referred to a thing that might be alive or dead, the term pointing first of all, as in Latin, to the matter and form of a human being. When employed to signify a cadaver, "corpse" needed, therefore, to be accompanied by a qualifying attribute: "this dede corps," Chaucer thus writes; "his breathless Corpes," we read in Shakespeare's *Henry IV, Part 2*.[4] Gradually, the Latinate expression lost all reference to a living being; it began to designate the physical shape of a deceased person and no more. Further epithets then became superfluous, the English form of the Latin *corpus* having acquired the meaning of "lifeless human being" or "shape of a dead person."

To this degree, the history of "corpse" differs from that of the word "cadaver," which, from its earliest uses, signifies a human body known to be lifeless. The ancient and medieval scholars of the Latin language explained this point by appealing to etymology. According to some, a *cadaver* is defined by the fact of "falling" (*cadere*), for it cannot stand upright; according to others, it is characterized by being in a state of lack (*carere*), not yet having been put to rest.[5] In ancient Roman usage, *cadaver* refers to a dead person deprived of burial rites. Among classical authors, the word appears, in this sense, for human remains that are abandoned on the battlefield, thrown to the beasts, or carried away by torrents, as well as for the bodily remains of those who suffer a most ignominious decease. The crucified, those killed in gladiatorial fights, dragged into the Tiber, or thrown into the sewer, all become *cadaveres.*[6] Long after such forms of execution had fallen into disuse, Latin authors continued to retain an awareness of the fact that a *cadaver* belongs above all to a dead person stained by indignity. In the sixth or seventh century, Isidore of Seville thus distinguishes the *funus*, "corpse," from the *cadaver*, explaining that a *cadaver* has not received the rites owed to the deceased. "Everyone who is dead is either a *funus*, or a *cadaver*," he writes, before adding: "It is a *funus* if it is being buried. . . . The term *cadaver*, on the other hand, is used if the body lies unburied, for *cadaver* comes from 'falling down' [*cadere*], because it can no longer stand upright."[7] Yet Isidore notes that the dead may also be called by simpler names. "In common usage, a cadaver is still spoken of as a body [*corpus*]," as in the *Georgics*: "Then the bodies [*corpora*] of those deprived of the light."[8]

The early Greek language suggests a different understanding of human remains. While modern English possesses a word for a dead person, "corpse," which once designated "the body" in general, whether alive or dead, the oldest corresponding form in Greek implies an inverse process: the classical term for "body" is first of all attested as an expression meaning "corpse." Bruno Snell called attention to this fact. "Aristarchus," he writes, "was the first to notice that in Homer the word *sōma* which subsequently came to mean 'body' is never used with reference to a living being; *sōma* is the corpse."[9] Homer's language possessed many terms for that thing "which is called 'body' by us": among others, *demas*, *guia*, and *melea*. Each of these words refers to some partial anatomical extension: "Instead of 'body' Homer says 'limbs'; *guia* are the limbs as moved by the joints, *melē*, the limbs in their muscular strength." Snell concludes that although endowed with a keen sense of the body's parts, the Homeric mentality "made no provision for the body as such."[10] "The early Greeks did not, either in their language or in the visual arts, grasp the body as a unit. . . . Of course the Homeric man had a body exactly like the later Greeks, but he did not know it *qua* body, but merely as the sum total of his limbs."[11] It is all the more remarkable that "the Homeric man" nonetheless admitted the existence of a moment in which the material human form emerges as a whole. Early Greek poetry suggests an understanding well worth considering: in death, a new unity arises from the many parts of the living being. *Sōma* becomes conceivable, body *qua* body, in the absence of a soul.[12]

This usage suggests that totality is crucial for the definition of the cadaver: the corpse alone is *a* body, rather than the multiple limbs, parts, or aspects of a living soul. When alive, one might wager, a person "has" a body; in decease, the person "is" one—and no more. Yet the history of words suggests that remains have also posed a further challenge: that of resemblance. Expressions for dead bodies evoking figures of similarity are legion. It is striking that the link between the expression of decease and likeness extends to what may be considered, in the European tradition, one of the designations of similarity par excellence. *Imago*, source of the modern "image" and its many foreign cognates, refers in its earliest uses neither to a visual aspect nor to a general representation; rather, it designates an "ancestor portrait" (*Ahnenbild*) and, more exactly, a wax portrait of the deceased.[13]

Romans kept such likenesses in their *atria*, employing them on important occasions, such as aristocratic funerals. Writing for a Greek audience unfamiliar with the customs of Latium, Polybius thus recounts that Romans placed *imagines* of the departed "in the most conspicuous position in the house, enclosed in a wooden shrine."

> The *imago* is a mask reproducing with remarkable fidelity both the features and the complexion of the deceased. On the occasion of public sacrifices, the Romans display these images, and decorate them with much care, and when any distinguished member of the family dies, they take them to the funeral,

> putting them on men who seem to them to bear the closest resemblance to the original in stature and carriage.[14]

Pliny the Elder was also familiar with such practices. "In the days of our ancestors," he recounts, Roman halls contained *imagines* on display: "Portraits modelled in wax [*expressi cera vultus*] were arranged, each in its separate niche, to be always in readiness to accompany the funeral processions of the family," thus assuring that "every member of the family that had ever existed was always present."[15] A word for this semblance of a dead ancestor, *imago* could by metonymy be employed to signify a "dead forefather." At further degrees of removal, the term came to mean "disguise," "representation," and, more generally, "copy" and "likeness."[16]

The link between corpse and similarity also persists in modern languages. While the Latin *imago*, as a term denoting likeness, derives from the name of the death mask, the Germanic branch of the Indo-European family suggests an inverse semantic relation: expressions for the dead human body appear to be formed from terms evoking similarity. Modern High German's ordinary word for "corpse," *Leiche*, is cognate with the modern English word *like*, according to a set of perplexing and yet linguistically indubitable lexical relations. Anglo-Saxon contains the word *līc*, "form, body," Old English counterpart of Old Norse *līk* and Gothic *leik*, signifying "body"; these words are in turn related to Dutch *lijk*, Danish *lig*, Swedish *lik*, which, like Modern High German *Leiche*, all signify "cadaver."[17] As with the passage from Latin *corpus* to modern English "corpse," or, inversely, from Homeric to classical Greek *sōma*, in modern languages, "body" and "dead body" are often difficult to tell apart. Repeatedly, perhaps systematically, words for the human shape mean "corpse."

Such expressions are also closely related to a host of terms denoting similarity, of which the modern English "like" is one obvious example. More generally, the extraordinarily productive suffixes *-like*, *-lik*, *-lich*, in the Germanic languages, which signify qualities of a common appearance, pertain to this semantic set.[18] Modern English "like," for example, derives from Anglo-Saxon *gelīc*, which literally means "the same body" (*ge* + *līc*): possessing "the same, or a common, body," and by extension, "the same form, shape, appearance."[19] Designations such as German *Leiche*, Swedish *lik*, and the now obsolete English words "lich," "like," or "lych," which signified "living body" and above all "dead body," suggest a common definition of the cadaver: it is a "resembling body." Admittedly, the exact relations among such expressions for body, shape, and similarity remain unclear. The *-like* suffix, in particular, may derive from a noun meaning "(physical) body," a noun meaning "generalized form," or some verbal adjective meaning "similar."[20] But there is no doubt that the words for "corpse," "shape," and "resemblance" in the Germanic languages are systematically related.

As an inquiry into the grounds of customs and the nature of appearances, philosophy could not fail to confront the challenges that lifeless bodies pose. In the Greek tradition, statements on corpses number among the major pronouncements of the earliest recorded philosophers. The most famous is perhaps also the most provocative: Heraclitus's apothegm, "Corpses should be thrown out more quickly than dung" (*nekues kopriōn ekblētoteroi*).[21] Charles H. Kahn comments that "no utterance of Heraclitus is better calculated to offend the normal religious sensitivities of an ancient Greek than this contempt for the dead, as every reader of *Antigone* will recognize."[22] The aphorism was often cited in antiquity.[23] Plato's Socrates marked out the difference between the living person and the dead body in terms that were no less sharp, though they did not challenge Greek funerary practices. Without lingering on the nature of the human cadaver, Socrates explains in the *Phaedo* that at the moment of decease, the soul (*psykhē*) abandons the body (*sōma*) with which it is united: "It departs pure, dragging with it nothing of the body."[24] Stated on the eve of Socrates's execution, that statement entails a consequence: after his death, nothing of the philosopher will remain in the physical form or matter that his soul until then enlivened.

For different reasons, the Epicureans and Cynics insisted on a related point, arguing that the bodies of the dead, be they animal or human, lack all sensation. Lucretius made of this thesis a crucial element in his teaching: since the dead can feel no pain, he explains, the living have nothing to fear from the loss of life.[25] Diogenes appears to have espoused a similar position in terms more idiosyncratic and extreme. According to Cicero, the Cynic philosopher made it known to his friends that after his death, they were to throw his body "anywhere," without troubling themselves to bury it. When they expressed concern about the danger that "birds and beasts" might pose to his exposed cadaver, he would add that he wished to have his staff set near him, so as to drive any such animals away. To their incredulous question, "How can you do that, given that you will not perceive them?'" Diogenes would respond: "How will I then be injured by them, if I have no sensation?"[26] Only occasionally did the Greek philosophers admit that there might be a continuity between a human being and the lifeless shape that resembles it after decease. Democritus, the ancient atomist, appears to have constituted such an exception. According to Aetius, he taught that "everything contains a sort of soul, even corpses [*kai ta nekra tōn sōmatōn*], which is why it is always apparent that they have a sort of warmth and perception, though most of it is breathed out."[27]

Perhaps no ancient philosopher returned as insistently as did Aristotle to the question of the nature of the lifeless human body. In his treatises on metaphysics, as well as on psychology, zoology, and biology, the philosopher and physician repeatedly evoked the example of the cadaver. It raised and also complicated some of the fundamental terms and distinctions in his doctrine. The first among them is the opposition between "form" and "matter," which seems, in many of the Aristotelian works, to define the structure of all earthly things.

According to the *Metaphysics*, matter is that from which something comes to be; form, by contrast, is that in accord with which any given matter is not only potential, but also actual.[28] To illustrate these concepts, Aristotle often employs examples drawn from the realm of *tekhnē*, "art" or productive knowledge, maintaining that they pertain to natural as well as artificial processes. At such times, Aristotle reasons that bronze may furnish the matter of a sculpted likeness of a person, being that "from which" the shaped image can be made. In the molded figure, matter and form remain distinct, while being hierarchically ordered. Form defines matter, which, in technical terms, it "informs." Aristotle holds that this structural distinction is also discernible among living things. "The soul [*psykhē*] is the primary substance," he states in the *Metaphysics*, "and the body [*sōma*] is matter." An animal is a compound of the two.[29] If one admits this analogy, one will reason that just as bronze, through the artisan's work, assumes the shape of a human figure, the mass of flesh and sinews that make up a "body" acquires the form proper to an animal through some natural process known only in part to us.

Yet there is an obvious limit to this analogy. The matter of a sculpture is "informed" contingently, and always so. No necessity demands that it be crafted in any particular shape; moreover, after it has acquired a certain form, it can take on another. Whatever matter and form are present in living beings are manifestly of a different nature. The parts and organs of a body can hardly be identified before life has begun. In addition, once the principle of life has departed from an animal, not only its form, but also its matter are absent; for "matter," according to Aristotle's definition, is potential, and a cadaver lacks all potentiality. The philosopher himself specifies this point: "We must not understand by that which is potentially capable of living what has lost the soul, but only what still retains it." "Seeds and fruits" are bodies that are "potential" in this sense.[30] Dried and cut leaves are of another nature. As J. L. Ackrill remarks, where animals are concerned, what resembles "matter" is therefore of a special kind. A living body is not contingently, but necessarily alive: "The material in this case is *not* capable of existing *except* as the material of an animal, as matter *so in-formed*."[31]

Aristotle himself drew the single consequence that these principles entail. Strictly speaking, a dead body is no "body" whatsoever, just as the severed parts of an animal, viewed from any rational perspective, cannot properly be considered "parts." More generally, a "dead person," Aristotle holds, may not rightly be called a person, even if he or she — or rather *it* — possesses "exactly the same configuration as a living person."[32] In the phrases "dead person" and "person," the repeated nouns are what Aristotle calls "homonyms": words that, while sharing a common form, correspond to beings whose definition is essentially distinct.[33] Aristotle expounds this principle repeatedly. In the *Meteorology*, he writes that "a dead person is a person in name alone" before adding that the same reasoning holds of the severed body part and the crafted likeness: "So the hand of a dead person, too, will in the same way be a hand in name only, just as stone flutes might still be called flutes; for these, too, seem to be instruments of a kind."[34] The identity between the living and the dead is one of mere name and image. In the *Metaphysics*, we read: "A living part cannot even exist if severed from the whole; for it is not a finger in any state that is the finger of a living thing, but the dead finger."[35] If the philosopher himself can speak of such things as the "dead person" and the "dead finger," it is by a figure such as catachresis, which lends a faulty designation to a thing that is nameable in no other way.

Homonym and semblance, from this perspective, are structurally equivalent: to the insubstantial self-identity of "person" in the two expressions, "person" and "dead person," there corresponds the resemblance of real to sculpted flute. Aristotle draws attention to the fact that linguistic usage, like art, is to this degree the source of an illusion. Suggesting that the living and the dead are equally susceptible to being called "persons" or "bodies," ordinary speech introduces a simulacrum into the field of representation. It is this likeness that the philosopher, in pursuit of intelligible identity, seeks to define and consequently to dismiss. Yet the impression that the dead body is a "body" cannot easily be dispelled. For even if one grants that the corpse is merely the image of the person who is not, one must confront a troubling question: What, then, is such a semblant thing? How may the dead person be defined, if it is no person whatsoever?

Nowhere does Aristotle confront this question directly. His successors, however, could hardly fail to encounter it. An early answer can be discerned at the edges of the Aristotelian logical doctrine as it was received and expounded by the master's late antique disciples. In *De interpretatione*, Boethius evokes the canonical ancient example, *ouk anthrōpos*, which he renders in Latin as *nonhomo*, "nonman" or "nonperson." He explains that to employ this curious name is in effect to deny its main component: "He who says 'nonman' removes 'man.'"[36] In his more extended interpretation of Aristotle, he goes further: "What is meant by 'nonman' is whatever is outside 'man,' once 'man' has been annulled."[37] Boethius proceeds to provide an example of such a "nonperson." It is what is denoted by "Sulla," the name of the famed Roman dictator. "If someone says of Sulla, who is not [*qui non est*], 'nonman,' then this signifies a certain thing that in reality and in the outside world does not last."[38] In the exposition of Aristotle's logic, the choice of example may seem incidental. Implicitly, however, the example also suggests a thesis on the status of the dead. In "not being" while nonetheless being "a certain thing," the exemplary "nonperson" (*nonhomo*) is the dead.

With the flowering of medieval Aristotelianism, later philosophers would find themselves obliged to provide more elaborate and explicit accounts of the dead. Psychology, medicine, and physics would all have roles to play. Even logic, the first of the branches of philosophy, reputedly the tool of all the others, offered answers to the question of the nature of the deceased. In *De interpretatione*, Aristotle alluded briefly to the falsity of claiming that "a dead person is a person."[39] Starting in the thirteenth century, philosophers would draw out the consequences that follow from the predication of "being dead" of any human being. The phrase "dead person" (*homo mortuus*) became the example of a fallacy to be investigated in detail: that of not distinguishing between the meanings of a term taken unqualifiedly (*simpliciter*) and in a certain sense (*secundum quid*). The philosophers reasoned that taken unqualifiedly, the "notion of person" (*ratio hominis*) includes the fact of being alive. A "dead person," for this reason, is not only no one and nothing, as Aristotle had explicitly held; more exactly, and in logical parlance, such a being is a contradiction in terms (*contradictio in adjecto*).

The medieval logicians provided an original analysis of the difficulty of predicating death of any person. They appealed to the apagogic mode of demonstration, whose form may be simply stated: from a manifestly inacceptable conclusion, drawn according to valid modes of inference, a faulty premise is detected. If qualified and unqualified terms are not strictly distinguished, one may infer, first, from the sentence "This is a dead person," "This is a person." Then, drawing out the meaning of the term "person," one may conclude, "This is a living person." By any reasonable rule of inference, that statement in turn entails: "This is nondead." Yet as long as one does not distinguish qualified and unqualified expressions, from the sentence "This is a dead person," one may also make a second inference, "This is dead," from which one may conclude, "This is nonliving." If one combines the two statements thus obtained by derivation, one reaches an inadmissible thesis: "This is a dead person" entails both "This is nondead" and "This is dead," "This is living" and "This is nonliving." Or, more simply: "The dead person is alive" (*homo mortuus est vivus*).[40] To avoid such a conclusion, the logical form of qualified and unqualified expressions must not be confused. In short: the "person" evoked in the phrase "dead person" must be understood to be a "person" relatively, rather than absolutely, speaking.

Theology, however, weighed most heavily on the question of the lifeless body. It did so in many ways. There was the issue of the condition of Christ's body after crucifixion. Was it the same as or different from the one that the Son of God possessed while still on earth? To hold a principle of simple identity could lead to heresy, because the thesis that Christ's body was unchanged at death could be understood to deny the reality of his decease. Yet a thesis of distinction between Christ's living and dead body could be taken to imply a position no less heterodox, suggesting that before resurrection, Christ's body was not yet divine.[41] General questions pertaining to human beings also demanded a rigorous treatment. The first among them involved the resurrection of the flesh, which Paul preached to the Corinthians. According to the apostle, human bodies, although "sown in corruption," would at the end of days be "raised incorruptible."[42] From the second to the fifth centuries, Christian thinkers elaborated the theory of this miraculous happening.[43] Its tenets were to be long lasting. Among the propositions condemned as heretical in Paris in 1277, there was the claim that after death, "the corrupted body does not return, one and the same, that is, does not rise numerically the same."[44] Finally, there remained the first, simplest, and perhaps most intractable of the challenges posed by the cadaver: that of its nature.

A systematic theologian, Thomas Aquinas treats all these questions, not least that of the exact status of human remains. Following Aristotle, as well as the church fathers, Thomas holds that the soul is the defining form of the human being. He maintains that at death, the soul departs from the matter that it has informed. His theory seeks to guarantee the identity of the soul, assuring its persistence from life to afterlife.[45] Yet in themselves, his theses do not resolve the questions posed by the cadaver. According to the Angelic Doctor's severer contemporaries, they may even imperil its identity. In a series of "corrections" addressed to Thomas, the thirteenth-century Franciscan William de la Mare argues that in his insistence on the soul as the sole form of the body, Thomas cannot but reduce the corpse to being an instance of the featureless substratum that is "prime matter" (*materia prima*): a being "neither a particular thing, nor a quantity, nor a quality, nor any of the other things [or categories] by which being is determined."[46] William draws out the absurd and ruinous consequence that such a reduction would entail. Were the Thomistic position correct, there would be, quite simply, no subject of death, for in the moment of decease, the living human body would be immediately replaced by indeterminate, unqualified matter. It would follow "that it was not the same body in number that died . . . and was buried." Rigorously formless, the apparent body of the dead would be no "body" at all, "prime matter" being insufficient to constitute a body.[47]

Thomas, however, is careful not to identify the living body with prime matter. As Antonia Fitzpatrick has shown, he accounts for the relative autonomy of the body from the soul by means of the Averroistic theory of "dimensive quantity" (*quantitas dimensiva*), a quasi-mathematical principle that supports organic form, assuring the body's persistent identity through nutrition, growth, and change.[48] Yet "dimensive quantity" is but a property of the living body, being an accidental form. For this reason, it cannot survive the moment of decease. In the section of his *Summa* devoted to the problems raised by the body, Thomas thus concludes, in conformity with Aristotle, that a corpse is in species and in number distinct from a living body.[49] That position continued to leave medieval philosophers and theologians dissatisfied.

Two challenges arose, as Thomas M. Ward has observed.[50] The cadaver seems to possess a shape that also resembles that of the living body. How, the philosophers asked, might one explain such a nonperson's form and likeness to the person? Thomas seems to have avoided such difficulties, yet they demanded a solution. Proposing his own account of the form of the soul in the late sixteenth century, Francisco Suárez still sought a doctrinal means to resolve these quandaries. He appealed to a divine intervention: at the moment of decease, and in the absence of any other efficient cause, he argued, "heaven or the author of nature" produces "the form of the cadaver" (*forma cadaveris*).[51] That hypothesis had obvious disadvantages. It posited an invisible occurrence: the miraculous substitution of one body by another, the inanimate double of the first. Moreover, in flagrant violation of Ockham's razor, it "multiplied beings" without reason; in cases where there would seem to be but one body, first alive and subsequently dead, it insisted on seeing two.

At the close of the thirteenth century, Duns Scotus advanced a different argument that was to be widely discussed in the Middle Ages, variously denied, adopted, and revised. Scotus held that there could be a plurality of forms within a single species, such as human beings. He argued that in addition to the soul, the substantial form known to Aristotle, there exists a "form of corporeality" (*forma corporeititas*) belonging to all animals. While the soul is the work of God, the "form of corporeality" is "drawn 'from the branch' [*ex traduce*]," deriving, in other words, from the parents of the individual animal.[52] Such a second form resolved several questions in the Scholastic doctrine of human being. Bodily properties such as extension, which appear to be at odds with an immaterial and unextended soul, found a sure foundation in this form. Above all, the apparent persistence of bodily dimensions beyond the moment of decease no longer appeared as an illusion in need of explanation or denial. Now, between "person" and "dead person" the pure homonymy for which Aristotle argued no longer held. Rather, in accordance with a profound and systematic impulse in Scotist philosophy, a new synonymy came into view.[53] According to the Subtle Doctor, one form of bodiliness belongs to the living as to the dead. It is the ground of the likeness of man and dead man, "person" and "nonperson."

That proposal offers a foundation for the suggestions made by words: the association of "corpus" and *corpse*, *līc* and *līk*, "body," and *lijk* and *Leiche*, "corpse," and the many terms indicating that the cadaver is a "like body" attest to such a form. There is little doubt that its notion was long productive in the Scholastic doctrine of the living soul. It remains so today in definitions of life as consisting of a conjunction of matter and substantial form.[54] Yet if one considers the consciousness and customs by which living persons tend regularly to the dead, it is, in a sense, all too obvious. Little is more manifest—if not also more unsettling—than the likeness of the dead body to the living. Moreover, the real difficulty confronted in mortuary traditions and practices is in a sense the inverse of the one that the Aristotelian philosophers repeatedly address. What is most urgently in need of resolution is not the question of how to dispel the illusory resemblance between the living and the dead, as Aristotle holds, or how to ground it, if one instead follows Scotus. It is, rather, the question of how to define the point at which the dead and the living body are distinguished. In their effort to confront a challenge bequeathed to thought by the ancients, the medieval philosophers leap past a major difficulty that all societies must in some way confront: When exactly is a person dead?

Through the end of the nineteenth century, the scientific, medical, and legal responses to this question varied considerably, not only across time, but even within single periods. Risks of errors in judgment remained constant. "Apparent death" and premature burial are not only predicaments evoked in literature, from the Hellenistic novel *Chaereas and Callirhoe* to Chrétien de Troyes's romance *Cligès*, from *Romeo and Juliet* to Poe's "The Fall of the House of Usher" and Zola's "The Death of Olivier Bécaille." Medical practice and legal discourse also foresaw the possibility of misidentified decease, seeking a host of measures by which to avert it. The foundation of the London Association for the Prevention of Premature Burial in 1899 and the United States Society for the Prevention of Premature Burial in 1900 testify to a shared concern. In time, it was to lead to the establishment of the public statutes that remain in force today, requiring that any declaration of decease be signed by a licensed physician.[55]

In the contemporary period, of course, the most familiar solutions to the problem of the moment of decease are legal rules developed on the basis of medical science. That such expedients are mutable is well known. In the early twentieth century, decease could be identified with the cessation of the beating of the heart and the breathing of the lungs. Within half a century, the situation had changed, following the development of the mechanical ventilator. "A person's heartbeat could now continue even when the patient had no discernible brain activity and respiration was mechanically sustained."[56] The possibility of organ transplantation further complicated the question of when to establish the time of death. Most organs begin to decay soon after the cessation of the heartbeat. If the moment of decease is established according to strictly cardiopulmonary standards, postmortem transplantation becomes extremely difficult, if not impossible, to perform.

New criteria soon emerged. In 1968, the Harvard Medical School proposed that decease be identified with the cessation of brain activity, while the Uniform Definition of Death Act, approved in the United States in 1981, identified death with the moment when a person has "sustained either irreversible cessation of circulatory and respiratory functions or irreversible cessation of all functions of the entire brain."[57] In our time, the "brain-death standard" is widely accepted. Yet this criterion, too, is also contested for several reasons. There is the fact that the decisive distinction is scarcely visible. To the naked eye, a "brain-dead" body may appear to be indistinguishable from a living one. The criterion of brain death, moreover, is foreign to many religious strictures, with which it may enter into veiled or open conflict. The progress of science, finally, may also furnish a cause of doubt. Contemporary technology is developing increasingly subtle means of measuring brain activity, thereby "calling into doubt the ability to measure brain death with any accuracy."[58]

It is not only the drawing of the line between the living and the dead, however, that raises difficulties. The nature of such a demarcation is also a problem in itself. What appears today as a border has also been represented as a threshold of a certain latitude: an expanse of variable magnitude into which the human body passes, not instantly, but gradually, as it approaches its departure from the community of the living. Anthropology has shone a bright light on such conceptions. In a groundbreaking essay published in 1905–1906, Robert Hertz was the first to reconstruct the "collective representations" in which death appears in social practice not as a punctual event, but as a "transitory state of a certain duration."[59] Focusing on the societies of Indonesia, and in particular those of the Dayak peoples of Borneo, Hertz studied the ways in which the living treat human remains in two successive moments: in the immediate aftermath of death and in the subsequent set of rites by which they later commit them to another world. He argued that such practices testify to the psychological and social foundations of mourning customs. "The brute fact of physical death is not enough to consummate death in people's minds. The image of the recently deceased is still part of the system of things of this world, and loosens itself from them only gradually by a series of internal partings."[60]

The Indonesian societies on which Hertz focused are familiar with an interval between the moment when life ceases and when the dead person is later laid to rest. This interval is a "middle state between death and the resurrection" in which certain procedures are performed, the most common among them being a first and provisional burial, to be followed by second mortuary practices at a later date.[61] Just as the human body gradually decays, its flesh being reduced, over time, to bones, persons are believed to loosen their tie to the community progressively. Among the peoples of the Malay Archipelago, Hertz noted, it is customary not to take the corpse to its burial place until "a more or less long period of time" has elapsed, during which the dead body has been placed, to decay, "in a temporary shelter." In older traditions from the region, the corpse is instead exposed outside, wrapped in bark and placed in the branches of a tree, before being buried.[62] "If a certain period is necessary to banish the deceased from the land of the living," Hertz explains, "it is because society, disturbed by the shock, must gradually regain its balance; and because the double mental process of disintegration and of synthesis that the integration of an individual into a new world supposes, is accomplished in a molecular fashion, as it were, which requires time."[63] Hertz argues that in their broad outlines, such "collective representations" are not unique. They suggest an account of the conditions of death rituals: "Mourning, at its origin, is the necessary participation of the living in the mortuary state of their relative, and lasts as long as that state."[64]

Since the corpse is not an inalterable object, but an organic being that decomposes over time, all societies must develop means to treat the stages of its persistence. Ancient Judaism furnishes a further example, which is in this regard also instructive. The Book of Numbers establishes the impure character of the human cadaver in clear terms: "He that toucheth the dead body of any man," one of its verses reads, "shall be unclean for seven days."[65] When the Rabbinic commentators of late antiquity sought to order the laws of scripture, they aimed to place this rule in a wider frame that would account for the duration in which human remains decay. Aware that from the moment of decease onward, the "dead body of any man" does not cease to change, the expositors elaborated a theory of the general conditions and consequences of the cadaver's transience: a "collective representation of death," in Hertz's terms, in which the corpse is the prime object.

Mira Balberg has proposed an illuminating analysis of the Rabbinic law of remains. "Openly and matter of factly discussing processes of decomposition and decay, in which the corpse rapidly loses its human form, dissolves into its surroundings, and eventually becomes almost indistinguishable from other matter, the rabbis construe the corpse as an entity in gradual transition from the human to the nonhuman, at the end of which it essentially disappears and becomes one with its environment."[66] It is common to assume that the "uncleanliness" of the biblical corpse derives from its removal from the living body.[67] Yet the Rabbinic sources suggest a different account, which is more subtle and less familiar. The Rabbis of the Mishnah propose a "graded system" of impurity, distinguishing among degrees of uncleanliness, in general and for the corpse and its parts.[68] In certain conditions, a dead body conveys impurity by its mere presence in an enclosed space, such as a tent; in other cases, a bodily part must be touched in order to produce uncleanliness; and in other circumstances, human remains are held to be incapable of transmitting any impurity whatsoever. Between these degrees of impurity, an order holds. It is the opposite of the one that the reader might well expect. According to the Rabbis, decomposition, in itself, produces no contamination; on the contrary, "the ability of the corpse parts to convey impurity is diminished as they disintegrate and become more fragmented."[69] In other words: "The greater the distance between a corpse part and the living body, the less capable this corpse part is of conveying impurity."[70]

The Babylonian collection known as the Tosefta offers a foundation for this rule. It distinguishes among dead bodies according to their degree of totality or fragmentation, establishing that those whose erstwhile integrity has been compromised, for example by a loss of a part or limb, are less strictly subject to legal regulation than "intact corpses."[71] Balberg has drawn the paradoxical thesis that subtends such reasoning: for the Rabbis, "the ultimate dead person is a living one."[72] A dictum attributed to Rabbi Eleazar presents this principle in startling terms: "The impurity of the living is greater than the impurity of the dead" (*merbah tum'at ha-hayim mi-tum'at ha-metim*).[73] The cadaver's most extreme uncleanliness lies in its greatest proximity to life in which nonperson and person, the dead body and the living body, can hardly be told apart. One might reason that what is most impure, in this sense, is less the "cadaver" in the Roman meaning of the term than the "corpse" that, in its novelty and its unviolated totality, seems no more than a *corpus*: something intensely similar the living person, although irreducible to it, a being of maximal — and maximally disquieting — resemblance.

In a brief but famous essay, Maurice Blanchot brought this likeness sharply into focus. Without any claim to contribute to anthropology, philology, or legal studies, and without evoking the Aristotelian problems of homonymy and the predication of decease, he raised the question of the semblance that distinguishes human remains. In an appendix to *The Space of Literature*, "Two Versions of the Imaginary," he names it "cadaverous resemblance," insisting on its singularity and importance.[74] "What we call mortal remains escapes common categories," he writes. "Something is there before us which is not really the living person, nor is it any reality at all. It is neither the same as the person who was alive, nor is it another person, nor is it anything else."[75] Blanchot defines this "something" as an "image" while immediately distinguishing it from the aesthetic object traditionally denoted by that name. "Classical art" is familiar with an image that "follows the object." It is "the object's aftermath, what comes later, what is left over and allows us still to have the object at our command when there is nothing left of it."[76] The image present in "mortal remains" is of a different nature. It is not "like" anything, being, rather, likeness itself: "If the cadaver is so similar, it is because it is, at a certain moment, similarity par excellence: altogether similarity, and nothing more. It is likeness, like to an absolute degree, overwhelming and marvelous."[77]

Death releases this "overwhelming and marvelous" resemblance, for it is solely in its power that a person begins to become "like to an absolute degree." "When the cadaverous presence is the presence of the unknown before us, the mourned deceased begins to *resemble himself*": to resemble not the "person he was when alive," but the "impersonal being, distant and inaccessible, which resemblance, in order to be the resemblance of someone, draws into the light."[78] The semblant body is in this sense a pure semblance. "The cadaver is its own image. It no longer entertains any relation with this world, where it still appears, except that of an image, an obscure possibility, a shadow ever present behind the living form which now, far from separating itself from this form, transforms it entirely into shadow.... That is why no living man, in fact, bears any resemblance yet."[79] Explicitly evoking André Breton while also alluding to Heidegger, Blanchot compares the cadaver to the presence of a "tool, once damaged." With its survival, a new being appears, "abandoned to the image": "the object's double."[80] Loosened from whatever thing of which it might have been the image, not "like something," but rather "like to an absolute degree," this double has no proper place. A "haunting presence," it is "something inaccessible from which we cannot extricate ourselves. It is that which cannot be found and therefore cannot be avoided. What no one can grasp is the inescapable."[81] Like the unburied Roman *cadaver*, like the corpses exposed in anticipation of their mortuary rites in Borneo or the untouchable shape of the dead person of Hebrew scripture, this nonperson "attacks the possibility of a *dwelling place* even for us who remain."[82]

This is why it must be removed from sight. "Eventually we have to put a term to the interminable," Blanchot writes. Otherwise "the *here*" risks falling "into the unfathomable nowhere.... And so the dear departed is conveyed into another place."[83] The statement might seem to be merely a gloss on the ancient Roman legal adage according to which "there is a public interest that corpses not lie about unburied." Yet Blanchot does more than recall the human necessity to which mortuary practices respond. He also gives an unexpected reason for the horror that the cadaver provokes, a reason distinct from decease in any of its familiar representations: as the absence of the soul from the body; as the presence of matter without any principle of form; or the cessation of organic activity, be it of the lungs, heart, or brain. Blanchot suggests that the source of unease lies elsewhere: in cadaverous resemblance. What is intolerable to the eye is what fascinates it, drawing it toward an "unfathomable nowhere": "similarity par excellence," "likeness . . . to an absolute degree, overwhelming and marvelous." The most impure of sights is that of the purely semblant body. In that thing, which was but is no longer any person, without, for that matter, not being a person, "impersonal being, distant and inaccessible," makes itself unavoidably perceptible. It is the remains that every language evokes and that none can name, if not by homonymy and its like.

CHAPTER ELEVEN

The Recurrent Voice

The period that extends from the instant of death to the moment when funeral rites have been completed may be long or brief, but it is in every case a highly structured social time in which the living adhere to a set of traditional rules and practices. The possibility of their infraction is never of minor importance. Negligence toward an unburied body can constitute more than a breach of proper conduct or an act of individual disrespect; it can also entail consequences that are threatening for the living, as well as for the deceased. When it is improperly handled, when it fails to receive the complete treatment that is owed to it, or when the rites accorded to it are, for one reason or another, illegitimate, the cadaver, a nonperson in itself, may become the source of other nonpersons, intermediary entities released from its own precariously transitional substance: beings that are not alive, yet that are also not fully dead or that, being alive as well as dead, confound the conditions of membership in a society.

Such entities are commonly known as ghosts. There is no society that is not familiar with their intermittent recurrence. Far from constituting essentially visual phenomena, as the Latin etymology of the term "specter" (from *specio*, "I look, view") suggests, such returning spirits are often—and sometimes first of all—acoustical in nature: "apparitions" to be heard, rather than beheld, like those "ghosts" that, according to Shakespeare's Calphurnia in *Julius Caesar*, "shriek and squeal about the streets."[1] Barely audible or all too perceptible, familiar or foreign, specters convey to the living tidings of intolerable survival and return. Their voices, once sounded, are not easily quieted.

These circumstances have been variously represented and illustrated, not only in domains of knowledge such as anthropology, sociology, and religious studies, but also in mythography and the writing of fiction. Lucius, the famously asinine narrator of Apuleius's *Metamorphoses*, learns of their substance and consequences at a dinner party in Thessaly, a country known in antiquity as a center of magic and the homeland of the most redoubtable of witches and sorcerers. In this territory of northern Greece, Lucius is told, "not even the dead are safe in their graves." There, the traditional relations between the living and the dead are disordered, to the detriment of all. "Human remains and body parts" (*reliquiae . . . et cadaverum praesegmina*) are "gathered from tombs and funeral pyres, and pieces are snipped from corpses," not only to defile the souls of the dead, but also "to destroy the living." And during the traditional preparations for funerals, "old hags of sorceresses . . . swoop down to snatch a body before its own people can bury it."[2]

In Apuleius's novel, a man named Thelyphron bears witness to these happenings. He recounts how, long before the festive evening at which Lucius meets him, he reached Larissa, the capital of the region, at "an evil hour," seeking some means to relieve his poverty. At the marketplace, he accepted the terms of a most unusual compact: he agreed to work as a bodyguard for a cadaver. He admits that he first greeted this proposition of employment with some skepticism: "Are corpses," he recalls asking the "tall old man" looking to hire someone, "here in the habit of running away?"[3] Yet he was immediately informed of his error. The danger to be averted lay not in the cadaver itself, but in the evil personages who stood to profit from its violation. "This is Thessaly you're in," he was told, "where witches regularly nibble pieces off the faces of the dead, to get supplies for their magic art."[4] Hence the task for the watchman. For one night, someone would be needed who would not shut his eyes, let his attention wander "for a second, or even steal a sidelong glance." He was to concentrate on the lifeless body.[5] For his labor, he would be paid a considerable sum: no less than a thousand sesterces. There was, however, a risk. The old man evoked it almost as an afterthought: "If the body is not intact when it is handed over in the morning, whatever has been removed or mutilated must be made good from the watcher's own person."[6]

Thelyphron recalls the bold terms with which, in response to the stranger's offer, he extolled his own merits: "You see before you a man of iron, who never sleeps, sharper-eyed than Lynceus or Argus, eyes all over him."[7] Thelyphron was hired, and soon he was in the home of the mourners. Admitted "through a small back door," he was led to a "small shuttered room" where he met a weeping woman, the wife of the deceased. She took him to another room, where he found himself before the dead body, then "draped in snow-white linen."[8] Once uncovered, the cadaver became the object of an inventory conducted by the widow in the presence of seven witnesses: "'Nose all there, eyes intact, ears entire, lips undamaged, chin in good shape. I ask you, fellow citizens, to note and attest this.'" The catalog of intact parts was committed to writing, inscribed on tablets and sealed.

Thelyphron was then left alone with the immobile body. "Dusk came, darkness fell, and time wore on until it was the dead of night," he recalls. "My fear was at its height when there suddenly glided in a weasel, which stood in front of me and fixed me with a piercing stare."[9] He ordered the intrepid beast away, insulting it, threatening to make it suffer for remaining near him and the cadaver. The animal did exactly as commanded. Yet Thelyphron saw little more. Suddenly he was "plunged," as he relates, "into a bottomless abyss of sleep." "The god of prophecy himself could not have told which of the two of us lying there was deader, so lifeless was I." With the benefit of hindsight, he remarks that it was he, the living man, who might that night have benefited from the presence of some guard. All he then remembered was waking at dawn. Anxiously, he rushed to the cadaver, uncovering its face. He "checked off all the features," ascertaining this extraordinary, if simple, fact: "They were there." Soon the "poor weeping widow" arrived to conduct her own examination. She reached the same results, told her steward to pay the guard for his work, and Thelyphron received his gold.[10] To his unexpected relief, he went on his way.

That the dead might stand to suffer from improper, lacunar, or botched mortuary practices was a troubling possibility well attested in ancient literature. When their bodies were denied the treatments they deserved, the souls of the dead were known, in Greek folklore and poetry, to return to haunt the living.[11] Each of the Homeric epics provides an example of such disquieting occurrences. When Achilles is slow to oversee the cremation of his beloved friend in the *Iliad*, the "soul of unhappy Patroklos" appears to him in his sleep. The Homeric ghost is an "image" or "likeness" (*eidōlon*) that possesses the dead man's stature, his "lovely eyes" and "voice," and although it is incorporeal, it is said to wear "such clothing as Patroklos wore on his body." The specter appears, stands over the hero's head, and speaks "a word" to him: "You sleep, Achilles; you have forgotten me."[12] The poet relates how the soul of the departed friend "comes back from death," without having joined the company of the deceased, to enjoin Achilles to cremate him. Only then will he be admitted into the kingdom of Hades. Gently, but firmly, the shade suggests that he will return again to Achilles if not granted the "rite of burning" that he deserves.[13]

On the threshold of his voyage to the underworld, Odysseus meets a similarly disturbed soul. In book 11 of the epic, the "man of many ways" is following Circe's advice to enter into communication with the bodiless spirits of the venerable dead, the first among them being that of Tiresias the Theban. Yet before Odysseus may converse with any spirit in Hades's realm, he meets the soul of unlucky Elpenor, the youngest of his company, "not terribly powerful in fighting nor sound in his thoughts."[14] Until this point in the unfolding of the epic action, Odysseus can presume that Elpenor has suffered the fate of many of his other men, who were transformed by Circe into swine. Now the hero learns that his companion's end was considerably less pacific: drunk, Elpenor climbed the roof of Circe's palace, slipped, and immediately rolled down to his death. His body was never found. Now the soul of the unhappily deceased marauder begs Odysseus and his men to grant him a proper burial, lest they suffer from his restlessness:

> Do not go and leave me behind unwept, unburied,
> when you leave, for I fear I might become the gods' curse upon you;
> but burn me there with all my armor that belongs to me,
> and heap up a grave mound beside the beach of the gray sea.[15]

Although they are able to make their demands for rites intelligible, the souls of the dead, in Greek representations, often speak otherwise than the living. Their voices repeatedly elude comprehension, being too subtle, too fleeting, or too insubstantial to be interpreted. When Achilles tries to embrace the image of Patroklos, it "goes underground, like vapour," making "a shrill cry" (*tetriguia*): a creaking, hissing, or squeaking sound, which is closer to the noises produced by insects and birds than human beings.[16] When Odysseus kills the iniquitous suitors at the end of the *Odyssey*, dispatching their souls to the netherworld, their company makes a like "gibbering." As Hermes herds the spirits toward their destination, they emit inarticulate, but audible noises, "as when bats in the depth of an awful cave flitter / and gibber [*trizousai poteontai*]."[17] *Trizein*, "to squeak" or "gibber," is the verb employed in both epics.[18] Other authors, such as Sophocles and Plutarch, choose a different figure, their dead producing a "buzzing" or "humming" (*bombos*, *bombein*).[19] Jan N. Bremmer has noted that these diverse sounds express a common incapacity: "The miserable sound of the souls of the dead is obviously caused by their inability to speak. Death is indeed called 'voice-robbing' by Hesiod (*Shield* 131) and Theognis (569) says that he will be as a 'voiceless stone' when he lies in the earth."[20] Developing this motif, the Roman poets represent the souls of the dead as "murmuring" (*susurrare*), "humming" or "buzzing" (*bombilare*), and, at the limit, as "silent" (*silentes*) and "mute" (*taciti*).[21] Yet their variegated wordlessness is never a simple absence of all sound. It is a silence that becomes perceptible even as it is kept.

There are many ways for a specter to be unable to speak its mind. Classical verse and prose linger on certain possibilities, while medieval literature explores others. The fourteenth-century *Treatise on the Ghost of Gui* by Jean Gobi is in this regard instructive. This Latin work recounts the unusual happenings to which its author, a Dominican monk, bore witness. The events occurred in the immediate aftermath of the death of one Gui or Guillaume de Corvo, a citizen of Alès, in southern France, in the winter of 1324 (or 1341, depending on the manuscripts). A legal record presents an abbreviated account of the case. "During the eight days following his burial," the spirit of the dead Gui is said to have returned: "He appeared, without any visible form, and solely by means of his voice, to his late wife, whom he sorely tormented."[22] "Extremely terrified," the woman sought assistance from ecclesiastical authorities. It fell to Jean Gobi, the prior of his order, to investigate the situation, determining the nature of the spirit alleged to appear, each night, in the dead man's dwelling.

Jean Gobi relates how for two consecutive nights he visited the house with three of his brethren, "more than a hundred laymen," and many other persons unknown to him. He began by asking the widow where exactly she perceived the spirit. She replied that it appeared in the bedroom she had shared with her late husband, where he had died. Jean Gobi and his three brethren then hasten to the room, where they sit on the bed of the deceased and begin to recite nine "lessons of the dead," followed by a litany. Jean Gobi recounts that as they concluded, the spirit made itself perceptible to them: "An invisible thing passed before us, and then moved toward the wife's bed, making the sound of a broom swept by itself."[23] Gui's widow seems never to have doubted the nature of the inscrutable being that the medieval manuscripts designate by the terms "thing" (*res*) and "voice" or "sound" (*vox*).[24] She was certain that it was her late husband's soul. Upon arriving in the house, Jean Gobi and his fellow churchmen, however, could not set aside the possibility that it might be the fruit of some "diabolical illusion." They aimed first to determine, therefore, whether it could be threatened by holy objects or repulsed by scriptural citations.

Establishing that the being was, as it itself claimed, "a good spirit," the monks put to it a question: "Who are you?" It answers with deceptive simplicity: "It is I."[25] Soon the spirit says much more, as Jean Gobi's *Treatise* relates. After claiming to be itself, the voice identifies itself as the dead man's soul: "Do not fear; I cannot harm you," it declares to the widow. "I am indeed the spirit of Gui, your late husband."[26] The scene is set for an extended "dialog with a ghost," in the words of Marie Anne Polo de Beaulieu, the text's editor. "It is nighttime, and each monk lights his lantern, while the rest of the house may be plunged into darkness. . . . As soon as the voice is heard, all the witnesses surround it. This closed circle functions, for two nights, to keep the spirit of the dead man in one place, supporting the project of interrogation and neutralization undertaken by Jean Gobi."[27] The one surviving pictorial representation of the narrative, dated to 1474, portrays this scene. In the chamber, a circle is formed: the widow and the prior face each other, while a notary and four others stand beside them. There is nothing to be seen inside the virtual frame that they compose, for a simple reason: the spirit's apparitions are exclusively acoustical.[28] Upon first perceiving this "voice" or "sound" (*vox*), Jean Gobi writes, everyone rushed to the bedroom, convinced that someone or something would soon unveil itself "before their own eyes." Yet the recurrent spirit remained obstinately unseen: "They saw nothing visible; they only heard a voice."[29] At first, all that could be perceived was "a strange sound," again "like that of a broom cleaning the floor."[30]

Gui's spirit had returned to speak because it was driven by the will to testify to the torment he suffered after death and Christian burial. Yet when the prior asks the voice, "by God's omnipotence, by the virtue of the body of Jesus Christ, by the milk and tears of the beatific Virgin Mary and the spirits of good," to state the reason for his suffering after decease, the spirit eludes the question. Gui's

Cy commence une vision
de lame dun honnourable
citoien de veronne en la
basse lombardie appellee
guy de thurno. Et pour
quoi lesperit apres son
trespas revenoit et tra
veilloit sa feme. Com
ment ung notable peur
coniura cel esperit. Des
demandes et responses
qui furent dentre lesprit
et le prieur. Et coment
le prieur en fin fist ung
beau don a lesperit en la
diminutio de sa penance

Prologue de lacteur.
Et la reverence
et honeur de nre
seigneur ihesus
voulons cy commencher et
exposer aucunes dispu
tations iadis faittes den
tre lesperit de ung home
trespasse Et de ung tres
notable clerc prieur des
freres prescheurs del ordre
monseigneur saint augu
stin. Et dist monseigneur
saint augustin ou livre
de la foy Que miracle ou
chose miraculeuse est chose

The ghost of Jean Gobi

Guy de Thurno, *The Soul's Vision*, miniature attributed to Simon Marmion (illumination) and David Aubert (writing), 1474, tempera. © Getty Museum, California.

soul limits itself to implicating the widow in some deed he dares not name. "Since you wish absolutely to know the reason," the returning spirit answers, "I will tell you that it is because of a great sin that we committed together in this place. We both confessed it, but since, in negligence, she did not do penance for the sin, God is now imposing this punishment on her."[31] Pressed by the clerics to say more, the ghost defends itself on doctrinal grounds, evoking a principle attributable to Augustine: "God does not wish one to reveal the sin that is effaced by confession."[32] Modern scholars have wondered as to the deed that the married couple may have committed. "A sexual sin? An infanticide?" Jean-Claude Schmitt asks, before commenting: "We will not know, because we are not to know. The theological reasons invoked are unanswerable; the spouses have admitted their sin in confession."[33] The *Treatise* also lends support to a second and more recent doctrine of the church. Confirming that the dead man's soul is both "good" and undergoing punishment after the instant of death, the *Treatise* adduces unequivocal evidence for the reality of purgatory: that "third place" that, as Jacques Le Goff has shown, becomes a crucial element of Latin theology in the twelfth century.[34]

In the representation of Gui's obstinately returning spirit, a narrative structure is discernible: some person's shade returns to the society of which that person, in life, was a member, to speak, obliquely and obscurely, of some matter that concerns the living no less than the dead. Often the configuration is at once clearer and more extreme: in such cases, the shade's tidings concern above all the living, rather than the departed. Spectral visitation, in any case, provides not only an image of the nature of the dead; it also affords an occasion for a revelation of another kind, by means of which the haunted hear of themselves, their past and future, and where they dwell. Ghosts bear a message for the living. They are their shades, in every sense.

Even where the nonpersons released from the dead seem far removed from the "thing" or "voice" heard in Jean Gobi's Alès, they often convey tidings of such a kind. Old Norse mythology and literature contain illuminating examples. In medieval Scandinavia, it was believed that a dead human being, especially one buried in unusual circumstances, could give rise to specters of a special sort: "not wraiths, disembodied spirits," as N. K. Chadwick has written, "but the incorporate spirits of the dead, animated corpses, solid bodies, generally mischievous, and greatly to be feared."[35] Such variegated beings appear throughout the Old Norse tradition, from the *Elder Edda* to the *Prose Edda*, the so-called "family sagas," and the "outlaw sagas."[36] Like the revenants of medieval Latin Europe, the Old Norse living dead intrude upon the societies in which they have no proper place not only to offer an image of existence after decease, but also to speak to the living of themselves.

An enigmatic Swedish shepherd of the *Saga of Grettir the Strong* offers perhaps the most enlightening instance of these "incorporate spirits of the dead." Glam is first introduced to the reader as a man "heavily built and strange in appearance, with eyes dark and wide open, wolf-grey in the colour of his hair."[37] He is hired by an Icelander to help defend his farm, which, as the narrator explains, "was subject to a lot of haunting" (*þar var reimt mjög*) by some "evil spirit" (*meinivættir*).[38] Yet before Glam can accomplish this task, he dies on Christmas Eve, shunning the fast respected by Christians and instead venturing outside in bad weather and, as the reader learns, "in rather a nasty mood." On Christmas Day, the farmers find his body in "a big area of trampled snow high up in the valley," lying "dead and blue as Hel and swollen up as an ox."[39] They infer that "the evil creature that had previously been there must have killed Glam, and that he must have caused it a great wound which had finished it off, for there has never been any trace of this evil creature since."[40] The farmers try twice to carry the dead shepherd's body to church for a proper funeral and burial, but it cannot be moved. On the third day after Christmas, a priest goes out to the field in search of the body, but it has disappeared. "Soon after," the saga relates, "people discovered that Glam was not resting in peace. This was a source of great affliction to people, so that many fell into a faint if they saw him, and some lost their wits. . . . People scarcely dared to go up into the valley even if they had good reason. This was thought in the district to be a source of great trouble."[41]

Glam is no longer alive, but he is also less, or perhaps more, than deceased. As if in precocious illustration of the logic of the Kantian infinite judgment, which defines an object by placing it in the endlessly "determinable," yet limited domain of everything that it is not, Glam is at this point in the saga neither alive nor not alive, neither dead nor not dead; instead, he is precisely "nondead," or, more idiomatically, "undead."[42] In Old Norse terms, he has become an *aptrangr* or *draugr*: a "revenant."[43] It is not his soul that has been loosened from his body, as in the traditions familiar to the Latin West, but rather his body that now survives its ordinary end.[44] Glam remains, at every point in the saga, a creature of flesh and blood. In conformity with the model of the Old Norse *draugr*, he is in death "larger, heavier, and, above all, stronger" than he was in life; his face and eyes are darker and "more terrifying" than they ever were.[45]

Grettir the Strong alone may vanquish him, in a battle that constitutes the crucial turning point of the saga. Grettir comes to the farm that Glam was once to have defended and that must now be protected from his intermittent visitations. At night, the revenant stealthily enters the farm. Grettir is waiting and pursues him. A terrible struggle ensues until Glam falls to the ground, "face upwards and backwards outside the building, with Grettir on top of him."[46] The saga lingers on this nocturnal scene: "There was bright moonlight outside and gaps in the heavy cloud. Sometimes it clouded over and sometimes it cleared away."[47]

Until this point in the saga, the undead man has moved outside all human community, and the reader cannot know whether, in his monstrous afterlife, he retains the ability to speak. Now the situation changes. The revenant addresses his adversary by name:

> At the moment Glam fell, the cloud cleared from the moon and Glam glared up at it. "You have displayed great zeal, Grettir," he said, "in seeking me out,

> and it will not seem surprising if you do not gain a great deal of good fortune from your encounter with me. But I can tell you this, that you have now acquired half the strength and development that was intended for you if you had not met me. I cannot now deprive you of the strength that you have already acquired, but I can ensure that you never become any stronger than you are now, and yet even now you are strong enough, as many will find out to their cost. You have become renowned up to now for your deeds, but from now on you will become guilty of crimes and deeds of violence, and nearly everything you do will lead to your misfortune and failure. You will be made outlaw and be compelled always to live in the open on your own. I also lay this upon you that these eyes of mine will be always before your sight, and you will find it hard to be alone and this will bring you to your death."[48]

With these words, the revenant at once confirms Grettir's status and lessens it. Glam, who is beyond the limit of natural life, specifies the thresholds of social and legal existence beyond which Grettir will now pass as he becomes an outcast and an outlaw.[49] Despite being congratulated and rewarded for his exploit, Grettir immediately knows that he has paid a price for his struggle with the undead man. The narrator comments:

> Grettir said there had been no improvement in his temper and said he was now much worse controlled than before, and he found it harder to bear being crossed. He noticed this great difference in himself, that he had become a person so afraid of the dark that he dared go nowhere on his own after it got dark; there appeared to him then all sorts of apparitions, and it has since been used as a saying that "Glam has lent someone his eyes" or "they have been given gloomsight" [*Glámur augna eða gefi glámsýni*] when things seem very different from what they are.[50]

Glam's words to Grettir have been read in several senses: as threat, prophecy, and curse. What is certain is that the revenant's utterance bears, from start to finish, on the living man, on whom it takes effect.

Later literary ghosts are rarely so prolix, and one impulse in the modern imagination seems to tend toward the figuration of specters ever more taciturn. That they bear some message for the living, however, is often all too certain, even when they are unable or perhaps unwilling to deliver it distinctly. The last of Henry James's ghost stories, "The Jolly Corner," proposes the most radically reconfigured example of such a narrative structure. In this tale, which was first published in 1908, a man finds himself in the company of a being no less spectral for being mute — and for being "somebody" other than any known variety of ghost. After twenty-three years in Europe, Spencer Brydon, aged fifty-six, is on his "so strangely belated return to America" to tend to his two properties in New York. One of them is his family residence: his "house on the jolly corner," "as he usually, and quite fondly, described it."[51] After his long absence, Brydon renews his long-standing affective ties with his "old friend," Alice Staverton, now "in the afternoon of life."[52] When Brydon tells her of his attachment to the house, of "the value of all he read into it, into the mere sight of the walls, mere shapes of the rooms, mere sound of the floors, mere feel, in his hand, of the old silver-plated knobs of the several mahogany doors," she wagers that he "may still, after all, want to live" in it.[53] Brydon assents to her suggestion, but he submits it to a syntactical and logical revision. Responding to her remark, he rewrites her present tense as an imperfect conditional, making of the future chance she evoked a past, unrealized possibility: that is, in logical terms, a past counterfactual. "'Oh,' he said, 'I *might* have lived here (since I had my opportunity early in life); I might have put in here all these years. Then everything would have been different enough."[54]

The action of the story follows from the materialization of that revision. In the walls of the house on the "jolly corner," what "might have been" assumes an increasingly definite shape. Miss Staverton is the first to perceive and designate it. In terms that hover between the literal and the figurative, she claims to have "seen" what or who her friend might have been had he never left New York City for Europe. The thought of that vision and its counterfactual subject fascinates Brydon. "'*He* isn't myself,'" he remarks. "'He's the just so totally other person. But I do want to see him,' he added. 'And I can. And I shall.'"[55]

Brydon is soon convinced that he has succeeded in his project, having discerned a "presence" moving through the house. The tale represents his thoughts, rendering his impressions by quotation marks, both suggesting and contesting the humanity of the shade that has captivated his imagination:

> His *alter ego* "walked" — that was the note of his image of him, while his image of his motive for his own odd pastime was the desire to waylay him and meet him. He roamed, slowly, warily, but all restlessly, he himself did . . . and the presence he watched for would roam restlessly too. But it would be as cautious and as shifty; the conviction of its probable, in fact its already quite sensible, quite audible evasion of pursuit grew for him from night to night, laying on him finally a rigour to which nothing in his life had been comparable.[56]

Brydon himself is the first to remark upon the unusual, if not unique character of this "*alter ego*," which is at once "the just so totally other person" and yet also himself as he might have been. The shade and image is somehow him, the man, yet also not. "People enough, first and last, had been in terror of apparitions, but who had ever before so turned the tables and become himself, in the apparitional world, an incalculable terror?"[57]

The "turning of the tables" results in a disorientation of several kinds.[58] Every night, Brydon walks through his house on regular "rounds" in pursuit of the "presence," even as he is overtaken by an "absolutely unmistakable" sentiment: that of "his being definitely followed, tracked at a distance carefully taken and to the express end that he should the less confidently, less arrogantly, appear to himself merely to pursue."[59] At first, "his fully dislocated thoughts of these manœuvres recalled to him Pantaloon, at the Christmas farce, buffeted and tricked from behind by ubiquitous Harlequin."[60] Soon, however, he reasons in terms of "combat," rather than comedy.[61] One evening, he notices that on the fourth floor, a door that he left open has been closed. He opens it, only to see that another door, which he had closed, has been opened. Knowing that he is in proximity to the being that he has sought, Brydon advances farther into the house. As he approaches the "presence," the text represents a vision: a shadow, a screen, and a figure on the threshold of being formed.

> The penumbra, dense and dark, was the virtual screen of a figure which stood in it as still as some image erect in a niche or as some black-vizored sentinel guarding a treasure.... He saw, in its great grey glimmering margin, the central vagueness diminish, and he felt it to be taking the very form toward which, for so many days, the passion of his curiosity had yearned.[62]

Brydon has met a being to which only an indistinctly expletive or impersonal pronoun "it" is adequate: "It gloomed, it loomed, it was something, it was somebody, the prodigy of a personal presence."[63] In a second moment, that wonder assumes a shape: "Rigid and conscious, spectral yet human, a man of his own substance and stature waited there to measure himself with his power to dismay."[64] The narrator comments: "The revulsion, for our friend, had become, before he knew it, immense."[65] Staring at the pair of hands that he sees raised before him, as if to conceal the stranger's face in a gesture of "dark deprecation," Brydon sees that the "spectral yet human" body has been inexplicably mutilated: one hand "had lost two fingers, which were reduced to stumps, as if shot away."[66]

> These hands, as he looked, began to move, to open; then, as if deciding in a flash, dropped from the face and left it uncovered and presented. Horror, with that sight, had leaped into Brydon's throat, gasping there in a sound he couldn't utter; for the bared identity was too hideous as *his*, and his glare was the passion of his protest. The face, *that* face, Spencer Brydon's? — he searched it still, but looking away from it in dismay and denial, falling straight from his height of sublimity. It was unknown, inconceivable, awful, disconnected from any possibility![67]

As "the stranger, whoever he might be, evil, odious, blatant, vulgar," advances threateningly, a struggle ensues. Brydon loses consciousness: "His head went round; he was going; he had gone."[68]

In the final section of the story, Brydon opens his eyes to find himself in the "ample and perfect cushion" that is Miss Alice Staverton's lap. From the confrontation with "the stranger," he has wrested a new knowledge, which he expresses in a single utterance: "There's somebody—an awful beast; whom I brought, too horribly, to bay. But he's not me." Three distinct theses are discernible in these dense phrases: a position of existence, by which "somebody," "an awful beast," hovering between the human and the nonhuman, is said to be; a claim about a completed action (the bringing of the "somebody" "to bay"); and a denial that establishes the substantial difference between the "somebody" and Brydon—or, in grammatical terms, between a third person ("it" or "him") and a first person ("me"). That it is the last of these three theses that matters most to Brydon is suggested by the words that he utters a page later, which define his relation to the "beast": "He's none of *me*, even as I *might* have been."[69]

The syntax of that two-part statement calls out for analysis, even as it resists it. A parallelism is established between a predicative being in the present indicative, which is a "being of" ("he's none of *me*"), and a transitive being of equivalence, which is a "being something," in the imperfect conditional ("I *might* have been"). How the two claims are to be related is difficult to decide, for the conjunctive "even as" suggests several possibilities. Absolute and relative being can hardly be told apart. "Even as" may be interpreted as one unit, such that "even as I *might* have been" means: "Even as I *might* have existed." But "even as" may also be anaphoric, indicating a truncation. The phrase then signifies: "He is none of *me*, even as I might have been [of him]." The sole certainty is the repeated affirmation of nonidentity. Brydon denies that he is himself the "horror," the "awful beast," the "brute" and "black stranger" with whom he has struggled.[70]

Critics of the tale have long sought to specify the exact nature of the "brute" that the narrator of "The Jolly Corner" fails, or perhaps refuses, to identify. Depending on the scholar, the mutilated "somebody" has been said to represent some modality of Brydon's mind or self, or James's; an unconscious proper to the character or to its author; the love or marriage that Brydon or James refused; or "American modernity" and its historical or most recent rapacious ambitions.[71] Nothing in "The Jolly Corner" excludes the possibility of these interpretations. Yet such glosses run the risk of avoiding the difficulty that the tale poses to the reader. "In this drama—this pantomime—of facts and figures, 'the one great fact,'" Deborah Esch notes, "has been and remains 'the incalculability,' the indeterminacy of the figure—the force that overwhelms Brydon when, in the story's climactic scene, he encounters his *alter ego* in all its identity and difference."[72] In that scene, Brydon first cannot see the face that stands before him; when, later, he succeeds in fixing his gaze upon it, it appears to him, in his own words, as "unknown, inconceivable, awful, disconnected from all possibility—!" The face, in short, is either masked or "inconceivable." In either case, it is unreadable, and the ghost, if that is what it is, remains strictly unidentifiable.

Whatever and whoever it may be, the "black stranger" walking through the upper floors of the Jolly Corner casts a pall over Spencer Brydon's life that his final awakening, felicitous as it may appear to be, cannot fully dispel. The reason is all too simple and follows from one of the basic conventions in ghost fictions. However diverse they may be in their shape and function, specters, revenants, and all manner of the undead share at least one task: they obstinately testify to a death. Implicitly but unmistakably, James's tale suggests a revision to this rule that vastly expands the field of the deceased. Here, in the movement from a present or future possibility to an imperfect conditional, in the passage from a "may still" to a "might have been," a life ends; something, someone, or "somebody" dies. The past counterfactual—the possibility that was not, yet could have been—becomes the semblant body, "spectral yet human," that emerges in the instant of decease to haunt, even to stalk, the living. But this reconfiguration of the fiction of the revenant immediately implies an obvious consequence. It follows ineluctably from the "farce" or "game of *ombres chinoises*"[73] that the narrative stages: if Brydon has a ghost, then either he himself or something in him must be deceased.

This consequence sets the tale's plot in a new perspective. In seeking to rid himself of his own ghost, the cultivated American steps forth in an astonishingly unsettling guise: he appears, in essence, as an animate cadaver who, long missing, now vainly strives to reclaim the home he once possessed. Yet from the structure of this Jamesian tale, one may also draw a second inference that is both darker and more comical than the first. If the "awful" *alter ego* appears to Brydon as a "man" of "substance and stature," it may be simply because "the black stranger" is, in truth, exactly what he seems to be — because, in other words, it is Spencer Brydon, and no one else, who is the roaming ghost.

The "horror," in such a reading, would lie in the discovery that the "brute" had been waiting, mutely but insistently, to deliver the most intolerable of news. Gesturing without words, manifestly silent while lacking neither reason nor language, the "awful beast" would inform the sophisticated American of the circumstance that he least dreamt of admitting: that he, despite appearances, was the nonman, the other "he," the "stranger," being the actual, if irreparably damaged man. Brydon's pronouncement, in this case, would still hold: "He" would be "none of *me*." Yet that thesis would sound in a sense contrary to the one with which the convalescent man reassures himself and his gracious interlocutor. The real reference of the personal pronouns would be opposed to the one that Bryon imagines: the "he," "unknown, inconceivable, awful," would point to the living human being, while the known, the conceivable, and the familiar — the "*me*," in all its illusory confidence and self-certainty — would designate the "beast," no less lifeless for possessing an apparently intact body.

With far less luck and decorum than Spencer Brydon, Thelyphron, in the *Metamorphoses* of Apuleius, learns a lesson of this kind. No sooner does he leave the place where he earned his pay as a corpse guard than the cadaver, too, departs. "As was traditional for a member of an aristocratic family," Thelyphron recalls in his tale, "it was being given a public funeral. The procession was passing through the city square when there appeared an old man in black, weeping and tearing his handsome white hair."[74] The elder Thessalian levels a serious charge: he alleges that the dead man was murdered by his wife "to please her lover and get her hands on the estate."[75] His allegation is met with various reactions. Shocked, some members of the procession rise up against the widow, who bursts into "well-studied" tears. The "crowd," in Thelyphron's words, begins to "turn ugly." Yet the old man has foreseen such strife, and he quickly proposes a means to resolve the discord. Leading forward "a young man dressed in a linen tunic and palm-leaf sandals with his head shaved bare," he introduces Zatchlas of Egypt, a priest capable of summoning the soul of the corpse from the underworld, thus restoring "his body to life."[76] Zatchlas proceeds to return the departed to the body that was his. The cadaver begins to speak: "Why, why, have you called me back for these few moments to life and its obligations, when I have already drunk the water of Lethe and embarked on the marshes of the Styx? Let me, I beg you, leave me to my rest."[77]

The soul of the dead man, however, prevaricates only briefly before dispelling the mystery of his untimely decease. "I died by the wicked arts of my new wife," the corpse explains. "Doomed to drink her poisoned cup, I surrendered my marriage bed to an adulterer before it had grown cold." The widow protests and, in the crowd, several views are soon heard. Some respect the veracity of the cadaver; others claim that a dead body that speaks "should," in principle, "not be believed." To defend his claims, the animated man has little choice but to provide incontrovertible evidence. The cadaver points at the astonished Thelyphron, declaring:

> There is the man who guarded my body. He performed his duties with the utmost alertness, so that the hags who were waiting to plunder my corpse, though they changed themselves into all sorts of shapes to achieve their purpose, failed to outwit his vigilance. At last they wrapped a cloud of sleep round him, and while he was buried in deep oblivion, they kept calling me by name, until my numbed limbs and chilled body made reluctant efforts to obey their magic summons. But at this point he heard his own name, which is the same as mine, and being in fact alive, though sleeping like the dead, he got up without knowing what he was doing and, like a lifeless ghost, walked

> mechanically over to the door. Though it had been carefully bolted, there was a hole in it, and through that they cut off first his nose and then his ears. Thus he suffered the mutilation that was meant for me. Then, so as not to give the game away, they made shapes of his missing ears and nose in wax and fitted them exactly in place. And there he stands, poor devil, paid not for his work but for his disfigurement.[78]

In Thelyphron these words inspire horror. He puts his hands to his face as the truth of the corpse's words becomes all too tangible: "I took hold of my nose, and it came off; I tried my ears, and so did they. Everybody was pointing at me, turning round to look at me, and there was a roar of laughter. Bathed in a cold sweat I slunk away through the crowd, and since then I have not been able to face returning home to be mocked, looking like this."[79] Listening to the cadaver's newfound voice, the living man comes to know what he could not see: he has been defaced. "Buried in deep oblivion," he missed the crucial moment, even as he remained dimly susceptible to the power of an address. Although he could not respond by speech to the voice that seemed to summon him by name, he also could not ignore it, and so he advanced, "like a lifeless ghost," to the edge of the space where, still sleeping, he would be irrevocably disfigured in place of another.

Such events would be unimaginable as well as unimagined were it not for a single fact, which the reader, like the guests of the Thessalian dinner party, discovers only at this point. A hidden bond joined the living to the deceased: that of homonymy. The dead and the living, in Apuleius's tale, bear a single name. When this circumstance of designation comes to light, the "tale of Thelyphron" shows itself to be a narrative of two individuals who are distinct in substance, yet indiscernible in appellation: "Thelyphron" the cadaver, who appears to rest in silence, to be guarded before burial, and "Thelyphron" the man, who seems the sole teller of his tale, before becoming the narrated subject of a story recounted by an unexpectedly loquacious cadaver. "The tables," in Henry James's narrator's terms, are thus "turned": the deceased, who seemed by definition speechless, discloses the decisive happenings in the first person, while the living, astonished, falls silent, becoming a third party.[80] From the voice of the body that was his namesake, Thelyphron, in this way, receives the tidings that no living being could have conveyed to him. He, and no one else, was the fragile subject of the vigil at which he could not stay awake. The rites were his and his alone, as he himself, unconscious and yet still not insensible, somehow knew. For Thelyphron, however, the lesson came too late.

CHAPTER TWELVE

Some Ones Left

Whatever the laws that govern their remains, whatever the rites performed in their memory, and whatever the beliefs concerning their physical and spiritual persistence, the dead, in human societies, always count. Yet beneath the evidence of that simple fact, several difficulties lie concealed. It may be granted that corpses are not to be "thrown out like dung," as Heraclitus boldly recommended; it may be admitted without controversy that cadavers are not nothing and, more generally, that the deceased, for the living, are never no one. A question nonetheless arises: What or who, then, are such individuals or things? What are they, in other words, if they are not persons or, for that matter, not *not* persons? From community to community, culture to culture, the terms with which one might seek to answer such questions may vary, but the challenge remains constant. Symmetrical considerations might be advanced concerning living persons, once it is recalled that in their practices, they are rarely indifferent to the afterlife of the deceased. What is the nature of a human society, one might then ask, if it is composed less of those alive than of those left alive in the absence of some others?

Nowhere do such questions resound more insistently than in the recurrent circumstances in which persons aim to secure some representation of their collective magnitude, determining their quantity: how many they may be. The difficulties of counting spare no one: the dead no less than the living. In such moments, problems of human arithmetic demand treatment. How persons are to be numbered, which persons are to be numbered, and for what duration any given count of persons may be considered to be valid—these are but some of the issues that any quantification of persons must confront. Such difficulties leave their mark not only on censuses and chronicles and the histories of nations and empires, but also on the writing of myth, literature, and some of the books that religious traditions have taken to be most holy.

The New Testament provides an instructive, if extraordinary narrative that attests both to the problems of how to number persons and to a uniquely wondrous solution brought to them. The episode, which appears in slightly differing detail in all three Synoptic Gospels, may be simply recounted.[1] Having crossed to the other side of the Sea of Galilee, reaching a land called Gerasa, Gadara, or Gergasa, Jesus meets a man who has become many, being possessed by indefinitely numerous demons. Jesus converses with him, exorcises the multitude of spirits that have tormented him, and thus returns him to sanity, health, and unicity.[2]

The most extended account of the encounter is in the Gospel of Mark, which presents the reader with what has been judged at once "the most 'stupendous'" and the "most scandalous" of the miracle stories in the New Testament.[3] Mark introduces the wild Gadarene by repeatedly remarking on the place he has taken as a residence. The demoniac has come from "out of the tombs" (*ek mnēmeiōn*); he has had "his dwelling in the tombs" (*en tois mnēmasin*); he has been spending day and night "in the tombs and in the mountains [*en tois mnēmasin kai en tois oresin*], crying out and cutting himself with stones."[4] The gospel suggests that while in life, this man has, in other words, begun to live as if among the dead. One scholar argues that the Gadarene's cries and self-inflicted wounds are best understood as a "*mourning ritual*—surely the most exhibitionist of rituals—which has got out of hand."[5] That they allude to traditional Jewish legal principles and practice is beyond doubt. As Rudolf Pesch observes, the Talmud identifies burial sites as "the favourite resort of unclean spirits (*bab. Nidda* 17a); and among the typical marks of a demoniac it includes: 'Being abroad at night, spending the night in a burial place, tearing his garments, destroying what people give to him (*jer. Terum.* 40b, 23).'"[6] The possessed man illustrates these traits.

In Mark, the Son of God heals the demoniac by the power of speech. Following what would appear to have been the traditional practice for ancient exorcism, Jesus utters the formula known as *apopompē*: he commands the "unclean spirit" to "come out of the man."[7] These words, however, seem insufficient to their task, for Jesus proceeds to make a further request—or perhaps to issue a second command, phrased in the interrogative mode. He asks the man: "What is thy name" (*ti onoma soi*)?[8] That query is exceptional, being the sole instance in the entire New Testament in which one person requests a name of another.[9] The answer that Jesus receives is no less remarkable. The demoniac responds without proposing any Hebrew, Greek, or Roman appellation. Instead, he claims for himself a common noun, woven into a complex and enigmatic proposition: "My name is Legion, for we are many" (*Legiōn onoma moi, hoti polloi esmen*).[10]

Rendering the same events, Luke presents a far less perplexing exchange. His demoniac says merely: "Legion." To this self-naming, the narrator of the gospel adds the following gloss: "Because many demons were entered into him."[11] In Luke, differences of number and place in the event of enunciation are clearly drawn. The individual names himself by a term generally employed to denote a multitude, but there is no confusion between unicity and plurality: the demoniac is one, even as he designates himself by the name "Legion." So, too, in Luke, speaker and commentator remain distinct; the Gadarene refers to himself as one person, even as the Evangelist interprets his words with reference to the mass of demons that has possessed him. Mark's rendition is denser and more equivocal. Singular and plural as well as speaker and commentator become rigorously indistinguishable: the demoniac identifies himself as at once "I" and "we," one and many. Paraphrasing the sense of this self-identification while retaining the nonsense of its syntax, one might say that in Mark, the Gadarene bears the name "Legion" because they are numerous.

In Mark, Luke, and Matthew, the demoniac's self-naming associates him with the Roman military formation in several senses, not least those of "belligerent multiplicity, hostile troop, occupying army, . . . invader and, perhaps, those who will crucify Christ."[12] Yet Mark takes a further step when he commits the possessed man to a statement that is not only surprising in meaning, but also aberrant in its grammatical structure. The declaration, "My name is Legion, for we are many," conjoins a phrase uttered in the first-person singular with a phrase uttered in the first-person plural, and what is more peculiar, it makes of the second phrase the explanation of the first.

Commentators have interpreted its shape in several ways. Herbert Preisker suggests that the transition from singular to plural alludes to the double status of the legion as both one and many, unit and plurality.[13] Joachim Jeremias holds instead that the sentence is to be explained by virtue of the differing vocabularies of the two languages closest to the Evangelists: *legiōna* in Aramaic means "soldier," yet it was rendered in Greek by the cognate *legiōn*, thereby prompting "the mistaken idea" that "the demoniac was possessed of a whole regiment of demons."[14] What is certain is that in Mark, the Gadarene's broken syntax achieves a remarkable effect. In a single utterance, the speaking subject shifts, as if to testify to a source of speech no longer in possession of itself. As Jean Starobinski remarks, "the same voice that says 'my name' (*onoma moi*) becomes a collective voice, and we are surprised here by the paradoxical effect of an anacoluthon."[15]

The next lines in Mark relate the discourse of the demoniac indirectly, referring it to some plural subject. "They," multiple, yet unspecified in their names and number, beg Jesus not to command them "to go out into the deep." "They" would rather enter into "an herd of many swine feeding on the mountain."[16] Without speaking any more words to the company of demons, Jesus grants them their request. The exorcism, however, leads them to their death: "Then went the devils out of the man, and entered into the swine: and the herd ran violently down a steep place into the lake, and were choked."[17] Having passed from man to animal and from the body of one to those of many, the unruly multitude perishes in a collective fall. Without explaining the basis for his assertion, Mark remarks that "they" — the swine, that is, or perhaps the mass of demons, if not both — "were about two thousand."[18] That many had been in the man, with him, acting and speaking in his stead.

Once relieved of their unruly plurality, the Gadarene regains his mind. He is then nameless, yet the syntax of the Gospel suggests that he is of a determinate number. Mark relates how "him that was possessed with the devil, and had the legion" is soon seen "sitting, clothed," in proximity to Jesus.[19] The man who was "many" (*polloi*) when residing among the dead has become one among the living. At the close of the episode, "he that had been possessed" asks his savior if he may remain in his presence.[20] Jesus, however, sends him away: "Go home to thy friends," he commands the man, "and tell them how great things the Lord hath done for thee, and hath had compassion on thee."[21] The "great things" done for him consist not only in the act of exorcism, but in the consequent alteration of his quantity: Jesus has assured that to one human body there corresponds one soul and no more. The "legion" has been dispersed, and the narrative moves on to other wonders.

Before the Gospels, the sacred books of the Hebrews insisted on the importance of counting persons one by one while alluding to the dangers inherent in that undertaking. In the first five books of the Hebrew Bible, God twice demands that the "children of Israel" be submitted to a census. Both times, his faithful servants are to oversee this count of heads. At the opening of the Book of Numbers, God speaks to Moses, "on the first day of the second month, in the second year after they were come out of the land of Egypt," issuing this order: "Take ye the sum of all the congregation of Israel [*se'u et-rosh kol-'adat beney-yisra'el*], after their families, by the house of their fathers, with the number of their names [*bemispar shemot*], every male by the polls. From twenty years old and upward, all that are able to go forth to war in Israel: thou and Aaron shall number them by their armies."[22] Six hundred thousand and three hundred and fifty persons will thus be numbered.[23] They are all men: women, children, and foreigners, if there are any in the desert, are excluded from this census. So, too, are the Levites, a holy class whose adult men are counted separately.

Later in the same book of the Bible, the children of Israel reach Shittim and begin "to commit whoredom with the daughters of Moab," "joining" themselves to the worship of Ba'al Peor. It is at this moment that Phinehas, the son of Aaron, kills two unnamed, yet infamously licentious offenders in an attempt to redress their sin. Despite this righteous execution, the anger of the Lord is kindled, and a mortal plague strikes the children of Israel. Hebrew scripture relates the exact number of persons who die: "Twenty and four thousand."[24] Echoing the terms of the law he gave to Moses, God then commands Aaron to oversee a second census of his people: "Take the sum of all the congregation of the children of Israel [*se'u et-rosh kol-'adat beney-yisra'el*], from twenty years old and upward, throughout their fathers' house, all that are able to go to war in Israel."[25] There follows an enumeration of the families taken into consideration, the Levites being once again counted separately. A second total count of Hebrew men is thus reached: "These are they that were numbered of the children of Israel, six hundred thousand and a thousand and seven hundred and thirty."[26]

Later in the sacred history of the Jews, the counting of persons plays a different role. Rather than following a plague, as in the second census in Numbers, the third numbering of the Hebrews precipitates one. This tally is recounted twice in Judaic historiography, in both Second Samuel and First Chronicles.[27] The difference between the two narratives is striking. Second Samuel relates that some years into the reign of David, "the anger of the Lord was kindled" against the king. In this account, God then issues an order to the overweening king: "Go, and number Israel and Judah" (*lekh meneh et-yisra'el ve'et-yehudah*).[28] First Chronicles sets a different scene. David is driven to begin numbering his people by another speaker: "Satan stood up against Israel," we read, "and provoked David to number Israel" (*vayyaset et-david, limnot et-yisra'el*)."[29] Depending on the biblical record to which one turns, the incitement to count persons is thus divine or satanic. What remains constant is the necessity: the people must be numbered. Between the second and the third census, there is, moreover, a common trait: the count of the living occurs in closest proximity to the count of those killed by the plague.

In Second Samuel as well as First Chronicles, Joab, the king's nephew and the commander of his army, seeks to dissuade David from carrying out the census. When the monarch orders Joab to take the count in Second Samuel, Joab responds with a question: "Why doth my lord the king delight in this thing?" First Chronicles suggests that Joab has some intuition of the perils of the project that he is to oversee: "Why doth my lord require this thing?" he asks in this account. "Why will he be a cause of guilt unto Israel?"[30] In both cases, the king's word prevails against Joab. The people are counted. In Second Samuel, David has no sooner taken the sum than he grasps his sin. He begs God, then, for forgiveness.[31] In First Chronicles, it is the Lord who first reacts to the census he has demanded: "God was displeased with this thing."[32] In both narratives, the wages of numbering is death. A pestilence strikes the children of Israel. The two accounts also concur on the arithmetic of loss: seventy thousand men perish from the plague.[33]

Why does the numbering of the living lead, both times, to so many deaths? Various answers have been proposed. According to the Talmudic tractate Yoma, any numbering of the Hebrews is strictly forbidden. Several ancient authorities are cited in support of this view. Rabbi Yitzhak explains: "It is forbidden to count the people of Israel." Rabbi Eleazar declares: "Whoever counts Israel transgresses a [biblical] prohibition, as it is said, *Yet the number of the children of Israel shall be as the sand of the sea, which cannot be measured*." Rav Nachman bar Yitzhak offers a fuller commentary: "He would transgress two prohibitions, for it is written, *Which cannot be measured nor numbered*."[34] Not all traditional exegetes, however, hold this position. The twelfth-century commentators Nahmanides and David Kimhi both contend that a census of the Jewish people is permissible, provided the circumstances demand it. King David errs not so much in numbering his subjects, these medieval rabbis contend, as in doing so in the absence of any justification: he counts "for no reason" (*shelo letzorekh*), incurring the divine punishment that his people will then bear.[35]

Yet there is also a further explanation. According to this reading, David's error is neither simply to count nor to count without a proper cause. It is to count, rather, without respecting the proper form by which persons are to be numbered. This is the reading advanced in the Talmudic tractate Berakhot, in which God announces that he will lead David to commit the most elementary of mistakes: "Rabbi Eleazar said: Said the Holy One, blessed be He, to David: Thou callest me a 'stirrer-up.' Behold, I will make thee stumble over a thing which even school-children know, namely, that which is written, *When thou takest the sum of the children of Israel according to their number, then shall they give every man a ransom for his soul unto the Lord.*"[36] In determining the number of the children of Israel and Judah, David "stumbles" by failing to observe a rule given to Moses for the census. Exodus establishes that "the sum of the children of Israel" is to be secured, in each case, by means of an offering: each man is to pay "a ransom for his soul unto the Lord" so "that there be no plague among them" through the fact of being numbered.[37] Every man to be counted must offer up "half a shekel, after the shekel of the sanctuary"; only after such a tax is levied may the census be taken.[38] How this "ransom" is to be understood, why the amount is fixed as this quantity, and why the threat of a plague stands over persons counted without observance of the tax is all today, in large part, obscure.[39] Yet in its structure, the practice dictated in Exodus is suggestive. If numbering is permitted once "half a shekel" has been paid, it may be because the counting then proceeds indirectly. Between those whose lives are tallied and the single number that they will compose, a third element will have intervened: the half shekel. It is not a multiplicity of living heads, but rather the "head" that is capital, in such conditions, that will have been summed. Perhaps this is how the counted are to be spared: where no one is directly numbered, no one is endangered.[40]

Even when the administration of a census does not run the risk of incurring a plague, the numbering of people disturbs the order of the living and the dead. The counting of persons has repeatedly led to the encounter with nonpersons—and with nonpersons of several varieties. Modern European literature contains what is perhaps its most extraordinary witness to such occurrences in Gogol's 1842 "poem" (*poema*), *Dead Souls*. Early nineteenth-century Tsarist demographic and fiscal practice furnish this novel with its basic conceit. The work is set in the age of the empire in which Russian landowners paid a yearly tax determined by the number of serfs or "souls" (*dushi*) belonging to their estate. That number was set by the state census. Since, however, years and even decades might elapse between one count and the next, serfs registered as alive in one numbering would often die after a census. Such peasants would continue, for a time, to count as alive for the purposes of the law. The administrative rule was on this point clear: landowners were to pay tax for all the "souls" recorded as in their possession during the last census, regardless of what might have happened to them from that point to the present moment.

Hence the ingenious plot that Pavel Ivanovich Chichikov, the "hero" of Gogol's work, devises to make the most of these legal circumstances. Being himself neither a serf nor a landowner, nor, for that matter, a censor, he intends to act upon the relations between persons, things, and the dead, profiting from the reality of persons who are at once definitively missing and yet taxable as if present. He proposes to relieve small and often impecunious landowners of the burden of their "dead souls." Chichikov goes so far as to offer to assume the weight of such persons at no cost whatsoever. Landowners need only agree, formally and in writing, to sign their dead hands away to him. When small gentry hesitate to accept his proposition, he suggests a more fully economic exchange: for a modest sum, to be established each time anew, he will purchase their "dead souls." A deed of sale will then be drawn up in the most regular of terms, as if the goods on which the legal contract bore were real things or living persons, rather than the far stranger and more macabre legal beings that they truly are: names of serfs once counted that, while valid in the law of taxation, correspond to no one alive.

Chichikov's unprecedented project bears on an institution that is in a certain sense a modern version of the "half a shekel" demanded in the Bible as a tax for every adult male. According to the Hebrew law, however, that quantity was owed once and only once, as a preliminary to one counting. The Tsarist tax was due yearly, being disjoined in time and periodicity from the administration of the census. The consequence was the divergence of the sums of persons represented in the law from life, a divergence embodied, so to speak, in "dead souls": legal ghosts in whom or which the categories of person and nonperson, life and death, grow difficult to tell apart.

The exact status of such spectral beings is well worth pondering. If the dead serf recorded as alive on the last census counts for the law as a person, that is, as a "head," it is because he is to be treated as a good of a certain value, that is, as a thing. Yet if he is to be reckoned as alive solely till the next census, it is because it is granted that such a person and thing may already be deceased, while taxable. The dead peasant's existence is a transient legal fiction that testifies to the demands of a modern administrative state.

Chichikov alone could conceive of a means to profit from such nonpersons. The reader meets him on his visits from one dilapidated country estate to another, during which time he stays in "N.," a provincial town remarkable for being without any particular charm. The prudent voyager introduces himself as carrying out "private business." He takes precautions not to offend his interlocutors or cause any scandals. It is during his visit to "the landowner Manilov, not at all an elderly man yet, with eyes that were as sweet as sugar, and who puckered them up every time he laughed," that Chichikov first reveals his unusual ambitions.[41] Having been well received at dinner in the company of Manilov's family, Chichikov finds himself at last alone with the small landowner in the "little corner" that his host calls his study.

As Manilov serves him some tea, Chichikov broaches the subject:

> "Allow me to make one request . . ." he said, in a voice about which there was a suggestion of a certain strange (or almost strange) intonation and immediately thereafter, for some unknown reason, glanced over his shoulder. Manilov also, for some unknown reason, glanced over his shoulder. "How long ago was it your pleasure to submit a tally of your serfs to the Bureau of Audits census?"
>
> "Why, a long time ago, by now; or it might be better to say that I can't recall when."
>
> "How many of your people have died since the last time you submitted a tally?"
>
> "Why, I can't tell; it would be better to ask the steward about this, I suppose."[42]

After the steward has been summoned and dispatched to determine the number of the dead serfs, making "a detailed list of them," as Chichikov adds, "with their names," the mysterious guest begins, in halting terms, to explain himself. Asked for what reasons he wishes to obtain a count of the serfs who have died since the last census, Chichikov replies:

> "For what reasons, you ask? Here are the reasons: I would like to buy some peasants —" said Chichikov, then stammered and did not finish what he was saying. . . . "No, it isn't the actual peasants I am after," said Chichikov. "What I wish to have is the dead ones —"
>
> "What, sir? Pardon me . . . I am somewhat hard of hearing; I thought I heard a most peculiar word —"
>
> "I proposed to acquire the dead people, who, however, would be designated as alive in the Bureau of Audits," said Chichikov.[43]

Many in the novel have difficulty grasping the terms of Chichikov's "proposition." After his driver loses his way one night in the woods, the frustrated traveler happens upon the humble residence of Nastasia Petrovna Korobochka, "widow of a collegiate secretary," as she introduces herself. No sooner has he woken up the next morning and drunk some of his mistress's fruit liquor than he proceeds to question her about her estate, this time doing so "at greater liberty," as the narrator remarks, "than with Manilov."[44] When Chichikov explains that he is traversing the countryside "on my own little business affairs," Korobochka wonders whether he means to buy honey or hemp. "No, mother, it's a different sort of goods I'm after." "Tell me, have any of your peasants been dying off?"[45] She admits to the loss of eighteen men. Chichikov reacts immediately: "'Let me have them, now, Nastasia Petrovna.'" But she is baffled. When, aiming to be more persuasive, he proposes to pay for them, she expresses only greater perplexity. "But how can one do such a thing? Really, I can't make head or tail of this. Or is it that you want to dig them up out of the ground?"[46] Her literalism betrays an ignorance of the legal institution that is the basis of the hero's plan. "Chichikov saw that the old woman had strayed far afield and that it was absolutely necessary to make clear to her just what was what. In a few words he explained to her that the transfer or purchase would be merely a paper transaction and that the souls would be listed as living."[47] He is searching not for physical bodies, but for "souls," yet those that interest him are of an exclusively formal and administrative existence. It is strictly paper persons that Chichikov wishes to acquire and amass.

Such persons are nonpersons of various kinds. They share, first, the fact of being deceased. Yet a second dimension of their nonpersonhood is also worth recalling. As serfs, they are legally diminished subjects: persons treated in some respects as things, in that they are susceptible to becoming the objects of possession. Chichikov's project presupposes that "dead souls" be nonpersons of both these varieties: those he wishes to acquire must be both deceased and diminished. Yet some dead souls in the novel are also nonpersons in a third sense, as the reader learns during Chichikov's visit to Pliushkin.

Here, the hero is overjoyed to discover among his host's possessions "a bit of paper, entirely crisscrossed with writing. The names of the peasants were as closely clustered on it as midges. There were all sorts of names on it: Paramonovs, and Pimenovs, and Panteleimonovs, and there was even peppered up a certain Grigorii

Doezhai-ne-doedesh (Try-to-get-there-but-you-won't); there were actually more than a hundred and twenty of them."[48] Now, to Chichikov's delight, Pliushkin announces that he is in possession of "runaways [*beglye*], too": "souls" of peasants who have gone missing. No trace of them remains.[49] As Chichikov is the first to grant, such serfs may, therefore, be considered for all practical purposes to be deceased.[50] "Our hero . . . was in the most cheerful spirits. Such an unexpected acquisition is a veritable gift. Really, no matter what you might say, there were not only the dead souls alone, but runaway souls as well, and two hundred odd creatures in all!"[51] Dead, diminished, and missing, such "souls" decline three fundamental cases of nonpersonhood while combining them.

All such beings draw their existence from civil and legal writing: paper deeds. Chichikov is a reader of such documents, but as the narrative unfolds, he also becomes their copyist and — for better and also for worse, as he will learn to his misfortune — their author. This much is, at first, a source of joy for "our hero." One scene finds the traveling buyer expectantly opening a chest in which he has stored his precious documents of possession. He has woken up, and after "lying for two minutes or so on his back," remembered "he now had just a little short of four hundred souls." Putting on his "morocco boots with fancy appliqués of variegated colors . . . clad only in a nightshirt that reached no farther down than a kilt and which made him look like a Scotsman, forgetting all about his dignity and his discreet middle age, he covered the room in two leaps, each time slapping his behind quite deftly with his heel":

> Then he immediately got down to business; as he stood before his traveling chest, he rubbed his hands with the same pleasant anticipation as that with which an incorruptible judge of a rural police court, out on the road for some investigation, rubs his on approaching a table set with all sorts of cold delicacies; save for this, Chichikov did not lose any time in taking certain papers out of it. He wanted to conclude everything as speedily as possible, without letting any grass grow under his feet. He had decided to formulate the title deeds himself, both original and duplicate, so as to avoid paying anything to the

> government clerks. He knew the correct form perfectly; he speedily wrote out in majuscules: 'In the Year One Thousand Eight Hundred and — "; then, immediately following, in minuscules, "So-and-so, a Landed Proprietor," and everything else that was required.
>
> In two hours all was in readiness. When, having finished, he glanced at these papers, at these muzhiks who, verily, had been muzhiks once upon a time, had worked, had plowed, drunk hard, driven horses, and fooled their masters, or, it may be, had been simply good muzhiks, some strange feeling that he himself could not comprehend immediately took possession of him. Every one of these memoranda seemed to have some sort of character of its own, and because of this, it seemed as if the muzhiks themselves took on their own characters.[52]

He rereads the names, nicknames, and summary accounts of the dead persons he has purchased and, lost in a reverie, imagines himself to be conversing with his new acquisitions, one after another.

The excitement that Chichikov feels for the names and descriptions recorded in his papers is comical, but it is also allegorical, and its force extends not only to the writer of the novel, but also to his readers. They are drawn into Chichikov's practice of reading, fascinated by names inscribed in the census and the inexistent beings that they evoke. Yet the readers of *Dead Souls* also find their reflected images in other persons in this work. Long ignorant of the reasons for Chichikov's undertaking, readers cannot but perceive something of their own puzzlement in that of the townspeople who learn of his project. "What was this riddle?" the inhabitants of the "town of N." wonder, in the narrator's rendition of their insistent voices. "Indeed, what was this riddle of the dead souls? There's no logic to dead souls; how, then, can one buy up dead souls? Where would you even dig up a fool big enough to buy them? And what sort of fairy-gold would he use to buy them? And to what end, for what business, could one utilize these dead souls?"[53] Soon the "Messieurs the bureaucrats" of the town "put to themselves a question which they should have put in the very beginning":

> They pondered and pondered and at last came to the decision to make thorough inquiries among those whom Chichikov had traded with and bought these souls from, in order to learn, at least, what the exact transaction had consisted of, and what, precisely, was the meaning of these dead souls, and whether he had not explained it to somebody — even though perhaps by mere chance, even though in some indirect, incidental way — his real intentions, and whether he had not told somebody just who he was in reality.[54]

It is only in the last pages of part 1 (the sole "part" that Gogol himself published) that the reasons for the hero's project come to light. At this point in the novel, Chichikov has bought a great number of souls and ordered their many papers. Moses or Aaron to his deceased, he has taken "the sum of their congregation." Chichikov considers their lives, such as they are, to be goods of great value. Admittedly, that worth is not directly convertible into money, for he cannot sell them; Chichikov is in the world of *Dead Souls* the sole merchant of obsolescent nonpersons. Yet he plans nonetheless to make of them a source of the virtual capital that is credit. In this period in Russian history, landowners could mortgage their serfs to the state treasury when in need of funds, and this is what Chichikov intends to do with his multitude of dead souls. "Suppose I were to acquire a thousand of them," he muses to himself, in feverish excitement, "and also, let's suppose, that the Tutelary Chambers were to give me two hundred rubles a soul on a mortgage, why, I'd have a capital of two hundred thousand right there!"[55] There is only one obstacle: in Tsarist Russia, it is illegal to buy or mortgage serfs without owning land, and Chichikov has none. Yet he quickly envisages a solution to that problem. If questioned as to the grounds of his acquisitions, he will contend that he has bought them "for relocation," to settle them in regions of the empire in which land is being "given away": the southern Ukraine and Crimea.

> That's precisely where I'll resettle all my dead souls! To the province of Kherson with them! Let 'em live there! And as for the resettlement, that can be put through in a legal way, all fitting and proper, through the courts. Should

> they want to verify those serfs, by all means, I'm not averse even to that. Why not? I'll submit an actual affidavit of verification signed by some Captain of the Rural Police in his own hand. The village might be called Chichikov Borough [*Chichikova Slobodka*], or by my Christian name—hamlet of Pavlovskoe [*sel'tso Pavlovskoe*]."[56]

Chichikov has devised what one might define as a speculative syllogism, a three-part reasoning on dead souls. He plans to pass from the transitory goods that are deceased serfs to the spectral capital that is credit by means of one intermediary stage: the acquisition of land. The triumphant consequence is to be the emergence of a new man: Chichikov the landowner, author of his title and his goods, master of his densely populated, if ghostly hamlet and "borough."

That the project fails to be completed seems all but certain. "The adventures of Chichikov," as Gogol published them, are unfinished. Although Gogol completed a draft of part 2, he burned it in 1845. In the drafts of the later portions of the narrative that remain today, Chichikov ruins himself. In one reader's words, "Authority and the ways of government are vindicated."[57] It seems that Gogol conceived of his ingenious hero's failure as a necessary step along an itinerary of salvation. "Transmuted into literature," Vladimir Nabokov writes, "the completed *Dead Souls* was to form three connected images: Crime, Punishment and Redemption."[58] The trilogy, to be sure, never reached that final form. In the pages that survive, Chichikov's fate is unresolved. His bright plans bear no fruit.

The impasse may be unavoidable. Even when goods and credit, tax and land are not the decisive questions, the time of persons is never that of the census. Gogol was not the sole nineteenth-century writer to have grasped the consequences of this fact, even if those that he drew from the administration of Tsarist Russia are in more than one sense incomparable. The people who lived in the age of the first modern censuses were keenly aware that whenever persons are to be counted, nonpersons crowd in upon them as the living and the dead enter into unexpected and often disquieting relationships.

In a poem published less than half a century before *Dead Souls*, "We Are Seven," William Wordsworth explored the ways in which the counting of even a small number of persons is fraught with uncertainty. He included the composition in *Lyrical Ballads*, which he published with Coleridge in 1798. As its arithmetical title suggests, his poem turns on the numbering of persons. Scholars have observed that it appeared in print the same year as Thomas Malthus's *Essay on the Principle of Population*, "at the height of Britain's census-taking debates," and only three years before the first British census in 1801.[59]

The poem is introduced by a speaker who calls to mind a girl, wondering what she may know:

—A simple Child,
That lightly draws its breath,
And feels its life in every limb,
What should it know of death?

I met a little cottage Girl:
She was eight years old, she said;
Her hair was thick with many a curl
That clustered round her head.[60]

In the fourth quatrain, the speaker puts a question to the "simple Child." It is that of number:

"Sisters and brothers, little Maid,
How many may you be?"
"How many? Seven in all," she said,
And wondering looked at me.

A pattern is set: the speaker asks; the girl responds. Both count persons. In a sense, the argument of the poem goes no further than these lines, in which the "simple Child" gives her sum of seven.

When the speaker asks where "they" may be, the child patiently enumerates six others: two "at Conway dwell," "two are gone to sea," and two "lie in the church-yard." The speaker infers that five, therefore, are living, while two are dead. He proceeds to tell the girl that she ought to revise her answer accordingly:

"You run about, my little Maid,
Your limbs they are alive;
If two are in the church-yard laid,
Then ye are only five."

The child, however, is unwavering in her estimation:

"Their graves are green, they may be seen,"
The little Maid replied,
"Twelve steps or more from my mother's door,
And they are side by side.

"My stockings there I often knit,
My kerchief there I hem;
And there upon the ground I sit,
And sing a song to them.

"And often after sun-set, Sir,
When it is light and fair,
I take my little porringer,
And eat my supper there."

When the "little Maid" again refers to the fact that her two siblings lie buried side by side, the speaker seeks to compel her to acknowledge that their spirits being now in heaven, those two must be excepted from the count. Yet she continues to stand by her initial sum:

"How many are you, then," said I,
"If they two are in heaven?"
Quick was the little Maid's reply,
"O Master! We are seven."

"But they are dead; those two are dead!
Their spirits are in heaven!"
'Twas throwing words away; for still

The little Maid would have her will,
And said, "Nay, we are seven!"[61]

It has been observed that in his interest in the number of the "little cottage Girl" and her siblings, the speaker of the poem presents himself as a census taker, with neither time nor interest to ask his young interlocutor for her given and family names.[62] The conditions in which he encounters the girl recall not only Wordsworth's own walking tours, but also the itinerary of an official British counter of inhabitants.[63] While Gogol's novel presupposed the census as an event that had come to pass, Wordsworth's poem consists of nothing but the numbering of persons, carried out and commented on through a dialogic exchange: one living being counts herself and her closest kin in the presence of another. Here, the adult and the child agree on a basic principle in the representation of human quantity: every person, adult or child, male or female, counts as one, immediately and without such a proxy as a tax or "ransom." Yet Wordsworth's two speakers differ on the conditions of personhood. For the adult, there is a certain point at which the numbers of people must end. To be "in heaven," in his view, is to be withdrawn from the set of the countable. This, of course, is why he takes his interlocutor and her siblings to be five. Rejecting that figure, the "little Maid" will not grant that death makes any difference. For her, persons retain their quantity, whether living or deceased. As Frances Ferguson has remarked, in the eyes of the "simple Child," a number is in this sense like a name; it establishes a relation between terms and persons that death cannot dissolve.[64]

While in Gogol's novel, the law of taxation and the administration of the census work to engender "dead souls," in Wordsworth's poem, the census taker labors, as if by an inverse obligation, to separate the living from the deceased. He must struggle, for he has entered the arithmetical dispute having made a perilous concession: he has admitted that in some circumstances, persons count as present even when they are not. He thus grants that two "at Conway," missing from the girl's place of residence, remain exactly two; he accepts, furthermore, that those who have "gone to sea," having removed themselves from any place on land, are nonetheless ones to be considered parts of the total sum. Having supposed that a person may be absent without ceasing to count as one, having tacitly accepted that even a missing person is still to be taken as present, he proceeds to make a demand no less dogmatic for being stated repeatedly. The adult would compel the "little Maid" to accept that other departed others, who did once count as two, may now only be reckoned to be none. In his numbering of persons, he has, in short, included the departed, yet excluded the deceased, without ever pausing to explain himself.

The truth is that the terms with which the adult first addresses the child announce the challenge that he sets himself: "Sisters and brothers, little Maid, / How many may you be?" In his opening question, the personal pronoun *you* is equivocal; it can refer to an individual or a plurality.[65] "Sisters and brothers, little Maid," moreover, may be read as composing a series, taken as one, or as a set of discrete elements, which count as many. With these words, the adult suggests what few speakers in a dialog are apt to grant: that a "you" may signify one or many, if not one as well as many, and that if "you" denotes a multitude, its number stands in need of definition. As the poem unfolds, the child obstinately offers the same answer to his question. He rejects it, certain that she has miscounted herself. Yet he is neither savior nor exorcist. Confronted by a "simple Child, / that lightly draws its breath," he lacks the authority and the power to drive out the legion that she takes herself to be. He can utter no *apopompē*. Hence the comedy of the exchange, in which words and figures continue to be "thrown away." Repeatedly sounding seven beats across two unequal lines,[66] the "little Maid" blithely rejects the difference between the living and the dead. For her, the two siblings in the earth, absent, but not nowhere, remain as countable as they are perceptible: "Their graves are green, they may be seen."[67] The most perplexing and the most infantile of consequences follow.

If this nameless girl of eight is seven, then she is one, yet also with three sets of two. Being many, she stands present before her censor, while being "at Conway," "gone to sea," and "in the church-yard laid." She is someone and also some ones, some of whom are dead. "The little Maid would have her will," and nameless, she would have her number, counting no one out.

Being *It*

Among the skills that children acquire without formal study or instruction, there is the capacity to submit any collection of things and persons to a procedure such that one among them may be singled out to play a part unlike that of the others. This procedure is both verbal and gestural. A speaker utters a set of phrases in rhyme and rhythm and, with each word, indicates the elements in the collection, one by one, by finger, fist, or hand, until reaching the one to be distinguished. In what is perhaps the first scholarly work devoted to the subject, the American chemist, bibliographer, and student of children Henry Carrington Bolton observed in 1888 that "the process is called in Scotland 'chapping out' and 'titting out'; but in England and America it is commonly known as 'counting out.'"[1] Contemporary American usage inclines toward the expression "choosing up."[2] The procedure is carried out in particular circumstances, of which Bolton gave a memorable account. One child assumes the role of "leader, generally self-appointed." He or she arranges the others "in a row, or in a circle about him, as fancy may dictate," and utters "a peculiar doggerel, sometimes with a rapidity which can only be acquired by great familiarity and a dexterous tongue, and pointing with the hand or finger to each child in succession, not forgetting himself (or herself), allots to each one word of the mysterious formula":

> One-ery, two-ery, ickery, Ann,
> Fillicy, fallacy, Nicholas, John,

Queever, quaver, English, knaver,
Stinckelum, stanckelum, Jericho, buck.[3]

That four-part series was but one of many that Bolton might have cited. Contemporary English speakers in North America and the United Kingdom may recall a briefer sequence that likewise functions to "count out" someone in a group: "One potato, two potato, three potato, four / Five potato, six potato, seven potato more."[4] In 1976, the formula was sufficiently popular for children in the United States to refer to any counting child as "the Potato Man" or "Potato Masher," no matter the doggerel employed.[5] Two folklorists describe the rules of this practice in the following terms:

> Before the Potato Masher begins to chant, each player places both fists in the center of a circle. As the rhyme is chanted, the Masher keeps time by tapping the fists of the players with his own fist. When he comes around the circle to himself, he hits himself on the left hand and then on his chin — in lieu of the fist he is using to keep time. The fist tapped as the rhyme comes to an end is withdrawn. When both of the child's fists have been withdrawn, he is out of the circle.[6]

Another well-attested formula from the United States is in four lines, the first of which is also the last:

Eenie, meenie, miney, mo.
Catch a tiger by the toe.
If he hollers, let him go.
Eenie, meenie, miney, mo.[7]

Children have also been known to draw from the elements of language simpler, yet formally homologous sequences:

A, B, C, D, E, F, G
H, I, J, K, L, M, N
O, P, Q, R, S, T, *You!*[8]

Numerals very often serve such ends, as Bolton's first example suggested. In addition to "One-ery, two-ery, ickory Ann," a recent anthology of such doggerel records rhymes beginning "One-ery, two-ery, ickery, E"; "One-ery, two-ery, ickery, on"; "One-ery, two-ery, six and seven"; "One-ery, two-ery, three-ery thumb"; and "One-ery, two-ery, tick-er-y ten."[9] Almost six hundred sequences of this kind have been documented in contemporary English.[10]

Bolton dubbed such formulae "counting-out rhymes." After proposing an account of their uses among children, he offered a catalog of their morphology and distribution in twenty languages of America, Europe, Asia, and Africa. Only three years later, in 1891, the Scottish reverend Walter Gregor, founding member of the Folklore Society, published a study of such sequences, which he took to constitute a "curious and interesting branch of Folklore, as well as of Philology."[11] "Most people know what counting-out rhymes are," he wrote in his introduction, "and for what purpose they are employed. They consist mostly of a jingle of words with swing and rhyme that have little or no meaning. They are met with in all parts of the world. They are used in this part of the country to find out who is to begin any game they engage in."[12]

Children having been "perhaps the first non-peasant group to be seriously studied by folklorists," these rhymes have been the subject of repeated discussion.[13] The circumstances in which they are recited seem fixed. One child either begins or ends with himself or herself, before or after moving in a row or circle among the other children, one by one, often starting with a word containing the number one (such as "one-ery"), up to the point where the rhyming sequence ends. The child on whom the last word or syllable falls is then considered to be "out." He or she will stand aside. That distinction, however, may bear two values. If the procedure is executed only once, the child denoted by the last word of the rhyme is immediately assigned a function. The selection process can then end. In most cases, however, the practice of recitation will be repeated as many times as there are children present — minus one. When all but one have been "chapped," "titted," or "counted out," the last among them will be accorded a crucial role: that child will be known as *it*.[14]

For a speaking being, to be to neither "I" nor "you," neither "he" nor "she" nor "they," but rather *it* is an exceptional condition that calls out for commentary. The pronominal form is in itself striking. It appears to be a peculiarity of English usage to attribute to a living person a neuter word generally denoting an inanimate object. Foreign languages are familiar with different conventions of designation in games. Where the terminology of "tag" in English requires that one child be known as *it*, French demands that such a player be named as "wolf" (*loup*), "cat" (*chat*) or "flea" (*puce*). German singles out one child as the "catcher" (*Fänger*). Italian usage is familiar with one who is "subjected," being said to "be under" (*sta sotto*). In all these languages, however, one player bears a special name that indicates his or her unique position with respect to some or many others, and in every case, there exist special rhymes, employed solely by children, that define the one to be thus "counted out."

Gregor alluded to the fact that such rhymes are "met with in all parts of the world," yet Bolton insisted on this circumstance, claiming to be in a position to contribute new evidence for its reality:

> The few authors who have noticed this branch of Folk-Lore have recognized the occurrence of this juvenile amusement in several countries of Europe, and lists of the doggerels have been compiled by native authorities, especially in Germany. We are able to demonstrate, however, in the following pages that the custom of counting-out and the use of sentences and doggerels for the purpose obtains around the world, and is a pastime with the children of civilized and semi-civilized races of the most diverse origin.[15]

Contemporary scholars of folklore are more cautious in their pronouncements. One recent study limits itself to asserting that "counting out as a method of deciding who is to be 'on it' is probably almost universal."[16] That sequences of the kind identified by Bolton and Gregor are extraordinarily widespread, however, can scarcely be doubted. Known in French as "little formulae of elimination" (*formulettes d'élimination*) or as "small counts" (*comptines*), a term with a clear cognate in Russian (*shchitalky*), familiar in Italian as "counts" (*conte*), in German as "counting rhymes" (*Anzählreime*) or "counting-off rhymes" (*Abzählreime*), these varieties of "peculiar doggerel" are found in the European languages and also beyond them. They put rhyme and rhythm at the service of a curious arithmetic: counting each and every element in a single series—up to the one who must count as none.

However peculiar they may be, such counts have an obvious practical utility. When a form of play demands that someone take on the role of "it" or that there be two sides, each composed of some number of players, children face the redoubtable difficulty of "selecting personnel."[17] Children's rhymes function as means to assign positions, deciding on the unknown according to some pattern set out in advance. For this reason, the first scholars of these rhymes discerned in them a childlike variety of divination: a drawing by lots, in Gregor's words, according to a practice "in use among nations of all degrees of civilization—from the most barbarous to the most civilized community."[18] He argued that in choosing by "choosing-out," children thereby assure the "survival of what was once the occupation of men in less advanced stages of civilization."[19]

Bolton held a similar position, asserting that as a means to determine roles, counting-out rhymes have their origin in the immemorial practice of "casting lots."[20] Moreover, he suggested that in their nonsense, such sequences derive from ancient spells and incantations.[21] The evidence that Gregor and Bolton adduced for those claims, however, is dubious at best, and such "survivalist" arguments are difficult to maintain today.[22] Yet their theses may also be contested for a different reason. Both nineteenth-century scholars assume that counting-out rhymes are sequences employed to reach a random distribution of roles, configuring the unknown according to some stochastic process. Yet the truth is that in children's rhymes, as in so many other domains, chance is far from being a simple datum. It may even be a mirage.

In 1971, Kenneth S. Goldstein made a significant contribution to the question, drawing on the ethnographic research in "speaking folklore" that he had conducted in a six-block area of Northwest Philadelphia between January 1966 and June 1967. Goldstein had done field work on children's practices of counting out. His informants consisted of sixty-seven girls and boys between the ages of four and fourteen. When asked about the reasons for choosing roles and sides based on counting-out rhymes, the children he questioned offered several answers. A small number suggested that their practice "removed friction." Goldstein relates their own words: "We don't fight about it"; "Less trouble." An even smaller number among them claimed that by counting out, they remitted all responsibility to some "supernatural" authority: "Fate decides," as they told him, or "God does the choosing." Yet the overwhelming majority of Goldstein's informants told him that selection by counting out has the merit of granting each player an equal opportunity: "Everybody has the same chance"; "It's more democratic."[23] In Goldstein's terms, the players viewed the counting-out process as "a game of chance." To this degree, they shared a view that has also been advanced by scholars who have sought to understand and classify the forms of play.[24]

Goldstein demonstrated, however, that the results of counting-out processes are far less random than children and adults might suppose. He showed how some "counters" vary rhymes according to the situation, adding or removing lines or altering their stress patterns to bring about a certain result. Children might also skip themselves when counting, if their elimination seemed imminent. Goldstein relates how one child had gone so far as to memorize all the first positions to be counted out according to the "One Potato, Two Potato" rhyme for all groups of ten or fewer members. By arranging the other children in a certain order, the ingenious boy could thus determine who would be excluded, and by rearranging the group after each elimination, he would continue to decide on the future course of the selection process. The nine-year-old, who "was considered something of a mathematic genius at school," had succeeded in developing a single "'changing position' strategy." This fact had not escaped his peers.

> One member of his play group, who was aware that some kind of manipulation was going on without knowing exactly what it was, would frequently thwart the change of position of the counter by changing his own position in the remaining group. Eventually, the precocious boy who had worked out the strategy began to count out the other youngster first so he would be free to make his further manipulations without interference.[25]

Such stratagems are far from being purely infantile. Elliott Oring has drawn attention to a passage of *The Jewish War* in which Flavius Josephus appears to suggest that he once saved himself by making a calculation of precisely this kind. In 67 CE, Josephus was defending the town of Yotapata in the Galilee from the Romans. When the invading army succeeded in entering the city and began slaughtering its inhabitants, he sought refuge in a cave. There he found forty Jewish soldiers in hiding. Despairing, they had resolved to take their lives. Josephus sought to dissuade them from their decision, but he failed. He then made them a proposition: "Since we are resolved to die, come let us leave the lot to decide the order in which we are to kill ourselves; let him who draws the first lot fall by the hand who comes next; fortune will thus take her course through the whole number and we shall be spared from taking our lives with our own hands."[26] They accepted his suggestion. Each drew a lot and "each thus selected presented his throat to his neighbor, in the assurance that his general [that is, Josephus] was forthwith to share his fate." Josephus recalls that he found himself in the position of the next to last to be killed. As he writes of himself: "He (should one say by fortune or the providence of God?) was left alone with one other; and anxious neither to be condemned by the lot nor, should he be left to the last, to stain his hand with the blood of a fellow countryman, he persuaded this man also, under a pledge, to remain alive."[27]

In his account of this progressive elimination of the members of this series, Josephus refrains from identifying the type of lots that the Jewish soldiers drew. He also says nothing of the exact arrangement by which the final selection was made. He limits himself to calling the reader's attention, in a parenthesis, to the question of whether he survived the selection process "by fortune or the providence of God." These occurrences, however, are also related in the Slavonic redaction of *The Jewish War*, which differs in several passages from the standard Greek text and which may derive from an older Greek recension that is now lost. The Slavonic version leaves little doubt as to the reasons for which Josephus recommended the procedure. "Commending his salvation to God the Protector," he writes, always referring to himself in the third person,

> he said, "Since it is well pleasing to God that we should die, let us be killed in turn. Let him whose turn comes last be killed by the second." And when he had thus spoken, he counted the numbers with cunning, and thereby misled them all [*i tako rek, pochte chisla s moudrostiu, i tem priblade vsa*]. And they were all killed, one by another, except one; and, anxious not to stain his right hand with the blood of a fellow-countryman, he besought this one, and they both went out alive.[28]

Counting "the numbers with cunning," Josephus appears to have employed a mathematical ruse much like the one mastered by the nine-year-old Philadelphian. "This passage suggests that the method to establish the order of victims was a form of counting-out, and that Josephus somehow could foresee and manipulate the order of selection so that he would be the last to remain."[29]

The cunning of the ancient Jewish military chronicler has often been recalled. In his 1612 *Pleasant and Delightful Problems Made by Numbers*, Claude-Gaspar Bachet, French poet, grammarian, and mathematician, drew attention to this episode in *The Jewish War*. He evoked it in his preface "To the Reader" as an indication that his own book might be "far from useless" and that the knowledge of arithmetical problems, more generally, might be on occasion most advantageous. Josephus's "is a truly remarkable story," he wrote, "that well teaches us that one ought not to despise such small subtleties, which sharpen the wit, training man for greater things and sometimes contributing an unexpected utility."[30] Bachet's twenty-third "problem" challenged the reader to provide a solution to the predicament that Josephus had confronted: "Given that a certain number of units distinct among each other has been provided, set and order these units in such a way that, always discarding the ninth, or the tenth, or the *n*th, as one wishes, up to a certain number, those to be left over will be the ones that one wants."[31]

Bachet also suggested that the chronicler's problem might admit of a more contemporary illustration. He evoked a maritime scenario: "Fifteen Christians and fifteen Turks finding themselves at sea in the same ship and a terrible tempest having arisen, the pilot declares that it is necessary to throw half the people on deck into the sea to save the rest."[32] It is agreed that Christians and Turks will be lined up in some order and the ninth person will be thrown overboard, until half the original thirty passengers are left. Hence Bachet's question: How ought one to arrange the set of travelers such that only the Christians will be left alive? In the twelfth century, Abraham Ibn Ezra had posed the same problem and a remarkably similar situation in his *Tachbula*, the difference being that the ship he evoked transported fifteen students and fifteen good-for-nothings, the second of whom being the ones to be eliminated. Variations of the problem can be found in the mathematics of Renaissance Europe and seventeenth-century Japan.[33] Its origins are far from clear. That it concerns the quandary faced by children in their counting-out rhymes, however, is difficult to deny.

Yet it is no less clear that a distance also separates Bachet's "pleasant and delightful problem" of pure arithmetic from the practice of children in their games. Language is the reason for a first divergence. As linguists have shown, counting-out rhymes are not only formulae that, when applied to a "a certain number of units distinct among each other," issue in the elimination of one member of a given set. Their discourse is also subtly and sometimes intensely patterned in its minimal parts. Consider

> Eenie, meenie, miney, mo
> Catch a tiger by the toe

If he hollers, let him go,
Eenie, meenie miney mo.

Almost every word exhibits phonological recurrences proper to poetic sequences: assonance, alliteration, and rhyme.[34] An analysis of the first line is in this sense exemplary. The first word, *eenie*, is part of the second, *meenie*; *meenie, miney* and *mo* alliterate; *mo* rhymes with *toe* and *go*; and, as a sequence, "the first line contains a progression from front-to-back middle vowels—*e, i, o*—as in the *fee, fi, fo* of *fee, fi, fo, fum*, or in the *ee, eye, oh* of 'Old McDonald had a Farm.'"[35] French *comptines*, in their apparent "gibberish," exhibit a similar "texturing of sound."[36] The mathematical puzzles evoked by Abraham Ibn Ezra and Bachet abstract from such verbal structures. All that remains in them is the problem that children face when assembled in a row or circle: where best to position themselves in the series, given a rule dictating the number of units to be counted before one is to be eliminated.

There is a second difference between children's practice and the piquant problem "made by numbers." It is perhaps not inconsequential that in the military scenario that Josephus lived to relate, elimination is final. Whatever their exact form, the rules of this drawing by lot dictate that whoever is selected will be *it* in a sense all too literal and macabre. Once a living, speaking person, he will become the nonperson that is the corpse. The least that one may state is that he will not step twice into the series of those waiting to be counted out. For the child, by contrast, the permutation demanded by the counting-out rhyme may be reiterated, first within a single process of selection and later with respect to other players, who in principle may all play again. Children's games make this fundamental demand of those who play them: none, including those who lose, are to be barred from playing again.

The limitless attraction of play derives from this indefinite recurrence. "Every profound experience longs to be insatiable, longs for return and repetition until the end of time," Walter Benjamin once wrote, quoting Goethe's rhyming formula: "All things would be resolved in a trice / If we could only do them twice" (*Es ließe sich alles trefflich schlichten, / Könnte man die Sache zweimal verrichten*). Yet Benjamin added that where children are concerned, only one more time is hardly better than never:

> The child is not satisfied with twice, but wants the same thing again and again, a hundred or even a thousand times. This is not only the way to master frightening fundamental experiences—by deadening one's own response, by arbitrarily conjuring up experiences, or through parody; it also means enjoying one's victories and triumphs over and over again, with total intensity. An adult relieves his heart from its terrors and doubles happiness by turning it into a story. A child creates the entire event anew and starts again right from the beginning.... Not a "doing as if" but a "'doing the same thing over and over again," the transformation of a shattering experience into habit—that is the essence of play.[37]

That insight places the arithmetical doggerel of children in an unexpected light. Counting without meaning to define any magnitude, rhyming without reason, children, in their nonsense sequences, turn the "shattering experience" of being *it* into habit. Their play accomplishes this conversion. Yet "play" may be a misleading term in this setting. As the first modern scholars of these infantile practices observed, counting-out rhymes serve less as play in the customary sense of the term than as prelude to play: they distribute a role or several roles, establishing how and in what manner to begin. Traversing a single series of persons in words and gesture, correlating those present with a word in a sequence, children find a way to assign the desirable and undesirable parts in the coming game. They succeed in deciding "who is to begin."[38] "Counting-out is one important way of getting into play," Roger D. Abrahams explains. "It provides a frame and a break between the stream of ordinary activity and the specially licensed behaviour we call playing."[39] If such rhymes constitute a game, the game is therefore "a game to begin a game": "before-play play."[40]

The mystery of the activity called "playing" is nowhere more evident than in such paradoxical formulations. By definition, there is no game that cannot be begun, yet the transition from the state of not playing to that of playing can scarcely be defined. A circle seems unavoidable. To initiate the game, one must presuppose it; preparing to "play," one engages in "before-play play." Yet "counting out" is more than a conceit devised to enter into the formal parameters of a game. It also offers an abbreviated image of the relations between persons and nonpersons.

Several of their principles appear distinctly in this miniature. First, those who count as less than others may be one or many, but whatever the rules of the game or system and whatever its terminology, nonpersons are never simply excluded. To be counted out is, for better or for worse, always to be taken into account. Second, the procedure of identification admits and even demands repetition, each counting being potentially a counting before a recount, a sequence whose recurrence is expected. Finally, the ways of being *it* are many; the scale of nonpersons is indefinitely variable. What is constant is this minimal demand: that there be at least some person who is scarcely one.

Yet children's patterned nonsense is also instructive for a further reason. Pointing to persons in quantifying things, designating living, speaking beings in naming numbers, counting-out rhymes respond to the challenge of our being numerous. They testify to human multiplicity and to the uncertain possibilities of its representation, laying bare an arithmetic of persons that is exemplary precisely in its patent unsteadiness. The "peculiar doggerel" of schoolyards admits positions for all those lined up and numbered in a row or circle, but it always also leaves a space for the absence and indeed the absenting of some others. There is the one who numbers — and who may thereby succeed in not numbering, or in varying the number — and there is the one who is numbered, but not as one: the "Potato Man" or "Potato Masher," in other words, and the one who, by cunning or by luck, is counted out. However many small persons partake of this "before-play play," there are always at least these two nonpersons. There are often many more. What is certain is the ineradicable possibility of being subtracted from the number of the whole. As children know all too well, to be someone is to be exposed, not exceptionally, but regularly, not once, but repeatedly, if not "over and over again," to the many ways of being *it*.

Notes

PREFACE

1. On the question of "nonman" and its legacy in the history of philosophy, see Daniel Heller-Roazen, *No One's Ways: An Essay on Infinite Naming* (New York: Zone Books, 2017).

ONE: THE REMOVAL

1. Nathaniel Hawthorne, "Wakefield," in *Tales and Sketches*, ed. Roy Harvey Pearce (New York: Library of America, 1982), p. 290.

2. *Ibid.*, p. 292.

3. *Ibid.*, p. 296.

4. *Ibid.*, p. 298.

5. *Ibid.*, p. 296.

6. *Ibid.*, p. 290.

7. Henry James, "Preface to 'The Altar of the Dead,'" in *The Art of the Novel: Critical Prefaces* (New York: Charles Scribner's Sons, 1934), p. 247.

8. Hawthorne, "Wakefield," p. 298.

TWO: LAWS OF LEAVING

1. Marcel Planiol, *Traité élémentaire de droit civil*, 3 vols., 3rd ed. (Paris: Pichon, 1904), vol. 1, § 611, p. 220. Throughout, unless otherwise noted, all translations in the text and notes are by the author. When published translations are cited, some have been silently modified.

2. Jeanne Louise Carriere, "The Rights of the Living Dead: Absent Persons in the Civil Law," *Louisiana Law Review* 50.5 (1990), p. 901.

3. Firmin Talandier, *Nouveau traité des absens* (Limoges: Th. Marmignon, 1831), p. 9.

4. Émile Tyan, "La condition juridique de 'l'Absent' (*Mafḳūd*) en droit musulman, particulièrement dans le Madhab Ḥanafite," *Studia islamica* 31 (1970), p. 249.

5. *Ibid.*, p. 250. Arabic in al-Kāsānī, *Kitāb badā'i' al-ṣanā'i' fī tartīb al-sharā'i'*, 7 vols. (1402; Beirut: dār al-kitāb al-'arabī, 1982), vol. 6, p. 196.

6. Charles Demolombe, *Traité de l'absence* (= *Cours de Code Napoléon*, vol. 2), 2nd ed. (Paris: Durand/Hachette, 1860), pp. 2–3.

7. Carriere, "The Rights of the Living Dead," pp. 902–903.

8. *Ibid.*, p. 905.

9. Ernst Levy, "Verschollenheit und Ehe in antiken Rechten," in Levy, *Gedächtnisschrift für Emil Secker* (Berlin: Julius Springer, 1927), p. 159.

10. The lack has been remarked upon more than once. See Demolombe, *Traité de l'absence*, p. 3; Carl Georg Bruns, "Die Verschollenheit," in Bruns, *Kleinere Schriften*, 2 vols. (Weimar: Hermann Bölau, 1882), vol. 1, p. 50; Levy, "Verschollenheit und Ehe in antiken Rechten," p. 160.

11. Levy, "Verschollenheit und Ehe in antiken Rechten," p. 159.

12. *Ibid.*, pp. 182–83.

13. See *ibid.*, p. 184.

14. For discussions, see *ibid.*, pp. 183–84, and Reuven Yaron, "The Missing Husband in Jewish Law," in *Mélanges à la mémoire de Marcel-Henri Prévost: Droit biblique, interprétation rabbinique, communautés et société* (Paris: Presses universitaires de France, 1982), pp. 133–40. For the translation quoted here, see p. 133.

15. Yaron, "The Missing Husband in Jewish Law," p. 135.

16. On the status of the *agunah*, see also Bluma Goldstein, *Enforced Marginality: Jewish Narratives on Abandoned Wives* (Berkeley: University of California Press, 2007), esp. pp. 1–9; Yael V. Levy, "The Agunah and the Missing Husband: An American Solution to a Jewish Problem," *Journal of Law and Religion* 10.1 (1993–94), pp. 49–71; J. David Bleich, "Survey of Recent Halakhic Periodical Literature: A 19th *Agunah* Problem and a 20th Century Application," *Tradition* 38.2 (2004), pp. 15–48.

17. Goldstein, *Enforced Marginality*, p. 4.

18. Yaron, "The Missing Husband in Jewish Law," p. 135.

19. *Ibid.*, pp. 135–40.

20. See Babylonian Talmud, Tractate Yebamoth 121a–121b; English in Isidore Epstein (ed.), *Hebrew-English Edition of the Babylonian Talmud*, various translators (New York: Soncino Press, 1960–).

21. David Santillana, *Istituzioni di diritto musulmano malichita, con riguardo anche al sistema sciafiita*, 2 vols. (Rome: Istituto per l'Oriente, 1925–38), vol. 1, § 29–33, pp. 162–67.

22. Tyan, "La condition juridique de l''Absent' (*Mafḳūd*) en droit musulman, particulièrement dans le Madhab Ḥanafite," pp. 250–51.

23. *Ibid.*, p. 255.

24. *Ibid.*

25. *Ibid.*, p. 251.

26. *Ibid.*, p. 256.

27. Rudolf Hübener, *A History of Germanic Private Law*, trans. Patrick S. Philbrick (Boston: Little, Brown, 1918), p. 49.

28. *Ibid.*, p. 50.

29. *Ibid.*

30. *Ibid.*, p. 51.

31. See Christina Deutsch, "Zwischen Leben und Tod: Die Verschollenen und ihre Hinterbliebenen im Spätmittelalter," *Trajekte* 14 (2007), p. 14.

32. See *ibid.*, p. 14.

33. *Ibid.*, p. 16.

34. 1604 Statute of Bigamy, 1 Jac 1 c 11, § 11.

35. Carriere, "The Rights of the Living Dead," pp. 908–909.

36. Cestui Que Vie Act, 1666 CHAPTER 11 18 and 19 Cha 2.

37. *Ibid.*

38. An Act declaring when the death of persons absenting themselves shall be presumed. Passed the 7th of March, 1797 (Rev 288), article 1. For a commentary, see Andrew W. Whinery, "Presumption of Death in New Jersey," *Mercer Beasley Law Review* 5.1 (1936), pp. 2–3.

39. Planiol, *Traité élémentaire de droit civil*, vol. 1, § 634, p. 227.

40. Code civil des Français du 21 mars 1804 (30 Ventôse de l'an XII), book 1, title 4, chapter 1, article 112, p. 30; English in *The Code Napoleon, or the French Civil Code* (London: William Benning, 1827), p. 34.

41. Planiol, *Traité élémentaire de droit civil*, vol. 1, § 634, p. 227. Cf. Talandier, *Nouveau traité des absens*, p. 19.

42. Planiol, *Traité élémentaire de droit civil*, vol. 1, § 612, pp. 220–21.

43. See Code civil des Français du 21 mars 1804, book 1, title 4, chapter 1, article 112.

44. See *ibid.*, book 1, title 4, chapter 1, articles 114 and 121.

45. Hernán Corral Talciani and María Sara Rodríguez Pinto, "Disparition de personnes et présomption de décès: Observations de droit comparé," *Revue internationale de droit comparé* 52.3 (2000), p. 562, basing themselves on Code civil des Français du 21 mars 1804, book 1, title 4, chapter 1, article 129.

46. Planiol, *Traité élémentaire de droit civil*, vol. 1, § 634, p. 227.

47. See Corral Talciani and Rodríguez Pinto, "Disparition de personnes et présomption de décès," pp. 557 and 561.

48. *Ibid.*, p. 561.

49. *Ibid.*

50. *Ibid.*, p. 558.

51. *Ibid.*, p. 559.

52. *Ibid.*, p. 565.

53. For an overview, *ibid.*, pp. 570–72.

54. *Ibid.*, p. 574.

55. Frances T. Freeman Jalet, "Mysterious Disappearances: The Presumption of Death and the Administration of the Estates of Missing Persons or Absentees," *Iowa Law Review* 54 (1986), p. 190.

56. Corral Talciani and Rodríguez Pinto, "Disparition de personnes et présomption de décès," p. 573.

57. D. Stone, "The Presumption of Death: A Redundant Concept?," *Modern Law Review* 44.5 (1981), p. 519.

THREE: FICTIONS OF THE RETURN

An earlier version of Chapter Three appeared as "Fictions of the Return," in *The Yearbook of Comparative Literature* 61 (2015), pp. 218–34.

1. Babylonian Talmud, Yebamoth 120a; English in Isidore Epstein (ed.), *Hebrew-English Edition of the Babylonian Talmud*, various translators (New York: Soncino Press, 1960–).

2. *Ibid.*

3. *Ibid.*

4. *Ibid.*

5. *Ibid.*

6. *Odyssey* 23.306–309; English in *The Odyssey*, trans. Richmond Lattimore (New York: Harper & Row, 1967), p. 506.

7. Dieter Beyerle, "Die Heimkehr des verschollenen Ehemannes bei Balzac, Zola, und Maupassant," *Romanistisches Jahrbuch* 27 (1976), p. 130.

8. See Natalie Zemon Davis, *The Return of Martin Guerre* (Cambridge, MA: Harvard University Press, 1983); cf. Robert Finlay, "The Refashioning of Martin Guerre," *American Historical Review* 93.3 (1988), pp. 553–71.

9. Michel de Montaigne, "Of the Lame or Crippel," in *The Essayes of Montaigne: John Florio's Translation*, introduction by J. I. M. Stewart (New York: Modern Library, 1933), p. 993; French in "Des Boyteux," in *Les essais*, ed. Jean Balsamo, Michel Magnien, and Catherine Magnien-Simonin (Paris: Gallimard, 2007), p. 1030. Davis points out that when he wrote these lines, Montaigne may not have read the confession of the presumed imposter, Arnaut de Tilh. See Davis, *The Return of Martin Guerre*, p. 199.

10. Honoré de Balzac, *Le Colonel Chabert*, in *La comédie humaine*, vol. 3, *Études de mœurs: Scènes de la vie privée, scènes de la vie de province*, ed. Pierre-Georges Castex et al. (Paris: Gallimard, 1976), p. 311. Cf. pp. 339, 351, and 355. It has been observed that Balzac's text announces Gogol's *Overcoat* in more ways than one: see Priscilla Meyer, *How the Russians Read the French: Lermontov, Dostoevsky, Tolstoy* (Madison: University of Wisconsin Press, 2008), pp. 26–33; Nils Åke Nilsson, "On the Origins of Gogol's 'Overcoat," in Elizabeth W. Trahan (ed.), *Gogol's "Overcoat": An Anthology of Critical Essays* (Ann Arbor: Ardis, 1982), pp. 61–72.

11. Balzac, *Le Colonel Chabert*, p. 323.

12. *Ibid.*, p. 328.

13. *Ibid.*, p. 333.

14. See Peter Brooks, "Narrative Transaction and Transference (Unburying *Le Colonel Chabert*)," *Novel* 15. 2 (1982), pp. 101–10.

15. Balzac, *Le Colonel Chabert*, pp. 315 and 311–12. On the legal status of Chabert's uncertain humanity, see Cathy Caruth, "The Claims of the Dead: History, Haunted Property, and the Law," in Austin Sarat, Lawrence Douglas, and Martha Merill Umphrey (eds.), *Law's Madness* (Ann Arbor: The University of Michigan Press, 2003), pp. 119–46, esp. pp. 121–23; Jacques Cardinal, "Perdre son nom: Identité, représentation et vraisemblance dans *Le Colonel Chabert*," *Poétique* 135.3 (2003), pp. 307–32.

16. Balzac, *Le Colonel Chabert*, pp. 323 and 321.

17. *Ibid.*, p. 365.

18. *Ibid.*, p. 367.

19. *Ibid.*, p. 372.

20. *Ibid.*, p. 372.

21. Guy de Maupassant, "Le Retour," in *Contes et nouvelles*, ed. Louis de Forestier, 2 vols. (Paris: Gallimard, 1974–1979), vol. 2, p. 206.

22. *Ibid.*, p. 212.

23. Émile Zola, "La mort d'Olivier Bécaille," in *Contes et nouvelles*, ed. Roger Ripoll with Sylvie Luneau (Paris: Gallimard, 1976), p. 803.

24. *Ibid.*

25. *Ibid.*, p. 829.

26. *Ibid.*, p. 830.

27. *Ibid.*

28. Émile Zola, "Jacques Damour," in *Contes et nouvelles*, pp. 896–929.

29. *Ibid.*, p. 903.

30. *Ibid.*

31. *Ibid.*, p. 904.

32. *Ibid.*, p. 905.

33. *Ibid.*, p. 906.

34. *Ibid.*, p. 920.

35. *Ibid.*, p. 923.

36. *Ibid.*, p. 929.

37. Luigi Pirandello, *Il fu Mattia Pascal*, ed. Giancarlo Mazzacurati (Turin: Einaudi, 1993), p. 96.

38. *Ibid.*, p. 219.

39. *Ibid.*, p. 257.

40. On *The Late Mattia Pascal* and Zola, see Manlio Lo Vecchio Musti, *L'opera di Luigi Pirandello* (Turin: G. B. Paravia, 1939), pp. 83–84, and more extensively, Piero Cudini, "'Il Fu Mattia Pascal': Dalle fonti chamissiani e zoliane alla nuova struttura narrativa di Luigi Pirandello," *Belfagor* 6 (1971), pp. 702–13, esp. pp. 705–709.

41. Pirandello, *Il fu Mattia Pascal*, p. 5.

42. *Ibid.*

43. *Ibid.*, p. 85.

44. *Ibid.*, pp. 91–93.

45. *Ibid.*, p. 280.

46. *Ibid.*, p. 279.

47. Cf. Roland Barthes's analysis of the sentence "I am dead" in a tale by Edgar Allan

Poe: "Analyse textuelle d'un conte d'Edgar Poe," in Claude Chabrol (ed.), *Sémiotique narrative et textuelle* (Paris: Larousse, 1973), pp. 29–54, esp. p. 47.

48. Franz Kafka, *Der Verschollene: Roman in der Fassung der Handschrift*, ed. Jost Schillemeit (Frankfurt am Main: Fischer, 1983), p. 7; English in *The Man Who Disappeared*, trans. Michael Hofman (London: Penguin Books, 1996), p. 30.

49. Franz Kafka, letter to Felice Bauer, November 11, 1912, in Kafka, *Briefe an Felice und andere Korrespondenz aus der Verlobungszeit*, eds. Erich Heller and Jürgen Born, with an introduction by Erich Heller (Frankfurt am Main: Fischer, 1967), p. 86.

50. Conrad Ernst Riesenfeld, *Verschollenheit und Todeserklärung nach gemeinem und preussischem Rechte, mit stäter Rücksicht auf die Vorschläge des Entwurfs eines bürgerlichen Gesetzbuchs für das deutsche Reich* (Breslau: Wilhelm Koebner, 1890), p. 7. In 1911, a year before Kafka began work on his first novel, his second cousin, Bruno Kafka, edited a textbook on Austrian family law by the jurist with whom Kafka himself had also studied: Horaz Krasnopolski, *Lehrbuch des österreichisches Privatrecht*, ed. Bruno Kafka, 5 vols. (Munich: Duncker & Humblot, 1910–1914), vol. 4, *Familienrecht*. As Hans Helmut Hiebel has shown, Kafka's novel echoes Austrian and German legal terminology in a number of ways: see Hiebel, "Parabelform und Rechtsthematik in Franz Kafkas Romanfragment *Der Verschollene*," in Theo Elm and Hans Helmut Hiebel (eds.), *Die Parabel: Parabolische Formen in der deutschen Dichtung des 20. Jahrhunderts* (Frankfurt am Main: Suhrkamp, 1986), pp. 219–54, esp. pp. 226–28.

51. Kafka, *Der Verschollene*, p. 17. On Kafka's America, see Mark Anderson, "Kafka and New York: Notes on a Traveling Narrative," in Andreas Huyssen and David Bathrick (eds.), *Modernity and the Text: Revisions of German Modernism* (New York: Columbia University Press, 1989), pp. 142–61. The word *verschollen* contains an index of sounding; as Sam Weber writes, "someone who is *verschollen* has dropped not so much out of sight as out of earshot: *schellen* means to resoud, resontate, reverberate. The *Verschollene* is one from whom nothing has been heard from a long time." See Weber, *Theatricality as Medium* (New York: Fordham University Press, 2004), p. 69. Stanley Corngold, by contrast, suggests that Kafka's title be rendered *The Boy Who Sank out of Sight*. See Corngold, *Complex Pleasure: Forms of Feeling in German Literature* (Stanford: Stanford University Press, 1998), pp. 121–38.

52. See Ulrike Vedder, "Die Figur des Verschollenen in der Literatur des 20. Jahrhunderts (Kafka, Burger, Treichel)," *Zeitschrift für Germanistik* 21.3 (2011), p. 552.

53. See Hiebel, "Parabelform und Rechtsthematik in Franz Kafkas Romanfragment *Der Verschollene*," p. 228. Kafka would have encountered the "father of a minor age" in

Krasnopolski's *Österreichisches Familienrecht*, p. 265. On Kafka and Krasnopolski, see Max Brod, *Über Franz Kafka* (Frankfurt am Main: Fischer, 1974), p. 45, and Klaus Wagenbach, *Kafka: Eine Biographie seiner Jugend* (Bern: Francke, 1958), p. 127. In Brod's edition of Kafka's novel, Karl Rossmann is said to be sixteen.

54. Vedder, "Die Figur des Verschollenen in der Literatur des 20. Jahrhunderts," p. 552.

55. Kafka, *Der Verschollene*, p. 388; *The Man Who Disappeared*, p. 481.

56. *Ibid.*, p. 402; p. 499. On Karl's final self-identification, see Heinz Politzer, *Franz Kafka: Parable and Paradox* (Ithaca: Cornell University Press, 1962), p. 161, and David Suchoff, *Kafka's Jewish Languages* (Philadelphia: University of Pennsylvania Press, 2012), pp. 127–28.

57. In a diary entry from 1916, Kafka calls Rossmann "the guiltless one," evoking an ending he does not appear to have composed: "Rossmann and K., the guiltless and the guilty, both executed without distinction in the end, the innocent one with a gentler hand, more pushed aside than struck down." See Kafka, *Tagebücher*, 3 vols., eds. Hans-Gerd Koch, Michael Müller, and Malcolm Pasley (Frankfurt am Main: Fischer, 2002), p. 757.

FOUR: THE TRANSIENT IMAGE

1. Quoted in Edward Higgs, *Identifying the English: A History of Personal Identification, 1500 to the Present* (New York: Continuum Books, 2011), p. 165.

2. Quoted in *ibid.*, p. 106.

3. Quoted in *ibid.*, pp. 106–107

4. Aeschylus, *Agamemnon*, lines 404–19; English in *Agamemnon*, vol. 1 of *The Complete Greek Tragedies*, ed. and trans. David Grene and Richmond Lattimore (Chicago: University of Chicago Press, 1959), p. 47.

5. Deborah Steiner, "Eyeless in Argos," *Journal of Hellenic Studies* 115 (1995), p. 178.

6. See George Thomson, *Æschylus and Athens: A Study in the Social Origins of Drama* (London: Lawrence and Wishart, 1916), p. 256; cf. Jean-Pierre Vernant, *Œuvres*, 2 vols. (Paris: Éditions du Seuil, 2007), vol. 2, pp. 1534–35.

7. *Cratylus*, 420a; English in *Plato in Twelve Volumes*, vol. 12, trans. Harold N. Fowler (Cambridge, MA: Harvard University Press, 1921). On *pothos*, see Vernant, *Œuvres*, vol. 2, pp. 1545–50.

8. For a discussion of the *stiboi* and the figure of the beloved's "traces," see Maurizio Bettini, *Il ritratto dell'amante* (Turin: Einaudi, 1992), pp. 18–20 and p. 23 n. 39.

9. Steiner, "Eyeless in Argos," pp. 175–76.

10. Pierre Chantraine, "Grec *kolossós*," *Bulletin de l'institut français d'archéologie orientale* 30 (1930), p. 449.

11. For the first hypothesis, see Charles Picard, "Le Cénotaphe de Midéa et les 'colosses' de Ménélas. *Ad Æsch. Agamemn.* v. 414 sqq," *Revue de philologie, de littérature, et d'histoire anciennes* 7 (1933), pp. 341–54; for the second, see Eduard Fraenkel, *Agamemnon*, 2 vols. (Oxford: Clarendon Press of Oxford University Press, 1950), vol. 2, pp. 218–19. On the passage, see also Carlo Brillante, "Metamorfosi di un'immagine: Le Statue animate e il sogno," in Giulio Guidorizzi (ed.), *Il Sogno in Grecia* (Rome: Laterza, 1998), pp. 17–33, esp. pp. 25–30. Cf. Jean Ducat, "Fonctions de la statue dans la Grèce archaïque: *Kouros* et *kolossos*," *Bulletin de correspondance hellénique* 100.1 (1976), p. 249.

12. Bettini, *Il ritratto dell'amante*, p. 17.

13. Chantraine, "Grec *kolossós*," p. 449.

14. The link of *kolossos* to *kolekanos* goes back to the historian Strattis. See Chantraine, "Grec *kolossós*," pp. 450–52.

15. Émile Benveniste, "Le sens du mot *kolossos*," *Revue de philologie, de littérature et d'histoire anciennes* 6 (1932), p. 124.

16. *Ibid.*, p. 133.

17. Herodotus, *Histories* 2.130; English in *Histories*, trans. A. D. Godley (Cambridge, MA: Harvard University Press, 1920), p. 433.

18. Benveniste, "Le sens du mot *kolossos*," pp. 120–21.

19. Herodotus, *Histories* 2.143; p. 451.

20. Benveniste, "Le sens du mot *kolossos*," p. 121.

21. See Herodotus, *Histories* 2.153, 2.175, 2.176.

22. See Steiner, "Eyeless in Argos," p. 176.

23. Deborah Steiner, *Images in Mind: Statues in Archaic and Classical Greek Literature and Thought* (Princeton: Princeton University Press, 2001), p. 10; cf. Steiner's earlier discussion in "Eyeless in Argos," p. 176. For the text, see A. Chaniotis et al. (eds.), *Supplementum Epigraphicum Graecum* 9. 72.117–21. The law has been repeatedly commented on: see, among others, Jean-Pierre Vernant, "The Figuration of the Invisible and the Psychological Category of the Double: The Kolossos," in Vernant, *Myth and Thought among the Greeks*, trans. Janet Lloyd with Jeff Fort (New York: Zone Books, 2006), pp. 321–32, esp. pp. 323–25; Christopher A. Faraone, *Talismans and Trojan Horses: Guardian Statues in Ancient Greek Myth and Ritual* (Oxford: Oxford University Press, 1992), pp. 81–82; and Robert Parker, *Miasma: Pollution and Purification in Early Greek Religion* (Oxford: Clarendon Press of Oxford University Press, 1983), p. 348.

24. Benveniste, "Le sens du mot *kolossos*," pp. 119–20.

25. Steiner, *Images in Mind*, p. 10.

26. Ulrich Wilamowitz-Möllendorf, "Heilige Gesetze: Eine Urkunde aus Kyrene," *Sitzungsberichte der Berliner Akademie* (1927), p. 169. Wilamowitz-Möllendorf suggests that the meaning of *kolossos* as a being "of immense dimensions" derives from the *kolossos* at Rhodes. Benveniste cites his article approvingly, "Le sens du mot *kolossos*," p. 119.

27. Louis Gernet, *The Anthropology of Ancient Greece*, trans. John Hamilton and Gregory Nagy (Baltimore: Johns Hopkins University Press, 1982), p. 170.

28. Translation in Steiner, *Images in Mind*, p. 9.

29. Vernant, *Myth and Thought among the Greeks*, p. 324 (translation modified). Cf. Gernet, *Anthropology of Ancient Greece*, pp. 170–71, and Steiner, *Images in Mind*, p. 9.

30. Pausanias 9.38.5. English in Pausanias, *Description of Greece*, trans. W. H. S. Jones and H. A. Ormerod, 4 vols. (Cambridge, MA: Harvard University Press, 1918).

31. Vernant, *Myth and Thought*, p. 331.

32. Pliny, *Natural History*, 35.15; English in Pliny the Elder, *Natural History*, trans. H. Rackam, 10 vols. (Cambridge, MA: Harvard University Press, 1938–1963), vol. 9, p. 271.

33. Pliny, *Natural History*, 35.151; English in *Natural History*, vol. 9, pp. 371–73.

34. Pliny, *Natural History* 35.156; English in *Natural History*, vol. 9, p. 377.

35. Bettini, *Il ritratto dell'amante*, p. 11.

36. *Ibid.*

37. Athenagoras, *Legatio pro Christianis*, in Jacques Paul Migne (ed.), *Patrologiae Cursus Completus*, Series Graeca 6: *Tou en hagiois patros hēmōn Ioustinou philosophou kai martyros ta heuriskomena panta* = S.P.N. *Justini philosophi et martyris opera quae exstant omnia* (Petit-Monrouge: Migne, 1857), coll. 923–24.

38. Steiner, *Images in Mind*, p. 3.

39. It has been noted that Pliny and Athenagoras say little of the shape of the body made by Boutades, assuming he is to have made one. See Bettini, *Il ritratto dell'amante*, p. 11; Victor I. Stoichita, *A Short History of the Shadow*, trans. Anne-Marie Glasheen (London: Reaktion Books, 1997), p. 17.

40. Stoichita, *Short History of the Shadow*, p. 17.

41. See *ibid.*, pp. 18–19.

42. See *Iliad*, 695–701; English in *Iliad*, trans. Richmond Lattimore (Chicago: University of Chicago Press, 1951). The scholia propose several glosses for the "house half-completed" (*domos hēmitelēs*). See R. O. A. M. Lyne, "Love and Death: Laodamia and Protesilaus in

Catullus, Propertius, and Others," *Classical Quarterly* 48.1 (1998), p. 201.

43. For the myth and its variations, see Bettini, *Il ritratto dell'amante*, pp. 12–13, and Laurel Fulkerson, "(Un)Sympathetic Magic: A Study of *Heroides* 13," *American Journal of Philology* 123.1 (2002), p. 64. On the appearances of bodies in dreams more generally, see Brillante, "Metamorfosi di un'immagine."

44. Fulkerson notes that throughout the *Heroides*, Ovid's "heroines are often 'incorrect' about the specific details of their stories." "(Un)Sympathetic Magic," p. 62.

45. Ovid, *Heroides*, trans. Harold Isbell (New York: Penguin Books, 1990), p. 122.

46. Fulkerson, "(Un)Sympathetic Magic," p. 82; cf. Howard Jacobson, *Ovid's Heroides* (Princeton: Princeton University Press, 1974), p. 211.

47. Fulkerson, "(Un)Sympathetic Magic," p. 81; cf. Jacobson, *Ovid's Heroides*, p. 208.

48. Bettini, *Il ritratto dell'amante*, p. 14.

49. On *pittura infamante*, see Robert Davidsohn, *Storia di Firenze*, 5 vols. (Florence: Sansoni, 1956), vol. 4, pp. 597–603; Gino Masi, "La pittura infamante nella legislazione e nella vita del comune fiorentino (sec. XIII–XVI)," in Masi, *Studi di diritto commerciale in onore di Cesare Vivante*, 2 vols. (Rome: Foro italiano, 1931), vol. 2, pp. 625–57; Gherardo Ortalli, *La pittura infamante nei secoli XIII–XVI* (Rome: Jouvence, 1979); Samuel Y. Edgerton, Jr., *Pictures and Punishment: Art and Criminal Prosecution during the Florentine Renaissance* (Ithaca: Cornell University Press, 1985).

50. *Digest* 50.13. 5.1; English in Alan Watson, ed., *The Digest of Justinian*, 4 vols. (Philadelphia: University of Pennsylvania Press, 1998), vol. 4, p. 444.

51. A. H. J. Greenidge, *Infamia: Its Place in Roman Public and Private Law* (Oxford: Clarendon Press of Oxford University Press, 1894), p. 18.

52. *Ibid.*, p. 36.

53. Ortalli, *La pittura infamante nei secoli XIII–XVI*, p. 26.

54. Edgerton, *Pictures and Punishment*, p. 68.

55. *Ibid.*, p. 69.

56. Ortalli, *La pittura infamante nei secoli XIII–XVI*, p. 15.

57. Original in Julius Ficker, *Forschungen zur Reichs- und Rechtsgeschichte Italiens*, 4 vols. (Innsbruck: Wagner, 1868–1874), vol. 4, pp. 513–14. See Ortalli, *La pittura infamante nei secoli XIII–XVI*, pp. 32–33. For a partial English translation of the documents, see David Freedberg, *The Power of Images: Studies in the History and Theory of Response* (Chicago: University of Chicago Press, 1989), pp. 254–55.

58. See Ortalli, *La pittura infamante nei secoli XIII–XVI*, p. 33.

59. See Edgerton, *Pictures and Punishment*, pp. 91–93.

60. Gherardo Ortalli, "Pittura infamante: Practices, Genres and Connections," in Carolin Behrmann (ed.), *Images of Shame: Infamy, Defamation and the Ethics of Oeconomia* (Berlin: De Gruyter, 2016), p. 31.

61. Edgerton, *Pictures and Punishment*, p. 75.

62. Freedberg, *The Power of Images*, p. 257.

63. See Ortalli, "Pittura infamante," p. 34, and, for a rich treatment of such documents, Wolfgang Brückner, *Bildnis und Brauch: Studien zur Bildfunktion des Effigies* (Berlin: Erich Schmidt, 1964), pp. 205–27.

64. Ortalli, *La pittura infamante*, p. 13 n.11.

65. Edgerton, *Pictures and Punishment*, p. 74.

66. Ortalli, *La pittura infamante nei secoli XIII–XVI*, p. 83.

67. Freedberg, *The Power of Images*, p. 250.

68. Helene Wieruszowski, "Art and the Commune in the Age of Dante," *Speculum* 19.1 (1944), p. 22.

69. Freedberg, *The Power of Images*, p. 253.

70. See the account in Brückner, *Bildnis und Brauch*, pp. 191–315, and from a different perspective, Freedberg, *The Power of Images*, pp. 263–82.

71. Brückner, *Bildnis und Brauch*, p. 198.

72. *Ibid.*, p. 203.

73. In this case, it appears that the "punishing" of the doll was intended not to humiliate the absentee, but to bear witness to the rigor of the legal authorities of Mecheln and their disapproval of the Meier. See *ibid.*, p. 224.

74. *Ibid.*, p. 250.

75. *Ibid.*, p. 249.

76. *Ibid.*

77. *Ibid.*, p. 262.

78. Freedberg, *The Power of Images*, p. 261.

79. Brückner, *Bildnis und Brauch*, p. 304.

80. *Ibid.*, pp. 306–307.

81. See Fredrik Grøn, "Über den Ursprung der Bestrafung in Effigie: Eine vergleichende rechts- und kulturgeschichtliche Untersuchung," *Tijdschrift voor Rechtsgeschiedenis / Revue d'histoire du droit* 13 (1934), p. 334.

FIVE: DECREASES OF THE HEAD

1. For a classical statement of this etymology, see Aulus Gellius 5.7; English in Gellius, *Attic Nights*, trans. J. C. Rolfe (Cambridge, MA: Harvard University Press, 2014); Boethius, *Contra Eutychen* 3; Latin in Boethius, *Liber contra Eutychen et Nestorium* (Turnhout: Brepols, 2010). For a modern study, see Maurice Nédoncelle, "Prosopon et persona dans l'antiquité classique: Essai de bilan linguistique," *Revue des sciences religieuses* 22.3–4 (1948), pp. 277–99.

2. Gaston Chabalet, *Droit romain de la capitis deminutio* (Cambrai: Deligne & Langlet, 1877), p. 5.

3. Émile Benveniste, "Problèmes sémantiques de la reconstitution," *Word* 10.2–3 (1954), pp. 251–64, rept. in *Problèmes de linguistique générale*, 2 vols. (Paris: Gallimard, 1966–1974), vol. 1, pp. 255–56.

4. Mario Bretone, "Capitis deminutio," *Novissimo digesto italiano* 2 (1958), p. 916. On *caput*, see also Carlo Gioffredi, "Caput," *Studia et documenta historiae et iuris* 11 (1945), pp. 301–13; Max Radin, "Caput et sōma," in Gabriel Le Bras (ed.), *Mélanges Paul Fournier* (Paris: Recueil Sirey, 1929), pp. 651–63.

5. Fernand Desserteaux, *Études sur la formation historique de la capitis deminutio*, vol. 1, *Ancienneté respective des cas et des sources de la capitis deminutio* (Paris: Champion, 1909), p. 6.

6. See, for example, *The Institutes of Justinian*, trans. J. B. Moyle, 2nd ed. (Oxford: Clarendon Press of Oxford University Press, 1889), section 16, and Cicero, *Topica*, ed. and trans. Tobias Reinhardt (Oxford: Oxford University Press, 2003), pp. 230–31.

7. For a summary of the debate, see Desserteaux, *Études sur la formation historique de la capitis deminutio*, vol. 1, pp. 7–8. For other accounts of *capitis deminutio*, see Max Cohn, "Zur Lehre von der capitis deminutio," in Cohn, *Beiträge zur Bearbeitung des römischen Rechts* 1 (Berlin: Weidmannsche Buchhandlung, 1878), pp. 41–400; Hugo Krüger, *Geschichte der capitis deminutio*, vol. 1 (Breslau: Wilhelm Koebner, 1887); Fridolin Eisele, "Zur Natur und Geschichte der capitis deminutio," in Eisele, *Beiträge zur römischen Rechtsgeschichte* (1896), pp. 160–216; Ugo Coli, *Capitis deminutio* (Florence: Vallecchi Editore, 1922); Max Kaser, "Zur Geschicte der 'capitis deminutio,'" *Iura* 3 (1952), pp. 48–89.

8. Cicero, *Topics* 18, in *Topica*, pp. 122–23; see the corresponding commentary on pp. 230–31.

9. Gaius, *Institutes* 1.159, in *The Institutes of Gaius*, trans. W. M. Gordon and O. F. Robinson, with the Latin text of Seckel and Kübler (London: Duckworth, 1988), pp. 102–103 (translation modified). The Veronese codex on which Seckel and Kübler based their

edition defines *capitis deminutio* as *prioris capitis deminutio*, not *prioris status permutatio*; the editors have emended the text.

10. Paulus, in *Digest* 4.5.11. English in Alan Watson, ed., *The Digest of Justinian*, 4 vols. (Philadelphia: University of Pennsylvania Press, 1998), vol. 1, p. 138.

11. *Ibid.* (translation modified).

12. Gaius 1.161; English in *The Institutes of Gaius*, pp. 104–105.

13. Rudolph Sohm, *The Institutes of Roman Law*, trans. James Crawford Ledlie (Oxford: Clarendon Press of Oxford University Press, 1892), p. 122. For a different, fuller account, see Karl Friedrich von Savigny, *Traité de droit romain*, trans. Charles Guenoux, 8 vols. (Paris: Firmin Didot Frères, 1840–1851), vol. 2, pp. 28–169.

14. William Warwick Buckland, *The Main Institutions of Roman Private Law* (Cambridge: Cambridge University Press, 1931), p. 70.

15. See Coli, *Capitis deminutio*; Kaser, "Zur Geschichte der 'capitis deminutio.'"

16. Buckland, *The Main Institutions of Roman Private Law*, p. 70.

17. See *Digest* 4.5; English in *The Digest of Justinian* vol. 1, pp. 138–40. Cf. "forfeiture of civil rights," the translation employed by Eleanor Stump in her edition of Boethius's commentary on the *Topics*: *In Ciceronia Topicis*, ed. and trans. Eleanor Stump (Ithaca: Cornell University Press, 1988), pp. 62–63.

18. Buckland, *The Main Institutions of Roman Private Law*, pp. 70–71.

SIX: RULES OF DIMINUTION

1. *Liber monstrorum*, Latin text and English translation in Andy Orchard, *Pride and Prodigies: Studies in the Monsters of the Beowulf-Manuscript* (Cambridge: D. S. Brewer, 1995), pp. 288–89. The entire text of the *Liber* can be found in *ibid.*, pp. 254–317. On the *Liber*, see also *Liber Monstrorum (secolo IX)*, ed. and trans. Franco Porsia (Naples: Liguori Editore, 2012), pp. 1–114.

2. *Liber monstrorum*, 1.15 and 1.16, pp. 268–69.

3. *Ibid.*, 1.17, pp. 268–69.

4. *Ibid.*, 1.24, pp. 272–73.

5. *Ibid.*, 1.40, pp. 280–81.

6. Euripides, *Iphigenia in Aulis* 1400, quoted in Aristotle, *Politics* 1.1.5, 1252b 5–10; English in Aristotle, *The Complete Works: The Revised Oxford Translation*, 2 vols., ed. Jonathan Barnes (Princeton: Princeton University Press, 1984), vol. 2, p. 1019.

7. *Institutes* 1.3; English in *The Institutes of Justinian*, trans. J. B. Moyle, 2nd ed. (Oxford:

Clarendon Press of Oxford University Press, 1889); *Digest* 12.6.64; English in Alan Watson, ed., *The Digest of Justinian*, 4 vols. (Philadelphia: University of Pennsylvania Press, 1998), vol. 1, p. 388.

8. Émile Benveniste, "Le nom de l'esclave à Rome," *Revue des études latines* 10 (1932), pp. 429–40; cf. his later treatment in *Le vocabulaire des institutions indo-européennes*, 2 vols. (Paris: Minuit, 1969), vol. 1, pp. 349–50.

9. Henri Lévy-Bruhl, "Théorie de l'esclavage," in Lévy-Bruhl, *Quelques problèmes du très ancient droit romain* (Paris: Domat-Montchrestien, 1934), pp. 15–33.

10. Alain Testart, *L'institution de l'esclavage: Une approche mondiale*, ed. Valérie Lécrivain (Paris: Gallimard, 2018), p. 67.

11. Benveniste, "Le nom de l'esclave à Rome," p. 434.

12. Benveniste, *Le vocabulaire des institutions indo-européennes*, vol. 1, p. 359. Testart takes the fact to be generalizable for "the West": *L'institution de l'esclavage*, p. 27.

13. Cicero, *De officiis* 3.107, in Marcus Tullius Cicero, *De officiis*, ed. Michael Winterbottom (Oxford: Clarendon Press of Oxford University Press, 1994), pp. 154–55; English in *On Duties*, ed. and trans. M. T. Griffin and E. M. Atkins (Cambridge: Cambridge University Press, 1991), p. 141.

14. See Daniel Heller-Roazen, *The Enemy of All: Piracy and the Law of Nations* (New York: Zone Books, 2009).

15. Orlando Patterson, *Slavery and Social Death: A Comparative Study* (Cambridge, MA: Harvard University Press, 1982), pp. 7–8.

16. M. I. Finley, *Ancient Slavery and Modern Ideology* (New York: Viking Press, 1980), p. 67.

17. *Ibid.*, p. 65.

18. For Aristotle's treatment of slavery, see *Politics* 1, especially chapters 3–7; cf. *Politics* 1278b32–8; *Nicomachean Ethics* 1160b28–32 and 1161a30–b10; *Eudemian Ethics* 1241b18–24 and 1242a28–32. An analysis, with reference to other Aristotelian passages on slavery, can be found in Peter Garnsey, *Ideas of Slavery from Aristotle to Augustine* (Cambridge: Cambridge University Press, 1996), pp. 107–27.

19. See Yan Thomas, "Imago naturae: Note sur l'institutionnalité de la nature à Rome," *Publications de l'école française de Rome* 147 (1991), p. 202.

20. *Ibid.*, pp. 202–203.

21. Gaius, *Institutes*, 1.3.9, in *Digest*, 1.5.3; English in *The Digest of Justinian*, vol. 1, p. 15.

22. On the status of Roman *res* as an "object of right," rather than a "thing," see Testart, "De quelques conceptions erronées à propos de l'esclavage, et de la façon dont elles

faussent toute comparaison avec l'esclavage dans les autres mondes," in *L'institution de l'esclavage*, pp. 305–13.

23. *Institutes*, 1.16.4; English in *The Institutes of Justinian*, p. 23.

24. Paulus, *Edict* 11, in *Digest* 4 5.3.1; English in *The Digest of Justinian*, vol. 1, p. 139.

25. William Warwick Buckland, *The Roman Law of Slavery: The Condition of the Slave in Private Law* (1908; Cambridge: Cambridge University Press, 1970), p. 3.

26. Ulpian, *Sabinus* 28, in *Digest* 50.17.22 pr.; English in *The Digest of Justinian*, vol. 4, p. 472.

27. Buckland, *The Roman Law of Slavery*, p. 3.

28. Ulpian, *Lex Julia et Papia* 4, in *Digest* 50, 17, 209; English in *The Digest of Justinian*, vol. 4, p. 483; cf. *Novellae* 22.9 and Gaius, *Institutes*, 3.101.

29. Ulpian, *Edict* 60, in *Digest* 28. 8. 1. pr.; English in *The Digest of Justinian*, vol. 2, p. 407.

30. Aristotle, *Athenian Constitution* 16.10; English in Aristotle, *The Complete Works*, vol. 2, p. 1503.

31. See Sviatoslav Dmitriev, "Athenian *ATIMIA* and Legislation against Tyranny and Subversion," *Classical Quarterly* 65.1 (2015), pp. 35–50.

32. Andocides, *On the Mysteries* 1.95–96; for a translation and commentary, see Dmitriev, "Athenian *ATIMIA* and Legislation against Tyranny and Subversion," p. 40.

33. Benjamin D. Meritt, "Greek Inscriptions," *Hesperia* 21.4 (1952), pp. 340–80; translation and commentary in Dmitriev, "Athenian *ATIMIA* and Legislation against Tyranny and Subversion," p. 40.

34. Dmitriev, "Athenian *ATIMIA* and Legislation against Tyranny and Subversion," p. 46. On *atimia*, see also Mogens Herman Hansen, *Apagoge, Endeixis and Ephegesis against Kakourgoi, Atimoi and Pheugontes: A Study in the Athenian Administration of Justice in the Fourth Century B. C.* (Odense: Odense University Press, 1976), pp. 75–90.

35. See Paul Usteri, *Ächtung und Verbannung in griechischen Recht* (Berlin: Weidmannsche Buchhandlung, 1903) for a comparative study, and Sara Forsdyke, *Exile, Ostracism, and Democracy: The Politics of Expulsion in Ancient Greece* (Princeton: Princeton University Press, 2005).

36. See Giuliano Crifò, "*Exilica causa, quae adversus exulem agitur*: Problemi dell'*aqua et igni interdictio*," in Crifò, *Du châtiment dans la cité: Supplices corporels et peine de mort dans le monde antique* (Rome: École française de Rome, 1984), pp. 453–97, esp. pp. 475–79.

37. See Giorgio Agamben, *Homo Sacer: Il potere sovrano e nuda vita* (Turin: Einaudi, 1995); English in *Homo Sacer: Sovereign Power and Bare Life*, trans. Daniel Heller-Roazen (Stanford: Stanford University Press, 1998).

38. See Testart, *L'institution de l'esclavage*, p. 68.

39. Crifò, "*Exilica causa, quae adversus exulem agitur*," pp. 472–73.

40. The term "lay sanction" is from Crifò: see *ibid.*, p. 481.

41. Max Kaser, "Zur Geschichte der 'capitis deminutio'," *Iura* 3 (1952), pp. 68–71; Dietmar Schanbacher, "Aqua et Igni Interdictio," in Hubert Cancik et al. (eds.) *Brill's New Pauly*, Brill Reference Online, https://referenceworks.brillonline.com/entries/brill-s-new-pauly/*-e130020.

42. Gaius, *Provincial Edict* 17, in *Digest* 28.1.8; English in *The Digest of Justinian*, vol. 2, p. 357.

43. Marcian, *Institutes*, 1, in *Digest* 48.19.17; English in *The Digest of Justinian*, vol. 4, p. 364. See Max Kaser, *Römische Privatrecht*, 2 vols. (Munich: Beck'sche Verlagsbuchhandlung, 1955–1958), vol. 1, *Das Altrömische, das Vorklassische und klassische Recht*, p. 251.

44. Brigitte Borgmann, "Mors Civilis: Die Bildung des Begriffs in Mittelalter und sein Fortleben im französischen Recht der Neuzeit," *Ius Commune* 4 (1972), pp. 81–157, esp. pp. 86–91.

45. Borgmann, "Mors Civilis," p. 106. On the monk as a slave, see Paulin M. Blecker, "The Civil Rights of the Monk in Roman and Canon Law: The Monk as *Servus*," *American Benedictine Review* 17 (1966), pp. 185–98.

46. Borgmann, "Mors Civilis," pp. 106–107.

47. *Ibid.*, pp. 107–108.

48. *Ibid.*, p. 108.

49. See *ibid.*, pp. 120–23.

50. Borgmann, "Mors Civilis," pp. 123–26. Cf. Jean Gaudemet, "Note sur l'excommunication," *Cristianesimo nella storia* 16 (1995), pp. 285–306; Giacomo Todeschini, *Visibilmente crudeli: Malviventi, persone sospette e gente qualunque dal Medioevo all'età moderna* (Bologna: Il Mulino, 2007), pp. 154–57.

51. See Giovanni Tarello, "Profili giuridici della questione della povertà nel francescanesimo prima di Occam," *Annali della Facoltà di Giurisprudenza dell'Università di Genova* 3 (1964), pp. 338–448; Roberto Lambertini, *La povertà pensata: Evoluzione storica della definizione dell'identità minoritica da Bonaventura ad Ockham* (Modena: Mucchi, 2000); Giorgio Agamben, *Altissima povertà: Regole monastiche e forma di vita* (Vicenza: Neri Pozza, 2011).

52. See Borgmann, "Mors Civilis," p. 132.

53. William Blackstone, *Commentaries on the Law of England*, 4 vols. (London: A. Strahan, 1825), vol. 4, pp. 380–81.

54. *Ibid.*, p. 388. Cf. J. G. Bellamy, *The Law of Treason in England in the Later Middle Ages* (Cambridge: Cambridge University Press, 1970), pp. 177–205.

55. See Franz Weithase, *Über den bürgerlichen Tod als Straffolge* (Berlin: Ernst-Reuter-Gesellschaft, 1966), pp. 6–7.

56. See Verena Hubmann, *L'image de la mort: Über die mort civile und ihre Abschaffung im französischen Recht und ihre Nachbildungen in den Kantonen Waadt und Wallis* (Zurich: Schulthess, 1990), pp. 15–24.

57. Jean Domat, *Les loix civiles dans leur ordre naturel*, 2 vols. (Paris: n. p., 1756), vol. 1, p. 15.

58. *Ibid.*, p. 93.

59. Pierre-François Muyart de Vouglans, *Institutes au droit criminel ou principes généraux sur ces matières, avec un traité particulier des crimes* (Paris: Le Breton, 1757), p. 413.

60. Daniel Jousse, *Traité de la justice criminelle en France*, 2 vols. (Paris: Chez Debure Père, 1771), vol. 1, n. 136 (p. 85).

61. François Richir, *Traité de la Mort civile, Tant celle qui résulte des condamnations pour cause de crime, que celle qui résulte des vœux en religion* (Paris: Thiboust, 1755).

62. *Ibid.*, p. iii.

63. *Ibid.*, p. 6.

64. *Ibid.*, p. 28.

65. Anne Simonin, *Le déshonneur dans la République: Une histoire de l'indignité* (Paris: Grasset, 2008), p. 319.

66. Richir, *Traité de la Mort civile*, p. 159.

67. Cesare Beccaria, *Dei delitti e delle pene*, chapter 26, in *Dei delitti e delle pene*, ed. Franco Venturi, 3rd ed. (Turin: Einaudi, 1973), p. 71; English in Richard Bellamy, ed., *On Crimes and Punishments and Other Writings*, trans. Richard Davies with Virginia Cox and Richard Bellamy (Cambridge: Cambridge University Press, 1995), pp. 58–59.

68. See Charles Schaub, *Dissertation sur la mort civile* (Geneva: A. I. Vignier, 1831), p. 26.

69. Simonin, *Le déshonneur dans la République*, p. 318.

70. Trophime Gérard de Lally-Tollendal, *Défense des émigrés français adressée au peuple français* (Paris: Chez Chochens 1797), p. 126, quoted in Simonin, *Le déshonneur dans la République*, p. 319 n. 2.

71. See Simonin, *Le déshonneur dans la République*, p. 320.

72. Miranda Frances Spieler, *Empire and Underworld: Captivity in French Guyana* (Cambridge, MA: Harvard University Press, 2012), p. 20.

73. See *ibid.*, pp. 26–34.

74. *Ibid.*, p. 84.

75. *Ibid.*, p. 86.

76. Simonin, *Le déshonneur dans la République*, p. 86.

77. Alphonse-Honoré Taillandier, *Réflexions sur les lois pénales de France et d'Angleterre* (Paris: B. Warée, 1824), p. 82, quoted in Hubmann, *L'image de la mort*, p. 286 n. 7.

78. See Hubmann, *L'image de la mort*, pp. 283–394, and, for the text of the abolition and a commentary, pp. 361–74.

79. Cited in G. A. Humbert, *Des conséquences de condamnations pénales relativement à la capacité des personnes en droit romain et en droit français* (Paris: Durand, 1855), p. 453.

80. Spieler, *Empire and Underworld*, p. 127.

81. *Ibid.*, pp. 131–32.

82. Simonin, *Le déshonneur dans la République*, p. 87.

83. United States Constitution, art. III, § 3, cl. 2.

84. See "Civil Death Statutes — Medieval Fiction in a Modern World,' *Harvard Law Review* 50.6 (1937), pp. 968–77.

85. Kim Lane Scheppele, "Facing Facts in Legal Interpretation," *Representations* 30 (1990), p. 50.

86. *Ibid.*, esp. pp. 50–51; see also pp. 71–72. Cf. Harry David Saunders, "Civil Death: A New Look at an Ancient Doctrine," *William and Mary Law Review* 11.4 (1970), pp. 988–1003, esp. 990–98.

87. Gabriel J. Chin, "The New Civil Death: Rethinking Punishment in the Era of Mass Conviction," *University of Pennsylvania Law Review* 160.6 (2012), p. 1798.

88. Howard Itzkowitz and Lauren Oldak, "Restoring the Ex-Offender's Right to Vote: Background and Developments," *American Criminal Law Review* 11 (1973), p. 721.

89. Alec C. Ewald, "'Civil Death': The Ideological Paradox of Criminal Disenfranchisement Law in the United States," *Wisconsin Law Review* (2002), p. 1046.

90. Chin, "The New Civil Death," p. 1790.

91. See Chin, "The New Civil Death." On the legacies of civil death in the United States, see also Luca Follis, "Resisting the Camp: Civil Death and the Practice of Sovereignty in New York State," *Law, Culture and the Humanities* 9.1 (2011), pp. 91–113; Follis, "Of Friendless and Stained Men: Grafting Medieval Sanctions onto Modern Democratic Law," in Simone Glanert (ed.), *Comparative Law — Engaging Translation* (London: Routledge, 2014), pp. 173–90; Sarah C. Grady, "Civil Death Is Different: An Examination of a Post-Graham Challenge to Felon Disenfranchisement under the Eighth Amendment," *Journal of Criminal Law and Criminology* 102.2 (2012), pp. 441–70; and Colin Dayan, *The Law Is a White Dog: How Legal Rituals Make and Unmake Persons* (Princeton: Princeton University Press, 2011).

SEVEN: OF IGNOMINIES

1. Jonathan Swift, *Gulliver's Travels*, ed. Claude Rowson, notes by Ian Higgins (Oxford: Oxford University Press, 2005), pp. 16–17.

2. *Ibid.*, p. 17.

3. *Ibid.*

4. *Ibid.*

5. *Ibid.*, p. 29.

6. *Ibid.*, p. 77.

7. *Ibid.*, p. 78.

8. Hugh Kenner, *The Counterfeiters: An Historical Comedy* (Bloomington: Indiana University Press, 1968), p. 129.

9. Swift, *Gulliver's Travels*, p. 88.

10. On extraordinary as well as all too ordinary sights and monsters in *Gulliver's Travels*, see Aline Mackenzie Taylor, "Sights and Monsters and Gulliver's *Voyage to Brobdingnag*," *Tulane Studies in English* 6 (1956), pp. 27–32, and Dennis Todd, "The Hairy Maid at the Harpsichord: Some Speculations on the Meaning of Gulliver's Travels," *Texas Studies in Literature and Language* 34.2 (1992), pp. 239–83.

11. On *ignominia*, see Léon Pommeray, *Études sur l'infamie en droit romain* (Paris: Sirey, 1937), pp. 11–39; Max Kaser, "Infamia und ignominia in den römischen Rechtsquellen," *Zeitschrift der Savigny-Stiftung für Rechtsgeschichte* 59 (1956), pp. 220–78; Joseph Georg Wolf, "Lo stigma dell'ignominia," in Alessandro Corbino, Michel Humbert, and Giovanni Negri (eds.), *Homo, caput, persona: La costruzione giuridica dell'identità nell'esperienza romana, dall'epoca di Plauto a Ulpiano* (Pavia: IUSS Press, 2010), pp. 491–550.

12. Elizabeth A. Meyer, *Legitimacy and Law in the Roman World* (Cambridge: Cambridge University Press, 2004), p. 93.

13. Nonius Marcellus, *De compendiosa doctrina* 24.5, quoted in Alfred Ernout and Ernest Meillet, *Dictionnaire étymologique de la langue latine: Histoire des mots*, 4th ed. (1932; Paris: Klincksieck, 2001), s.v. "ignominia."

14. Georges Pieri, *L'histoire du cens jusqu'à la fin de la République romaine* (Paris: Sirey, 1968), p. 114.

15. Pommeray, *Études sur l'infamie en droit romain*, pp. 25–26. For further analyses of ignominy and infamy, see the studies by Kaser and Wolf cited above, as well as Clément Bur, *La citoyenneté dégradée: Une histoire de l'infamie à Rome (312 av. J.-C.–96 apr. J.-C.)* (Rome: École française de Rome, 2018). On medieval and early modern legacies of infamy and ignominy,

see Giacomo Todeschini, *Visibilmente crudeli: Malviventi, persone sospette e gente qualunque dal Medioevo all'età moderna* (Bologna: Il Mulino, 2007), esp. pp. 43–78.

16. Nathaniel Hawthorne, *The Scarlet Letter*, in *Collected Novels* (New York: Library of America, 1983), p. 165.

17. *Ibid.*

18. *Ibid.*, p. 171.

19. *Ibid.*, p. 168.

20. *Ibid.*, p. 204.

21. *Ibid.*, p. 175.

22. *Ibid.*, p. 214, also p. 245.

23. *Ibid.*, p. 192.

24. *Ibid.*, p. 181.

25. *Ibid.*, p. 185.

26. *Ibid.*, p. 219

27. *Ibid.*, p. 331.

28. *Ibid.*, p. 335.

29. *Ibid.*, p. 171. See also pp. 185, 261, 291.

30. *Ibid.*, p. 338. For other references to the lovers' "stigma," see pp. 292, 331, 340, 344.

31. *Ibid.*, p. 339.

32. *Ibid.*, p. 345.

33. On *boni mores*, see Félix Senn, "Des origines et du contenu de la notion de bonnes mœurs," *Recueil d'études sur les sources du droit en l'honneur de François Gény*, 3 vols. (Paris: Sirey, 1934), vol. 1, pp. 53–67.

34. On memory sanctions in ancient Rome, see Harriet I. Flower, *The Art of Forgetting: Disgrace and Oblivion in Roman Political Culture* (Chapel Hill: University of North Carolina Press, 2006).

35. George Orwell, *Nineteen Eighty-Four* (London: Penguin Books, 2013), p. 51.

36. *Ibid.*, p. 53; cf. p. 182.

37. George Orwell, "How the Poor Die," in *The Collected Essays, Journalism, and Letters of George Orwell*, ed. Sonia Orwell and Ian Angus, 4 vols. (New York: Harcourt & Brace, 1968), vol. 4, p. 224.

38. *Ibid.*

39. *Ibid.*, p. 226.

40. *Ibid.*, pp. 227–28.

41. On Goffman's "non-person" and its relation to Orwell, see Andrew Travers, "Non-Person and Goffman: Sociology under the Influence of Literature," in Travers, *Goffman and Social Organization: Studies in a Sociological Legacy* (London: Routledge, 1999), pp. 156–76.

42. Erving Goffman, *Communication Conduct in an Island Community* (PhD diss., University of Chicago, 1953), p. 1. In his dissertation, Goffman identifies the island only as "Bergland."

43. *Ibid.*, p. 217.

44. *Ibid.*, p. 218.

45. *Ibid.*, pp. 218–21.

46. *Ibid.*, p. 222.

47. *Ibid.*, pp. 222–23.

48. *Ibid.*, p. 226.

49. *Ibid.*, p. 226.

50. *Ibid.*, pp. 223–24.

51. Erving Goffman, *The Presentation of Self in Everyday Life* (Edinburgh: University of Edinburgh, 1956), p. iii.

52. *Ibid.*, pp. 87–95.

53. *Ibid.*, p. 95.

54. *Ibid.*

55. *Ibid.*, p. 96.

56. Erving Goffman, *Behavior in Public Places: Notes on the Social Organization of Gatherings* (New York: The Free Press, 1963), p. 83.

57. *Ibid.* On staring, see, more recently, Rosemarie Garland-Thomson, *Staring: How We Look* (Oxford: Oxford University Press, 2009).

58. Goffman, *Behavior in Public Places*, p. 84.

59. *Ibid.*

60. *Ibid.*

61. Travers, "Non-Person and Goffman," pp. 164–65.

62. For Goffman's account of "spoiled identity," see Erving Goffman, *Stigma: Notes on the Management of Spoiled Identity* (Englewood Cliffs: Prentice Hall, 1963).

63. See Erving Goffman, "Footing," originally published in *Semiotica* 25 (1979), pp. 1–29, in Goffman, *Forms of Talk* (Philadelphia: University of Pennsylvania Press, 1981), pp. 124–59. As Goffman indicates in *Forms of Talk* (p. 144), the point was already made by Dell Hymes

in *Foundations in Social Linguistics: An Ethnographic Approach* (Philadelphia: University of Pennsylvania Press, 1974), p. 54.

64. James D. McCawley, "Speech Acts and Goffman's Participant Roles," *Eastern States Conference on Linguistics* 1 (1984), p. 260. Cf. McCawley's later account, "Participant Roles, Frames, and Speech Acts," *Linguistics and Philosophy* 22.6 (1999), pp. 595–619.

65. See Goffman, *Forms of Talk*. For an assessment of Goffman's contributions to the study of language, see, in addition to the articles by McCawley cited above, Stephen G. Levinson, "Putting Linguistics on a Proper Footing: Explorations in Goffman's Concepts of Participation," in Paul Drew and Anthony Wootton (eds.), *Erving Goffman: Exploring the Interaction Order* (Boston: Northeastern University Press, 1988), pp. 161–227.

66. Swift, *Gulliver's Travels*, p. 28.

67. *Ibid.*, p. 86.

68. *Ibid.*, p. 208.

69. *Ibid.*, p. 209.

70. *Ibid.*

71. *Ibid.*, p. 215.

72. *Ibid.*, pp. 208–209.

73. *Ibid.*, p. 214. Cf. the "Horror and detestation" with which he meets the image of his face, p. 260.

74. *Ibid.*, p. 219.

75. On the Houyhnhnms as exemplary "rational animals," see R. S. Crane, "The Houyhnhms, the Yahoos, and the History of Ideas," in Joseph Anthony Mazzeo (ed.), *Reason and the Imagination: Studies in the History of Ideas 1600–1800* (New York: Columbia University Press, 1962), pp. 231–53; William H. Halewood and Marvin Levich, "Houyhnhnm Est Animal Rationale," *Journal of the History of Ideas* 26.2 (1965), pp. 273–81.

76. Swift, *Gulliver's Travels*, p. 249. On Houyhnhnm rationalism, see Mary P. Nichols, "Rationality and Community: Swift's Criticism of the Houyhnhnms," *Journal of Politics* 43.4 (1981), pp. 1153–69.

77. Swift, *Gulliver's Travels*, p. 240.

78. *Ibid.*, p. 258.

79. *Ibid.*, p. 218.

80. *Ibid.*, p. 223.

81. *Ibid.*, p. 257.

82. *Ibid.*, p. 218. On the Houyhnhnm language, see Marjorie W. Buckley, "Key to the

Language of the Houyhnhnms in *Gulliver's Travels*," in A. Norman Jeffares (ed.), *Fair Liberty Was All His Cry: A Tercentenary Tribute to Jonathan Swift, 1667–1745* (London: Palgrave Macmillan, 1967), pp. 270–79, and on foreign languages in *Gulliver's Travels*, Ann Cline Kelly, "After Eden: Gulliver's (Linguistic) Travels, *ELH* 45.1 (1978), pp. 33–54, and H. D. Kelling, "Some Significant Names in Gulliver's Travels," *Studies in Philology* 48.4 (1951), pp. 761–78.

83. Swift, *Gulliver's Travels*, p. 219.

84. *Ibid.*, pp. 260–61.

85. *Ibid.*, p. 261.

86. *Ibid.*

87. See Nicolás Panagopoulos, "Gulliver and the Horse: An Enquiry into Equine Ethics," in Harold Bloom (ed.), *Jonathan Swift's Gulliver's Travels* (New York: Infobase, 2009), p. 152.

88. Swift, *Gulliver's Travels*, p. 262.

89. *Ibid.*, p. 262. On the reasons for Gulliver's expulsion, see also W. B. Carnochan, "The Complexity of Swift: Gulliver's Fourth Voyage," *Studies in Philology* 60.1 (1963), pp. 30–31.

90. Swift, *Gulliver's Travels*, p. 263.

91. *Ibid.*, p. 264.

92. *Ibid.*, p. 265.

93. *Ibid.*, p. 271.

94. *Ibid.* On Gulliver as Odysseus, see Kenner, *The Counterfeiters*, pp. 140–41.

95. Swift, *Gulliver's Travels*, p. 271.

96. *Ibid.*, p. 277.

EIGHT: FICTIONS OF PERSISTENCE

1. The link between the Greek and Vedic phrases was first made by Adalbert Kuhn in 1853: see Kuhn, "Ueber die durch nasale erweiterte verbalstämme," *Zeitschrift für vergleichende Sprachforschung* 2 (1853), p. 467. For later accounts, see Gregory Nagy, *Comparative Studies in Greek and Indic Meter* (Cambridge, MA: Harvard University Press, 1974); Edwin D. Floyd, "*Kleos aphthiton*: An Indo-European Perspective on Greek," *Glotta* 58 (1980), pp. 133–57; Calvert Watkins, "An Indo-European Theme and Formula: Imperishable Fame," in Watkins, *How to Kill a Dragon* (Oxford: Oxford University Press, 1995), pp. 173–78.

2. For Thersites, see *Iliad* 2.212; for Elpenor, see *Odyssey* 10 and *Odyssey* 12.10–15. English in Homer, *The Odyssey*, trans. Richmond Lattimore (New York: Harper & Row, 1967) and *Iliad*, trans. Richmond Lattimore (Chicago: University of Chicago Press, 1951).

3. Chrétien de Troyes, *Le conte du graal, ou le roman de Perceval*, ed. Charles Méla (Paris: Librairie Générale Française, 1990), line 3582.

4. Chrétien de Troyes, *Lancelot, Le chevalier de la charrette*, ed. Mario Roques (Paris: Classiques français du Moyen Âge, 1958), line 4487.

5. Chrétien de Troyes, *Le chevalier au lion, ou le Roman d'Yvain*, ed. David F. Hult (Paris: Librairie Générale Française, 1994), lines 2806–30.

6. See Christiane Marchello-Nizia with Régis Boyer et al., eds., *Tristan et Yseut: Les premières versions européennes* (Paris: Gallimard, 1995).

7. Gottfried von Straßburg, *Tristan: Text, Nacherzählung, Wort- und Begriffserklärungen*, ed. Gottfried Weber (Darmstadt: Wissenschaftliche Buchgesellschaft, 1967), lines 2017–18.

8. On the varieties of medieval Icelandic outlawry, see G. Turville-Petre, "Outlawry," in Einar G. Pétursson and Jónas Kristjánsson (eds.), *Sjötíu ritgerðir helgaðar Jakobi Benediktssyni I* (Reykjavik: Stofnun Árna Magnússonar á Íslandi, 1977), pp. 769–78; Andreas Heusler, *Das Strafrecht der Isländersagas* (Leipzig: Duncker & Humblot, 1911), pp. 124–90.

9. Jesse L. Byock, s.v. "Outlawry," in *Medieval Scandinavia: An Encyclopedia*, ed. Phillip Pulsiano (New York: Garland, 1993).

10. Turville-Petre, "Outlawry," p. 778. On the terms *vargr* and its cognates, see Michael Jacoby, *Wargus, vargr 'Verbrecher', Wolf: Eine Sprach- und rechtsgeschichtliche Untersuchung* (Uppsala: Almquist & Wiksell, 1974); cf. review by John Lindow, *Speculum* 52.2 (1977), pp. 382–85; Mary Roche Gerstein, *Warg: The Outlaw as Werewolf in Germanic Myth, Law and Medicine*, PhD diss., University of California at Los Angeles, 1972; Georg Christoph von Unruh, "Wargus: Friedlosigkeit und magisch-kultische Vorstellungen bei den Germanen," *Zeitschrift der Savigny-Stiftung für Rechtsgeschichte* 74 (1959), pp. 1–40.

11. See *Grettis Saga Ásmundarsonar: Bandamanna saga; Odds þáttar Ófeigssonar*, ed. Guðni Jónnson (Reykjavik: Hið Íslenzka fornritafélag, 1936); *Vestfirðinga sögur*, ed. Björn K. Þórólfsson and Guðni Jónnson (Reykjavik: Hið Íslenzka fornritafélag, 1958), *Harðar saga*, ed. Þórhallur Vilmundarson and Bjarni Vilhjálmsson (Reykjavik: Hið Íslenzka fornritafélag, 1991); English in J. M. Dent (ed.), *Three Icelandic Outlaw Sagas: The Saga of Gisli, The Saga of Grettir, The Saga of Hord*, trans. J. M. Dent (London: University College, 2004).

12. A. Arazi, s.v. "Ṣu'lūk," in *Encyclopedia of Islam*, ed. H. A. R. Gibb et al., 13 vols. (Leiden: Brill, 1960–2009).

13. Francesco Gabrieli, *Shànfara: Il bandito del deserto* (Florence: Fussi Editore, 1947), p. 11. For an English translation of the Lamiyya, see Warren T. Treadgold, "A Verse

Translation of the Lamiyah of Shanfara," *Journal of Arabic Literature* 6 (1975), pp. 31–34. For a philological commentary as well as a further translation, see Alan Jones, *Early Arabic Poetry: Edition, Translation and Commentary*, 2 vols. (Oxford: Ithaca Press Reading for the Board of the Faculty of Oriental Studies, 1992–1996), vol. 1, *Marāthī and Ṣu'lūk Poems*, pp. 139–204. On al-Shanfarā, see also Michael Cooperson, s.v. "al-Shanfara," in Michael Cooperson and Shawkat M. Toowara (eds.), *Arabic Literary Culture, 500–925* (Detroit: Thomas Gale, 2005). The antiquity and authenticity of the poem have been much debated.

14. Al-Shanfarā, "Lamiyya," lines 26–37; English in Treadgold, "A Verse Translation of the Lamiyah of Shanfara," p. 32.

15. *Ibid.*, line 5; p. 31.

16. *Ibid.*, line 6; p. 31.

17. Adelbert von Chamisso, *Peter Schlemihls wundersame Geschichte*, in *Sämtliche Werke*, 2 vols., ed. Jost Perfahl (Munich: Winkler, 1975), vol. 1, p. 14; English in *Peter Schlemihl, The Shadowless Man*, trans. Joseph Jacobs (London: George Allen, 1899), p. 1 (translation modified).

18. *Ibid.*, p. 15; p. 2.

19. *Ibid.*, p. 18; p. 7.

20. *Ibid.*, p. 24; p. 25 (translation modified).

21. *Ibid.*, pp. 24–25; p. 26 (translation modified).

22. See Pierre Péju, "L'ombre et la vitesse," in Adelbert von Chamisso, *Peter Schlemihl*, trans. Hippolyte von Chamisso (Paris: Éditions Corti, 1994), pp. 109–10. Schlemihl has three dreams, of which this is the first. See also Colin Butler, "Hobson's Choice: A Note on 'Peter Schlemihl,'" *Monatshefte* 69.1 (1977), p. 13; Enrico De Angelis, introduction to Adelbert von Chamisso, *Storia straordinaria di Peter Schlemihl* (Milan: Garzanti, 1995), p. xiv.

23. Ralph Flores, "The Lost Shadow of Peter Schlemihl," *German Quarterly* 47.4 (1974), p. 570.

24. Chamisso, *Sämtliche Werke*, vol. 1, p. 18; *Peter Schlemihl*, p. 9.

25. *Ibid.*, p. 22; p. 19.

26. *Ibid.*, p. 23; p. 22. On this scene and its illustrations, see Victor I. Stoichita, *A Short History of the Shadow*, trans. Anne-Marie Glasheen (London: Reaktion Books, 1997), pp. 167–85.

27. Chamisso, *Sämtliche Werke*, vol. 1 p. 23; *Peter Schlemihl*, p. 23.

28. *Ibid.*, pp. 30–31; p. 44.

29. *Ibid.*, p. 37; p. 64.

30. *Ibid.*, p. 39; p. 71.

31. *Ibid.*, p. 40; p. 72.

32. *Ibid.*, p. 41; p. 76.

33. Thomas Mann, "Chamisso," in *Gesammelte Werke*, 13 vols. (Frankfurt am Main: Fischer, 1960–1974), vol. 9, p. 56.

34. Martin Swales, "Mundane Magic: Some Observations on Chamisso's *Peter Schlemihl*," *Forum for Modern Language Studies* 12 (1976), p. 250. For a fuller and more recent discussion, see Richard T. Gray, *Money Matters: Economics and the German Cultural Imagination, 1770–1850* (Seattle: University of Washington Press, 2008), pp. 236–37. On the interpretations of the shadow, see also Jean-Pierre Danès, "Peter Schlemihl et la signification de l'ombre," *Études germaniques* 35 (1980), pp. 444–48; Gero von Wilpiert, *Der verlorene Schatten: Varianten eines literarischen Motifs* (Stuttgart: A. Kröner, 1978), pp. 30–42; Wolfgang Neubauer, "Zur Schatten-Problem bei Adelbert von Chamisso," *Literatur für Leser* 9 (1986), p. 24.

35. See Julius von Negelein, "Bild, Spiegel und Schatten im Volksglauben," *Archiv für Religionswissenschaft* 5 (1902) pp. 1–37; Fritz W. Pradel, "Der Schatten im Volksglauben," *Mitteilungen der schlesischen Gesellschaft für Volkskunde* 12 (1904), pp. 1–36; E. L. Rochholz, "Ohne Schatten, Ohne Seele: Der Mythus vom Körperschatten und vom Schattengeist," *Germania* 5 (1860), pp. 69–94. See Stith Thompson, *Motif-Index of Folk-Literature: A Classification of Narrative Elements in Folktales, Ballads, Myths, Fables, Mediaeval Romances, Exempla, Fabliaux, Jest-Books, and Local Legends*, 6 vols. (Bloomington: Indiana University Press, 1955–1958), vol. 3, F1038.

36. Alice A. Kuzniar, "Spurlos . . . verschwunden: 'Peter Schlemihl' und sein Schatten als der verschobene Signifikant," *Aurora* 45 (1985), p. 194.

37. Rolf Günter Renner, "Schrift der Natur und Zeichen des Selbst: *Peter Schlemihls wundersame Geschichte* im Zusammenhang von Chamissos Texten," *Deutsche Vierteljahrschrift für Literaturwissenschaft und Geistesgeschichte* 65.4 (1991), p. 654.

38. Gray, *Money Matters*, p. 240.

39. Chamisso, *Peter Schlemihl*, trans. Hippolyte von Chamisso, p. 8. The citations are from René Just Haüy, *Traité élémentaire de physique*, 2 vols., 3rd ed. (Paris: Courcier, 1821), vol. 2, § 1002 and § 1006.

40. Michael Lommel, "Peter Schlemihl und die Medien des Schattens," *Athenäum* 17 (2007), pp. 47–48.

41. Chamisso, *Peter Schlemihl*, trans. Hippolyte von Chamisso, p. 9.

42. Hitzig translates "le solide" as *körperlichen Raum*, while in a recent translation into

German, Alexander Roesler opts for *das Wirkliche* or *etwas Wirkliches*: see Adelbert von Chamisso, *Peter Schlemihls wundersame Geschichte*, with a commentary by Thomas Betz and Lutz Hagerstedt (Frankfurt am Main: Suhrkamp, 2003), pp. 107–108. See Lommel, "Peter Schlemihl," pp. 48–49 n. 27. For an analysis of Chamisso's appeal to the physics of shadows, see Stoichita, *Brief History of the Shadow*, pp. 167–72. Cf. Péju, "L'ombre et la vitesse," p. 157.

43. E. T. A. Hoffmann, "Die Abenteuer der Silvesternacht," in *Fantasiestücke: In Callot's Manier, Werke 1814*, vol. 2, part 1 of *Sämtliche Werke*, ed. Wulf Segebrecht et al., 6 vols. (Frankfurt am Main: Deutscher Klassiker Verlag, 1985–2004), p. 358; "A New Year's Eve Adventure," in *The Best Tales of Hoffman*, ed. E. F. Bleiler (New York: Dover, 1967), p. 128.

44. Hoffmann, "Die Abenteuer der Silvesternacht," pp. 358–59; "A New Year's Eve Adventure," p. 128.

45. Nathaniel Hawthorne, "A Virtuoso Collection," in *Tales and Sketches*, ed. Roy Harvey Pearce (New York: Library of America, 1982), p. 711.

46. *Ibid.*

47. Friedrich Nietzsche, *Menschliches, Allzumenschliches I und II*, vol. 2 of *Sämtliche Werke: Kritische Studienausgabe*, ed. Giorgio Colli and Mazzino Montinari, 15 vols. (New York: De Gruyter, 1999), p. 537; English in *Human, All Too Human: A Book for Free Spirits*, trans. R. J. Hollingdale (Cambridge: Cambridge University Press, 1986), p. 301.

48. Luigi Pirandello, *Il fu Mattia Pascal*, ed. Giancarlo Mazzacurati (Turin: Einaudi, 1993), p. 221.

49. *Ibid.*, p. 222.

50. On Chamisso and Faust, see Hermann J. Weigand, "Peter Schlemihl," in A. Leslie Willson (ed.), *Surveys and Soundings in European Literature* (Princeton: Princeton University Press, 1966), pp. 209–10. Chamisso wrote a *Faust* fragment, dated 1803: see *Sämtliche Werke*, vol. 1, pp. 500–509.

51. Chamisso, *Sämtliche Werke*, vol. 1, pp. 43–44; *Peter Schlemihl*, p. 82.

52. *Ibid.*, p. 44; p. 82.

53. *Ibid.*, p. 57; p. 120.

54. *Ibid.*, p. 59; pp. 126–27.

55. *Ibid.*, p. 60; p. 130.

56. On Schlemihl's scientific activities and their relation to Chamisso's, see Marko Pavlyshyn, "Gold, Guilt and Scholarship: Adelbert von Chamisso's *Peter Schlemihl*," *German Quarterly* 55.1 (1982), pp. 50–52.

57. Chamisso, *Sämtliche Werke*, vol. 1, p. 63; *Peter Schlemihl*, p. 138.

58. *Ibid.*, p. 64; p. 139.

59. *Ibid.*, p. 64; p. 141.

60. *Ibid.*, p. 64; pp. 140–41.

61. Péju, "L'ombre et la vitesse," p. 125.

62. Chamisso, *Sämtliche Werke*, vol. 1, p. 66; *Peter Schlemihl*, p. 146.

63. Heinrich Heine, *Romanzero*, in *Sämtliche Werke*, ed. Jost Perfahl and Werner Vordtrieder, 4 vols. (Munich: Winkler, 1969–1972), vol. 1, p. 609; English in *Complete Poems of Heinrich Heine: A Modern English Version*, trans. Hal Draper (Cambridge, MA: Suhrkamp/Insel, 1982), p. 673.

64. Quoted in Karl Fulda, *Chamisso und seine Zeit* (Leipzig: C. Reissner, 1881), pp. 133–34. On Chamisso's use of the name, see also Max Zeldner, "A Note on 'Schlemihl,'" *German Quarterly* 26.2 (1953), pp. 115–17.

65. On the Jewishness and non-Jewishness of Chamisso's Schlemihl, see Richard Block, "Queering the Jew Who Would Be German: Peter Schlemihl's Strange and Wonderful History," *Seminar* 40.1 (2004), pp. 93–110.

66. Numbers 1:4.

67. Numbers 1:6.

68. Numbers 2:12, 7:36, 7:41, 10:19.

69. Numbers 7:36.

70. Numbers 25:1.

71. Numbers 25:6–8.

72. Numbers 25:14–5.

73. Babylonian Talmud, Sanhedrin 82b. For an English translation, see Isidore Epstein, ed., *Hebrew-English Edition of the Babylonian Talmud*, various translators (New York: Soncino Press, 1960–).

74. For accounts of the history of the term and figure of *schlemiehl*, see Sidra DeKoven Ezrahi, s.v. "Schlemiehl," in Dan Diner (ed.), *Enzyklopädie jüdischer Kultur und Geschichte*, 7 vols. (Stuttgart: J. B. Metzler, 2011–); Dov Sadan, "Lesugia: Shelumiel," *Orlogin* 1 (1950), pp. 198–203; Arthur Norman, "The 'Schlemiehl' Problem," *American Speech* 27.2 (1952), pp. 149–50.

75. Heinrich Heine, "Jehuda ben Halevy," in *Sämtliche Werke*, vol. 1, p. 611; English in *Complete Poems of Heinrich Heine*, p. 675.

76. Heine, *Romanzero*, p. 609; *Complete Poems of Heinrich Heine*, p. 673.

77. *Ibid.*, p. 611; p. 675. On Heine's account of "Schlemihldom," see Hannah Arendt, "The

Jew as Pariah," in Jerome Kohn and Ron H. Feldman (eds.), *The Jewish Writings* (New York: Schocken Books, 2007), pp. 275–97, esp. pp. 277–83; Rochelle Tobias, "Writers and 'Schlemihls': On Heine's *Jehuda ben Halevy*," in Aris Fioretos (ed.), *Babel: Für Werner Hamacher* (Basel: Urs Engeler, 2009), pp. 362–70.

NINE: RETURNING TO RIVA

1. Franz Kafka, *Tagebücher*, 3 vols., ed. Hans-Gerd Koch, Michael Müller, and Malcolm Pasley (Frankfurt am Main: Fischer, 2002), pp. 810–11; English in Franz Kafka, *The Great Wall of China and Other Texts*, ed. and trans. Malcolm Pasley (New York: Penguin Books, 2002), pp. 51–52.

2. Franz Kafka, *Nachgelassene Schriften und Fragmente*, ed. Jost Schillemeit, 2 vols. (Frankfurt am Main: Fischer, 1993), vol. 1, pp. 305–306; English in *Great Wall of China and Other Texts*, p. 47.

3. *Ibid.*, pp. 306–307; pp. 47–48.

4. *Ibid.*, p. 307; p. 48.

5. *Ibid.*, p. 309; p. 49.

6. *Ibid.*

7. *Ibid.*, p. 309; pp. 49–50.

8. *Ibid.*, pp. 310–11; p. 50. The passage may belong to a different "fragment" from the preceding one, for in Kafka's *Oktavheft* it is interrupted by an apparently unrelated text.

9. *Ibid.*, p. 378; p. 52.

10. For three versions, see Erwin S. Steinberg, "The Three Fragments of Kafka's 'The Hunter Gracchus,'" *Studies in Short Fiction* 15.3 (1978), pp. 305–17; for five versions, see Hartmut Binder, "'Der Jäger Gracchus': Zu Kafkas Schaffensweise und poetischer Topographie," *Jahrbuch der deutschen Schillergesellschaft* 15 (1971), pp. 375–440.

11. See the discussion in *The Great Wall of China and Other Texts*, pp. 47–55.

12. On Kafka and Flaubert, see Marthe Robert, "Kafka et Flaubert," *L'Arc* 79 (1980), pp. 26–30; Jeanne Bem, "Flaubert lecteur de Kafka, ou l'écriture de l'existence," *Revue d'histoire littéraire de la France* 81.4–5 (1981), pp. 677–87; Uta Degner, "What Kafka Learned from Flaubert: 'Absent-Minded Window Gazing' and 'The Judgment,'" in Stanley Corngold and Ruth V. Gross (eds.), *Kafka for the Twenty-First Century* (Rochester: Camden House, 2011), pp. 75–88.

13. Kafka, *Nachgelassene Schriften und Fragmente*, vol. 1, p. 378; English in *Great Wall of China and Other Texts*, p. 52.

14. *Ibid.*, pp. 383–84; p. 55.

15. *Ibid.*, p. 312; p. 51.

16. *Ibid.*

17. *Ibid.*, p. 311; p. 50.

18. Franz Kafka, *Oxforder Oktavhefte 1 &2*, ed. Roland Reuß and Peter Staengle, 4 vols. (Basel: Stroemfeld/Roter Stern, 2006), *Oktavheft* 2, 9 verso.

19. Roland Reuß, "Running Texts, Stunning Drafts," in Corngold and Gross, *Kafka for the Twenty-First Century*, p 31.

20. Dietrich Krusche, "Die kommunikative Funktion der Deformation klassischer Motive: 'Der Jäger Gracchus'. Zur Problematik der Kafka-Interpretation," *Textanalyse* 25.1 (1973), pp. 128–40, esp. pp. 133–40. For an account of the biographical dimensions of the Gracchus texts, see Binder, "'Der Jäger Gracchus.'"

TEN: THE SEMBLANT BODY

1. Papinian, *Digest* 11.7.43; English in Alan Watson, ed., *The Digest of Justinian*, 4 vols. (Philadelphia: University of Pennsylvania Press, 1998), vol. 1, p. 355.

2. See, among others, Julian Thomas, "Death, Identity and the Body in Neolithic Britain," *Journal of the Royal Anthropological Institute* 6.3 (2000), pp. 653–68; J. C. Barrett, "The Living, the Dead and the Ancestors: Neolithic and Early Bronze Age Mortuary Practices," in J. C. Barrett and I. A. Kinnes (eds.), *The Archaeology of Context in the Neolithic and Bronze Age* (Sheffield: Department of Archaeology and Prehistory, 1988), pp. 30–41.

3. Herodotus 3.38, in *Histories*, trans. A. D. Godley (Cambridge, MA: Harvard University Press, 1920).

4. *Oxford English Dictionary*, 2nd ed., prepared by J. A. Simpson and E. S. C. Weiner, 20 vols. (Oxford: Clarendon Press of Oxford University Press, 1989), s.v. "Corpse."

5. See Yan Thomas, "Corpus aut ossa aut ceneres: La chose religieuse et le commerce," *Micrologus* 7 (1999), p. 91.

6. *Ibid.*

7. Isidore of Seville, *Etymologiae sive Originum*, ed. W. M. Lindsay, 2 vols. (Oxford: Clarendon Press of Oxford University Press, 1957), 11.2.35, English in *The Etymologies*, trans. Stephen A. Barney, W. J. Lewis, J. A. Beach, and Oliver Berghof (Cambridge: Cambridge University Press, 2006), p. 243. In Greek, the term *ptōma* had a similar force: see Jackie Pigeaud, "La question du cadavre dans l'antiquité gréco-romaine," *Micrologus* 7 (1999), p. 55. See also Servius's account of Roman funeral terminology: "*Funus* is the corpse when it is already burning; while

it is carried, we call it *exsequias*; when it is already burnt, *reliquias*; when it is already buried, *sepulchrum*" (*funus enim est iam ardens cadaver: quod dum portatur exsequias dicimus: crematum iam reliquias: conditum iam sepulcrum*): commentary to *Aeneid* 2.539. See the discussion in Hildegard Cancik-Lindemaier, "Corpus: Some Philological and Anthropological Remarks upon Roman Funerary Customs," in Albert I. Baumgarten, Jan Assmann and Guy G. Stroumsa (eds.), *Self, Soul and Body in Religious Experience* (Leiden: Brill, 1998), p. 419.

8. Virgil, *Georgics* 4.255.

9. Bruno Snell, *The Discovery of the Mind: The Greek Origins of European Thought*, trans. T. G. Rosenmeyer (Oxford: Basil Blackwell, 1953), p. 5.

10. *Ibid.*, p. 6.

11. *Ibid.*, pp. 7–8.

12. On Snell's theses and their reception, see Brooke Holmes, *The Symptom and the Subject: The Emergence of the Physical Body in Ancient Greece* (Princeton: Princeton University Press, 2010), pp. 4–9.

13. On Roman *imagines*, see Harriet I. Flower, *Ancestor Masks and Aristocratic Power in Roman Culture* (Oxford: Clarendon Press of Oxford University Press, 1996).

14. Polybius 6.53, in *Histories*, 6 vols., trans. W. R. Paton (Cambridge, MA: Harvard University Press, 1922–1927), vol. 3, p. 389.

15. Pliny the Elder, *Natural History* 35.2; English in *The Natural History*, trans. John Bostock (London: Taylor and Francis, 1855), p. 225.

16. See Flower, *Ancestor Masks and Aristocratic Power*, pp. 32–35.

17. Walter W. Skeat, *A Concise Etymological Dictionary of the English Language* (Oxford: Clarendon Press of Oxford University Press, 1901), p. 295.

18. See James A. Walker, "Gothic *-leik-* and Germanic **lik-* in the Light of Gothic Translations of Greek Originals," *Philological Quarterly* 28 (1949), pp. 274–93; Kristin Killie, "On the Source(s) and Grammaticalization of the Germanic -lik Suffix," *Neuphilologische Mitteilungen* 108.4 (2007), pp. 659–82.

19. Eric Partridge, *A Short Etymological Dictionary of Modern English*, 3rd ed. (London: Routledge, 1961), s.v. "Like."

20. See Killie, "On the Source(s) and Grammaticalization of the Germanic -lik Suffix."

21. Hermann Diels, *Die Fragmente der Vorsokratiker*, 3 vols., 6th ed. by Walther Kranz (Berlin: Weidmann, 1951), fragment 96; M. Marcovich (ed.), *Heraclitus, editio maior* (Merida: Los Andes University Press, 1967), fragment 76; English as well as Greek in Charles H. Kahn, *The Art and Thought of Heraclitus: An Edition of the*

Fragments with Translation and Commentary (Cambridge: Cambridge University Press, 1979), pp. 68–69.

22. Kahn, *The Art and Thought of Heraclitus*, p. 212.

23. Marcovich, *Heraclitus, editio maior*, pp. 407–10.

24. *Phaedo* 80e. The myth of Er in the *Republic* suggests a different theory, as Pigeaud has observed, "La question du cadavre," p. 56.

25. Lucretius, *De rerum natura* 3.870–87, 3.888–93. As Cancik-Lindemaier ("Corpus," p. 418) has observed, the argument is also to be found in Augustine, *De civitate dei* 1.12.

26. Cicero, *Tusculan Disputations* 1.43; English in *Tusculan Disputations*, trans. J. E. King (Cambridge, MA: Harvard University Press, 1927). The anecdote is one of the central threads in Thomas W. Laqueur's wide-ranging study, *The Work of the Dead: A Cultural History of Mortal Remains* (Princeton: Princeton University Press, 2015).

27. Ps-Plutarch, *Epitome* 4. 4. 7 = Aetius 4.4.7.; English in C. C. W. Taylor (ed.), *The Atomists: Leucippus and Democritus, Fragments, a Text and Translation*, trans. C. C. W. Taylor (Toronto: University of Toronto Press, 2010), p. 107. Democritus is known also to have pointed to the "growth of hair and nails after burial." Tertullian, *De Anima* 51.2.

28. See Aristotle, *Metaphysics*: Zeta 7.7. 1032b30–1033a1.

29. *Ibid.*, 11.1037a5–6.

30. Aristotle, *De Anima* 2.1.412b25–27; English in Aristotle, *The Complete Works: The Revised Oxford Translation*, 2 vols., ed. Jonathan Barnes (Princeton: Princeton University Press, 1984), vol. 1., p. 901.

31. J. L. Ackrill, "Aristotle's Definitions of Psuche," *Proceedings of the Aristotelian Society*, n. s., 73 (1972–1973), p. 126.

32. Aristotle, *De partis animalium* 1.1,640b30–641a16; English in Aristotle, *The Complete Works*, vol. 1, pp. 5–6.

33. For Aristotle's definition of homonyms, see *Categories* 1.1,1a1–1a5. On Aristotle's homonymy in general, see T. H. Irwin, "Homonymy in Aristotle," *Review of Metaphysics* 34.3 (1981), pp. 523–44; Julie K. Ward, *Aristotle on Homonymy: Dialectic and Science* (Cambridge: Cambridge University Press, 2008). On homonymy and the Aristotelian body, see Marc. S. Cohen, "Hylomorphism and Functionalism," in Martha C. Nussbaum and Amélie Oksenberg Rorty (eds.), *Essays on Aristotle's De Anima* (Oxford: Clarendon Press of Oxford University Press, 1992), pp. 57–74; Jennifer Whiting, "Living Bodies," in Nussbaum and Rorty, *Essays on Aristotle's De Anima*, pp. 75–91; Christopher V. Mirus, "Homonymy and the Matter of a Living Body," *Ancient Philosophy* 21 (2001), pp. 357–73.

34. Aristotle, *Meteorology* 4.12.389b25–390b2; English in Aristotle, *The Complete Works of Aristotle*, vol. 1, p. 86.

35. Aristotle, *Metaphysics* 7.10.1035b4–1035b31; English in Aristotle, *The Complete Works of Aristotle*, vol. 2, p. 103.

36. Boethius, *Commentarii in librum Aristotelis Peri hermeneias*, ed. Karl Meiser, 2 vols. (Leipzig: Teubner, 1877–1880), vol. 1, p. 52.15: "Qui vero dicit non-homo hominem tollit."

37. *Ibid.*, vol. 2, p. 62.14–16: "Sublatio enim homine quidquid praeter hominem est, hoc significat non-homo."

38. *Ibid.*, p. 62.7–10. For a commentaries, see L. M. De Rijk, "The Logic of the Indefinite Names in Boethius, Abelard, Duns Scotus and Radulphus Brito," in H. A. G. Braakhuis and C. H. Kneepkens (eds.), *Aristotle's Peri hermeneias in the Latin Middle Ages: Essays on the Commentary Tradition* (Groningen: Ingenium, 2003), pp. 212–13, and Daniel Heller-Roazen, *No One's Ways: An Essay on Infinite Naming* (New York: Zone Books, 2017), pp. 40–41.

39. Aristotle, *De interpretatione* 11.21a21.

40. See Sten Ebbesen, "The Dead Man Is Alive," *Synthese* 40 (1979), pp. 43–70.

41. For the locus classicus for the debate, see Peter Lombard's *Sententiae in libri IV distinctae*, ed. Ignatius Grady, 4 vols. (Grottaferrata: Editiones Collegii S. Bonaventurae ad Claras Aquas, 1979–1981), vol. 3, d. 22, ch. 1, pp. 135–36. For accounts of the medieval debates concerning these problems, see Tullio Gregory, "Per una fenomenologia del cadavere," in *Speculum naturale: Percorsi del pensiero medievale* (Rome: Edizioni di storia e letteratura, 2007), pp. 121–50, esp. pp. 129–39; Dennis Des Chene, *Life's Form: Late Aristotelian Concepts of the Soul* (Ithaca: Cornell University Press, 2000), pp. 67–113.

42. Paul, First Letter to the Corinthians 15:42.

43. See Caroline Walker Bynum, *The Resurrection of the Body in Western Christianity, 200–1336* (New York: Columbia University Press, 1995), esp. chapters 1 and 2.

44. *Chartularium universitatis Parisiensis*, ed. Henri Denifle and Émile Chatelain, 4 vols. (Paris: Delalain, 1889–1897), vol. 1, proposition 17, p. 544.

45. On Thomas's account of body and soul, see Antonia Fitzpatrick, *Thomas Aquinas on Bodily Identity* (Oxford: Oxford University Press, 2017).

46. For this definition of *materia prima*, see Jean Hamesse, ed., *Les auctoritates Aristotelis: Un florilège medieval. Étude historique et édition critique* (Louvain: Publications universitaires, 1974), 128 (161), quoted in Fitzpatrick, *Thomas Aquinas on Bodily Identity*, p. 65.

47. William de la Mare, *Correctorium Fratis Thomae*, in Palémon Glorieux (ed.), *Le Correctorium Corruptorii 'Quare'* (Kain: Le Saulchoir, 1927), a 31, p. 129. For a discussion of this

critique, see Fitzpatrick, *Thomas Aquinas on Bodily Identity*, pp. 10–11.

48. See Fitzpatrick, *Thomas Aquinas on Bodily Identity*, p. 21. For a presentation of the doctrine of dimensive quantity, see *Summa Theologica*, part 3, question 76, article 2. On dimensive quantity in Averroes, see Silvia Donati, "The Notion of *Dimensiones Indeterminatae* in the Commentary Tradition of the *Physics* in the Thirteenth and in the Early Fourteenth Century," in Clees Leijenhorst, Christoph Lüthy, and Johannes M. M. H. Thijssen (eds.), *The Dynamics of Aristotelian Natural Philosophy from Antiquity to the Seventeenth Century* (Leiden: Brill, 2002), pp. 189–223.

49. Thomas Aquinas, *Summa theologiae* 3.50.5.

50. Thomas M. Ward, *John Duns Scotus on Parts, Wholes, and Hylomorphism* (Leiden: Brill, 2014), pp. 536–37.

51. Francisco Suárez, *Disputationes metaphysicae*, disputation 18, section 2, § 28, pp. 608–609. See the discussion in Dennis Des Chene, *Physiologia: Natural Philosophy in Late Aristotelian and Cartesian Thought* (Ithaca: Cornell University Press, 1996), pp. 122–67, esp. pp. 146–51; cf. Ward, *John Duns Scotus on Parts, Wholes, and Hylomorphism*, pp. 537–38.

52. See Des Chene, *Life's Form*, p. 86, who notes that these terms can also be found in Descartes.

53. For an extended treatment, see Ward, *John Duns Scotus on Parts, Wholes, and Hylomorphism.*

54. Ward has made this case compellingly in *John Duns Scotus on Parts, Wholes, and Hylomorphism.*

55. See Ray D. Maddoff, *Immortality and the Law: The Rising Power of the American Dead* (New Haven: Yale University Press, 2010), pp. 34–40.

56. *Ibid.*, p. 36.

57. *Ibid.*, p. 37.

58. *Ibid.*, p. 38.

59. Robert Hertz, "Contribution à une étude sur la représentation collective de la mort," *Année sociologique* 10 (1905–1906), p. 129; English in *Death and the Right Hand*, trans. Rodney and Claudia Needham, with an introduction by E. E. Evans-Pritchard (Glencoe: The Free Press, 1960), p. 81. For an evaluation of the merits and limits of Hertz's study, see Peter Metcalf, "Meaning and Materialism: The Ritual Economy of Death," *Man*, n. s., 16.4 (1981), pp. 563–78, esp. pp. 564–67.

60. Hertz, "Contribution à une étude sur la représentation collective de la mort," p. 129; English in *Death and the Right Hand*, p. 81.

61. *Ibid.*, p. 130; p. 82 (translation slightly modified). Hertz alludes here to Archibald Campbell's *The Doctrines of a Middle State between Death and the Resurrection* (London: W. Taylor, 1721).

62. Hertz, "Contribution à une étude sur la représentation collective de la mort," pp. 50–51; English in *Death and the Right Hand*, pp. 29–30.

63. *Ibid.*, p. 130; p. 82.

64. *Ibid.*, p. 137; p. 86.

65. Numbers 19:11.

66. Mira Balberg, *Purity, Body and Self in Early Rabbinic Literature* (Berkeley: University of California Press, 2014), p. 99.

67. See Julia Kristeva, *The Powers of Horror: An Essay on Abjection*, trans. L. S. Roudiez (New York: Columbia University Press, 1982), p. 109.

68. See Balberg, *Purity, Body and Self*, pp. 100–104.

69. *Ibid.*, p. 103.

70. *Ibid.*, p. 113.

71. *Ibid.*, pp. 113–14.

72. *Ibid.*, p. 116.

73. Quoted in *ibid.*, p. 117.

74. Maurice Blanchot, *L'espace littéraire* (Paris: Gallimard, 1955), pp. 270–73; English in *The Space of Literature*, trans. Ann Smock (Lincoln: University of Nebraska Press, 1982), pp. 257–60.

75. *Ibid.*, p. 268; p. 256.

76. *Ibid.*, p. 273; p. 260.

77. *Ibid.*, p. 271; p. 258 (translation slightly modified).

78. *Ibid.*, p. 270; p. 257 (translation slightly modified).

79. *Ibid.*, p. 271; p. 258 (translation slightly modified).

80. *Ibid.*, p. 271; pp. 258–59.

81. *Ibid.*, p. 271; p. 259.

82. *Ibid.*, p. 272; p. 259.

83. *Ibid.*

ELEVEN: THE RECURRENT VOICE

1. William Shakespeare, *Julius Caesar*, ed. Arthur Humphreys (Oxford: Clarendon Press of Oxford University Press, 1984), 2.2.24.

2. Apuleius, *The Golden Ass*, trans. E. J. Kenny (London: Penguin Books, 1998), 2.20, p. 32 (translation slightly modified).

3. *Ibid.*, 2.21, p. 33.

4. *Ibid.*

5. *Ibid.*, 2.22, p. 33.

6. *Ibid.* (translation slightly modified).

7. *Ibid.*, 2.23, p. 34.

8. *Ibid.* 2.23–24, p. 34.

9. *Ibid.*, 2.25, p. 35.

10. *Ibid.*

11. See Sarah Iles Johnston, *Restless Dead: Encounters between the Living and the Dead in Ancient Greece* (Berkeley: University of California Press, 1999); D. Felton, "The Dead," in Daniel Ogden (ed.), *A Companion to Greek Religion* (Malden: Blackwell, 2007), p. 99.

12. Homer, *Iliad*, 23.68–69, trans. Richmond Lattimore (Chicago, University of Chicago, Press, 1951), p. 452.

13. *Ibid.*, 23.75–76, p. 452. On this passage, see R. S. J. Garland, "Geras Thanonton: An Investigation into the Claims of the Homeric Dead," *Bulletin of the Institute of Classical Studies* 29 (1982), pp. 69–80.

14. *Odyssey* 10.551–53, trans. Richmond Lattimore (New York: Harper & Row, 1967), p. 166.

15. *Odyssey* 11.72—75, p. 170.

16. See Henry George Liddell and Robert Scott, *A Greek-English Lexicon*, 8th ed. (New York: American Book Company, 1901), s.v. "trizō."

17. *Odyssey* 24.6–7, p. 345.

18. See Hendrik Wagenvoort, *Inspiratie door bijen in de droom* (Amsterdam: Koninklijke Nederlandse Akademie van Wetenschappen, 1966), pp. 86–88.

19. For Sophocles, see Bruno Snell, *Tragicorum Graecorum fragmenta*, 5 vols. (Göttingen: Vandenhoek & Ruprecht, 1977), vol. 4, *Sophocles*, ed. Stefan Radt, fragment 879, p. 568. For Plutarch, see *Moralia* 567E.

20. Jan N. Bremmer, *The Early Greek Concept of Soul* (Princeton: Princeton University Press, 1983), p. 85. On the ancient "phonosphere" more generally, see Maurizio Bettini, *Voci: Antropologia sonora del mondo antico* (Turin: Einaudi, 2008).

21. See Virgil, *Aeneid* 6.264.709; see also Ovid *Fasti* 2.609, 5.481. See also Corrado Bologna, "Il linguaggio del silenzio," *Studi storico-religiosi* 2 (1978), pp. 305–34.

22. Jean Gobi, *Dialogue avec un fantôme*, ed. Marie Anne Polo de Beaulieu, preface by Jean-Claude Schmitt (Paris: Les Belles Lettres, 1994), p. 72.

23. *Ibid.*, p. 52.

24. See *ibid.*, p. 58, and the corresponding note 16, p. 156.

25. *Ibid.*, p. 58.

26. *Ibid.*, p. 74.

27. Marie Anne Polo de Beaulieu, "Paroles de fantôme: Le cas du revenant d'Alès (1323)," *Ethnologie française*, n.s., 33.4 (2003), p. 567.

28. The image is reproduced on page 188 above and in Polo de Beaulieu, "Paroles de fantôme," p. 567, the source being Guy de Thurno, *La vision de l'âme*, with the miniature attributed to Simon Marmion for the illumination and David Aubert for the text (1474). On the "noncorporeality" of the ghost, see Polo de Beaulieu, "Paroles de fantôme," pp. 38–42.

29. Gobi, *Dialogue avec un fantôme*, p. 75.

30. *Ibid.*, p. 95.

31. *Ibid.*, p. 96. For the Augustinian echo, see p. 159, n. 49.

32. *Ibid.*, p. 97.

33. Jean-Claude Schmitt, preface to Gobi, *Dialogue avec un fantôme*, p. xxv.

34. Jacques Le Goff, *La naissance du purgatoire* (Paris: Gallimard, 1981).

35. N. K. Chadwick, "Norse Ghosts (A Study in the *Draugr* and the *Haugbúi*)," *Folklore* 57.2 (1946), pp. 50–65, and Chadwick, "Norse Ghosts II," *Folklore* 57.3 (1946), pp. 106–27; here, "Norse Ghosts," p. 50.

36. In addition to Chadwick, see Hans-Joachim Klare, "Die Toten in der altnordischen Literatur," *Acta Philologica Scandinavica* 8 (1933–1934), pp. 1–56; Claude Lecouteux, *Fantômes et revenants au Moyen Âge*, postface by Régis Boyer (Paris: Imago, 1986); William Sayers, "The Alien and the Alienated as Unquiet Dead in the Sagas of the Icelanders," in Jeffrey Jerome Cohen (ed.), *Monster Theory: Reading Culture* (Minneapolis: University of Minnesota Press, 1996), pp. 242–63; Ármann Jakobsson, "Vampires and Watchmen: Categorizing the Medieval Icelandic Undead," *Journal of English and Germanic Philology* 100.3 (2011), pp. 281–300.

37. *Grettis Saga Ásmundarsonar: Bandamanna saga; Odds þáttar Ófeigssonar*, ed. Guðni Jónsson (Reykjavik: Hið Íslenzka fornritafélag, 1936), p. 109; English in J. M. Dent, ed. and trans., *Three Icelandic Outlaw Sagas: The Saga of Gisli, The Saga of Grettir, The Saga of Hord* (London: University College, 2004), p. 141.

38. *Ibid.*, pp. 108–109; p. 140.

39. *Ibid.*, p. 112; p. 142

40. *Ibid.*, p. 112; p. 143.

41. *Ibid.*, p. 113; p. 143.

42. For the "undead" as exemplary of the logic of the infinite judgment, see Slavoj Žižek, *Tarrying with the Negative: Kant, Hegel, and the Critique of Ideology* (Durham: Duke University Press, 1993), p. 113.

43. On these terms, see the authors above, as well as Aron Gurevich, *Historical Anthropology of the Middle Ages* (Cambridge: Polity Press, 1992), pp. 116–21. On the *draugar* in relation to other medieval varieties of "returning dead," see Nancy Mandeville Caciola, *Afterlives: The Return of the Dead in the Middle Ages* (Ithaca: Cornell University Press, 2016), pp. 212–15.

44. On "revenants" in the medieval Latin West, see Jean-Claude Schmitt, *Les revenants: Les vivants et les morts dans la société médiévale* (Paris: Gallimard, 1994).

45. Sayers, "The Alien and the Alienated as Unquiet Dead in the Sagas of the Icelanders," p. 242.

46. *Grettis Saga Ásmundarsonar*, p. 121; *Three Icelandic Outlaw Sagas*, p. 149.

47. *Ibid.*, p. 121; p. 149.

48. *Ibid.*

49. On the scene, see Robert Cook, "Reading for Character in *Grettis Saga*," in John Tucker (ed.), *Sagas of the Icelanders: A Book of Essays* (New York: Garland, 1989), pp. 226–40; Kathryn Hume, "The Thematic Design of 'Grettis Saga,'" *Journal of English and Germanic Philology* 73.4 (1974), pp. 469–86; Lotte Motz, "Withdrawal and Return: A Ritual Pattern in the *Grettis Saga*," *Arkiv for Nordisk Filologi* 88 (1973), pp. 91–110; Janice Hawes, "The Monstrosity of Heroism: Grettir Ásmundarson as an Outsider," *Scandinavian Studies* 80.1 (2008), pp. 19–50.

50. *Grettis Saga Ásmundarsonar*, p. 123; *Three Icelandic Outlaw Sagas*, p. 150. As the translator notes, "the name Glam is etymologically related to gloom and gloaming, though these words are not derived from the name" (*ibid.*, n. 40).

51. Henry James, "The Jolly Corner," in *Complete Stories*, 5 vols. (New York: Library of America, 1996–1999), vol. 5, *1898–1910*, pp. 697–98.

52. *Ibid.*, p. 699.

53. *Ibid.*, p. 704.

54. *Ibid.*

55. *Ibid.*, p. 708.

56. *Ibid.*, p. 711.

57. *Ibid.*, p. 712.

58. On the figure of the "turned tables," see Deborah Esch, "A Jamesian About-Face: Notes on 'The Jolly Corner,'" *ELH* 50.3 (1983), pp. 587–605, esp. pp. 591–92.

59. James, "The Jolly Corner," p. 714.

60. *Ibid.*, p. 714.

61. *Ibid.*, p. 715.

62. *Ibid.*, p. 724.

63. *Ibid.*

64. *Ibid.*

65. *Ibid.*, pp. 724–25.

66. *Ibid.*, p. 725.

67. *Ibid.*

68. *Ibid.*, p. 726.

69. *Ibid.*, pp. 729 and 730.

70. *Ibid.*

71. See, among others, Russell J. Reising, "Figuring Himself Out: Spencer Brydon, 'The Jolly Corner' and Cultural Change," *Journal of Narrative Technique* 19.1 (1989), pp. 116–29; Eric Savoy, "The Queer Subject of 'The Jolly Corner,'" *Henry James Review* 20.1 (1999), pp. 1–21; Andrew Miller, *The Burdens of Perfection: On Ethics and Reading in Nineteenth-Century British Literature* (Ithaca: Cornell University Press, 2008), pp. 205–17.

72. Esch, "A Jamesian About-Face," p. 600.

73. James, "The Jolly Corner," p. 710.

74. Apuleius, *The Golden Ass* 2.27; English, p. 36.

75. *Ibid.*

76. *Ibid.* 2.28; p. 36.

77. *Ibid.* 2.29; p. 37.

78. *Ibid.* 2.30; pp. 37–38 (translation slightly modified).

79. *Ibid.* 2.30; p. 38 (translation slightly modified).

80. See John J. Winkler, *Auctor and Actor: A Narratological Reading of Apuleius's "The Golden Ass"* (Berkeley: University of California Press, 1985), pp. 113–14.

TWELVE: SOMES ONES LEFT

1. Matthew 8:28–34; Luke 8:26–39; Mark 5:1–20.

2. On the setting of the episode, see Charles Masson, "Le démoniaque de Gérasa," in *Vers les sources d'eau vive: Études d'exégèse et de théologie du Nouveau Testament* (Lausanne: Payot,

1961), pp. 20–37, esp. pp. 20–21; Rudolf Pesch, "The Markan Version of the Healing of the Gerasene Demoniac," *Ecumenical Review* 23.4 (1971), pp. 352–53. Cf. Jean Starobinski, "Le démoniaque de Gérasa: Analyse littéraire de Marc 5. 1–20," in Roland Barthes, François Bovon, J. Leenhardt, Robert Martin-Archard, and Jean Starobinski, *Analyse structurale et exégèse biblique: Essais d'interprétation* (Neuchâtel: Delachaux & Niestlé, 1972), pp. 68–69.

3. Pesch, "The Markan Version of the Healing of the Gersaene Demoniac," p. 349.

4. Mark 5.2–5.

5. J. Duncan M. Derrett, "Spirit-Possession and the Gerasene Demoniac," *Man*, n.s., 14.2 (1979), p. 287.

6. Pesch, "The Markan Version of the Healing of the Gerasene Demoniac," p. 356, who refers the reader to Paul Billerbeck and Hermann Strack, *Kommentar zum neuen Testament aus Talmud und Midrasch*, 4 vols. (Munich: C. H. Beck'sche Verlagsbuchhandlung, 1922–1928), vol. 1: *Das Evangelium nach Matthäus erläutert aus Talmud und Midrasch*, p. 491. The scriptural passage (and indeed the entire episode) may also allude to Isaiah 65:3–4, as suggested by John F. Craghan, "The Gerasene Demoniac," *Catholic Biblical Quarterly* 30.4 (1968), p. 526.

7. Mark 5:8.

8. Mark 5:9.

9. Craghan, "The Gerasene Demoniac," p. 525.

10. Mark 5:9.

11. Luke 8:30.

12. Starobinski, "Le démoniaque de Gérasa," p. 75.

13. Herbert Preisker, s.v. "Legiōn," in Gerhard Kittel (ed.), *Theologisches Wörterbuch zum Neuen Testament*, 10 vols. (Stuttgart: Kohlhammer, 1942–).

14. Joachim Jeremias, *Jesus' Promise to the Nations*, trans. S. H. Hooke (Naperville: A. R. Allenson, 1958), p. 30. Cf. Masson, "Le démoniaque de Gérasa," p. 31.

15. Starobinski, "Le démoniaque de Gérasa," p. 75.

16. Mark 5:31–32.

17. Mark 5:33.

18. Mark 5:13.

19. Mark 5:15.

20. Mark 5:18.

21. Mark 5:19.

22. Numbers 1:2–3.

23. Numbers 1:46; cf. the figure given by Moses at Numbers 11:21.

24. Numbers 25:9.

25. Numbers 26:2.

26. Numbers 26:51.

27. Second Samuel 24:2; First Chronicles 21:5.

28. Second Samuel 24:1.

29. First Chronicles 21:1.

30. First Chronicles 21:3.

31. Second Samuel 24:10.

32. First Chronicles 21:7.

33. First Chronicles 21:14; Second Samuel 24:15.

34. Yoma 22b; English in Isidore Epstein, ed., *Hebrew-English Edition of the Babylonian Talmud*, various translators (New York: Soncino Press, 1960–).

35. Nahmanides, commentary to Numbers 1:3; David Kimhi, commentary to First Samuel 15:4, quoted in David Golinkin, "Does Jewish Law Permit Taking a Census?," *Modern Issues in Jewish Law*, 3.4 (2008).

36. Berakhot 62b; English in Epstein, *Hebrew-English Edition of the Babylonian Talmud.*

37. Exodus 30:11–16.

38. Exodus 30:13.

39. On the Biblical censuses, see M. Barnouin, "Remarques sur les tableaux numériques du livre des nombres," *Revue biblique* 76 (1969), pp. 351–64; George E. Mendenhall, "The Census Lists of Numbers 1 and 26," *Journal of Biblical Literature* 77.1 (1958), pp. 52–66.

40. See Yoma 22. On the danger of the census in the Bible and elsewhere, see James George Frazer, *Folk-lore in the Old Testament: Studies in Comparative Religion, Legend, and Law*, 3 vols. (London: Macmillan, 1919), vol. 2, pp. 555–63.

41. Nikolai Vasil'evich Gogol', *Polnoe sobranie sochineniĭ i pisem*, 23 vols., vol. 7, part 1: *Mertvye dushi* (Moscow: Nasledie, 2012), p. 17; English in Nikolai Gogol, *Dead Souls*, trans. Bernard Guilbert Guerney, rev. Susanne Fusso (New Haven: Yale University Press, 1996), p. 11.

42. *Ibid.*, p. 33; p. 27.

43. *Ibid.*, pp. 33–34; p. 28.

44. *Ibid.*, p. 47; p. 43.

45. *Ibid.*, p. 49; p. 45.

46. *Ibid.*, p. 49; p. 45.

47. *Ibid.*, pp. 49–50; pp. 45–46.

48. *Ibid.*, p. 119; pp. 120–21.

49. *Ibid.*, p. 121; p. 123.

50. *Ibid.*, p. 130; p. 133.

51. *Ibid.*, p. 123; p. 125.

52. *Ibid.*, pp. 127–28; p. 130.

53. *Ibid.*, pp. 177–78; p. 186 (translation slightly modified).

54. *Ibid.*, p. 184; pp. 192–93.

55. *Ibid.*, p. 225; pp. 240–41.

56. *Ibid.*, p. 226; p. 241.

57. Richard Peace, *The Enigma of Gogol* (Cambridge: Cambridge University Press, 1981), p. 245.

58. Vladimir Nabokov, *Nikolai Gogol* (New York: New Directions, 1961), p. 136. Cf. James B. Woodward, *Gogol's "Dead Souls"* (Princeton: Princeton University Press, 1978).

59. See Hollis Robbins, "'We Are Seven' and the First British Census," *English Language Notes* 48.2 (2010), p. 202. On Wordsworth and the census, see also Frances Ferguson, "Malthus, Godwin, Wordsworth, and the Spirit of Solitude," in Elaine Scarry (ed.), *Literature and the Body: Essays on Populations and Persons* (Baltimore: Johns Hopkins University Press, 1988), pp. 106–24; James M. Garrett, *Wordsworth and the Writing of the Nation* (Burlington: Ashgate, 2008), esp. pp. 13–41.

60. William Wordsworth, *Poetical Works*, ed. Thomas Hutchinson, rev. Ernest de Sélincourt (New York: Oxford University Press, 1936), p. 66.

61. *Ibid.*

62. Frances Ferguson, "Historicism, Deconstruction, and Wordsworth," *diacritics* 17.4 (1987), p. 42.

63. Robbins, "'We Are Seven' and the First British Census," p. 203.

64. Ferguson, "Historicism, Deconstruction, and Wordsworth," p. 41. It is striking, as Ferguson notes, that the dead siblings alone are given names.

65. See *ibid.*, p. 40.

66. *Ibid.*, p. 42.

67. On this line, see Alan Bewell, *Wordsworth and the Enlightenment: Nature, Man, and Society in the Experimental Poetry* (New Haven: Yale University Press, 1989), esp. p. 196; cf. James Shokoff, "Wordsworth's Duty as a Poet in 'We Are Seven' and 'Surprised by Joy,'" *Journal of English and Germanic Philology* 93.2 (1994), pp. 228–39.

BEING *IT*

1. Henry Carrington Bolton, *The Counting Out Rhymes of Children: Their Antiquity, Origin and Wide Distribution: A Study in Folk-Lore* (London: Elliot Stock, 1888), p. 1.

2. Roger D. Abrahams, "Introduction: Getting to *It*, or A Special Way of Beginning," in Roger D. Abrahams and Lois Rankin (eds.), *Counting Out Rhymes: A Dictionary* (Austin: University of Texas Press, 1980), p. xi.

3. Bolton, *The Counting Out Rhymes of Children*, p. 1.

4. See Abrahams and Rankin, *Counting Out Rhymes*, no. 206, pp. 164–65.

5. Mary Knapp and Herbert Knapp, *One Potato, Two Potato. . . . : The Secret Education of American Children* (New York: W. W. Norton, 1976), p. 25.

6. *Ibid.*

7. For an analysis, see David C. Rubin, Violeta Ciobanu, and William Langston, "Children's Memory for Counting-Out Rhymes: A Cross-Language Comparison," *Psychonomic Bulletin and Review* 4.3 (1997), pp. 421–24. The variants for the rhyme appear in Abrahams and Rankin's dictionary as no. 133, pp. 58–61, with "nigger" in place of "tiger"; as they indicate, the racist dimension of that rhyme has been discussed since 1850. See Knapp and Knapp, *One Potato, Two Potato*, pp. 197–98.

8. Abrahams and Rankin, *Counting Out Rhymes*, no. 6, from Iona and Peter Opie, *Children's Games in Street and Playground* (Oxford: Oxford University Press, 1969), p. 30.

9. Abrahams and Rankin, *Counting Out Rhymes*, no. 402, pp. 161–62; cf. rhymes nos. 400 and 403–34, pp. 162–84.

10. See Abrahams and Rankin, *Counting Out Rhymes.*

11. Walter Gregor, *Counting-Out Rhymes of Children* (London: David Nutt, 1891), p. 4. As Gregory indicates in his foreword, he completed the research by May 1, 1889, when he presented it "at a meeting of the Buchan Field Club in Peterhead."

12. Gregor, *Counting-Out Rhymes of Children*, p. 5.

13. Elliott Oring, "On the Tradition and Mathematics of Counting-Out," *Western Folklore* 56.2 (1997), p. 139.

14. For the greater frequency of the second use of the counting-out practice, see N. G. N. Kelsey, *Games, Rhymes, and Wordplay of London Children*, ed. Janet E. Alton and J. D. A. Widdowson (London: Palgrave Macmillan, 2019), p. 12.

15. Bolton, *The Counting Out Rhymes of Children*, p. 9.

16. Kelsey, *Games, Rhymes, and Wordplay of London Children*, p. 11. For a discussion of the conditions in which the universality of such claims might be tested, see Andy Arleo,

"Counting-out and the Search for Universals," *Journal of American Folklore* 110.438 (1997), pp. 391–407.

17. Kenneth S. Goldstein, "Strategy in Counting Out: An Ethnographic Field Study," in Elliott Oring (ed.), *Folk Groups and Folklore Genres: A Reader* (Logan: Utah State University Press, 1989), p. 187.

18. Gregor, *Counting-Out Rhymes of Children*, p. 6.

19. *Ibid.*, p. 9.

20. Bolton, *The Counting Out Rhymes of Children*, pp. 26–34.

21. See, for example, *ibid.*, p. 44.

22. See Oring, "On the Tradition and Mathematics of Counting-Out," pp. 139–41.

23. Goldstein, "Strategy in Counting Out," p. 188.

24. *Ibid.*, p. 189. See Roger Caillois, *Man, Play, and Games*, trans. Meyer Barash (New York: The Free Press of Glencoe, 1961), p. 36; Brian Sutton-Smith, *The Games of New Zealand Children* (Berkeley: University of California Press, 1959), pp. 89–90.

25. Goldstein, "Strategy in Counting Out," p. 193.

26. Flavius Josephus, *The Jewish War, Books I–III*, 2 vols., trans. H. St. J. Thackeray (Cambridge, MA: Harvard University Press, 1927), book 3, chapter 8, paragraph 7, p. 685.

27. *Ibid.*, p. 687.

28. *Ibid.*, p. 654. For the Slavonic text, see *La prise de Jérusalem de Josèphe le Juif*, 2 vols., ed. V. Istrin, dir. André Vaillant, trans. Pierre Pascal (Paris: Institut des études slaves, 1934), book 3, chapter 8, paragraph 7, p. 236.

29. Oring, "On the Tradition and Mathematics of Counting-Out," p. 144.

30. Claude-Gaspar Bachet, *Problèmes plaisants et délectables qui se font par les nombres*, 5th ed. (1612; Paris: Gauthier-Villars, 1884), p. 9.

31. *Ibid.*, p. 118. The problem stretches from p. 118 to p. 121.

32. *Ibid.*, p. 118.

33. Oring, "On the Tradition and Mathematics of Counting-Out," p. 142.

34. Rubin, Ciobanu, and Langston, "Children's Memory for Counting-out Rhymes," pp. 421–24.

35. *Ibid.*, p. 421.

36. See Arleo, "Counting-out and the Search for Universals," p. 396.

37. Walter Benjamin, "Spielzeug und Spielen: Randbemerkungen zu einem Monumentalwerk," in *Gesammelte Schriften*, ed. Rolf Tiedemann and Hermann Schweppenhäuser, 7 vols., vol. 3: *Kritiken und Rezensionen* (Frankfurt am Main: Suhrkamp, 1991), p. 131; English

in *Walter Benjamin, Selected Writings, Volume 2, Part 1: 1927–1930*, ed. Michael W. Jennings (Cambridge, MA: Harvard University Press, 2005), p. 120.

38. Bolton, *The Counting Out Rhymes of Children*, p. 1; Gregor, *Counting-Out Rhymes of Children*, p. 1.

39. Abrahams and Rankin, *Counting Out Rhymes*, p. xi.

40. *Ibid.*, pp. xiv and xvii.

Works Cited

Abrahams, Roger D. and Lois Rankin, eds., *Counting Out Rhymes: A Dictionary* (Austin: University of Texas Press, 1980).

Ackrill, J. L., "Aristotle's Definitions of Psuche," *Proceedings of the Aristotelian Society*, n. s., 73 (1972–1973), pp. 119–33.

Aeschylus, *Agamemnon*, vol. 1 of *The Complete Greek Tragedies*, ed. David Grene and Richmond Lattimore (Chicago: The University of Chicago Press, 1959).

Agamben, Giorgio, *Homo Sacer: Il potere sovrano e nuda vita* (Turin: Einaudi, 1995).

———, *Homo Sacer: Sovereign Power and Bare Life*, trans. Daniel Heller-Roazen (Stanford: Stanford University Press, 1998).

———, *Altissima povertà: Regole monastiche e forma di vita* (Vicenza: Neri Pozza, 2011).

Anderson, Mark, "Kafka and New York: Notes on a Traveling Narrative," in Andreas Huyssen and David Bathrick (eds.), *Modernity and the Text: Revisions of German Modernism* (New York: Columbia University Press, 1989), pp. 142–61.

Anon., "Civil Death Statutes — Medieval Fiction in a Modern World," *Harvard Law Review* 50.6 (1937), pp. 968–77.

Apuleius, *The Golden Ass*, trans. E. J. Kenny (London: Penguin Books, 1998).

Arazi, A., s.v. "Ṣu'lūk," *Encyclopedia of Islam*, ed. H. A. R. Gibb et al., 13 vols. (Leiden: Brill, 1960–2009).

Arendt, Hannah, *The Jewish Writings*, eds. Jerome Kohn and Ron H. Feldman (New York: Schocken Books, 2007).

Aristotle, *The Complete Works: The Revised Oxford Translation*, 2 vols., ed. Jonathan Barnes (Princeton: Princeton University Press, 1984).

Arleo, Andy, "Counting-out and the Search for Universals," *The Journal of American Folklore* 110.438 (1997), pp. 391–407.

Athenagoras, *Legatio pro Christianis*, in Jacques Paul Migne (ed.), *Patrologiae Cursus Completus*, Series Graeca 6: *Tou en hagiois patros hēmōn Ioustinou philosophou kai martyros ta heuriskomena panta* = S.P.N. *Justini philosophi et martyris opera quae exstant omnia* (Petit-Monrouge: Migne, 1857).

Bachet, Claude-Gaspar, *Problèmes plaisants et délectables qui se font par les nombres*, 5th ed. (1612; Paris: Gauthier-Villars, 1884).

Balberg, Mira, *Purity, Body and Self in Early Rabbinic Literature* (Berkeley: University of California Press, 2014).

Balzac, Honoré de, *Le Colonel Chabert*, in *La comédie humaine*, vol. 3, *Études de mœurs: Scènes de la vie privée, scènes de la vie de province*, ed. Pierre-Georges Castex et al. (Paris: Gallimard, 1976), pp. 291–373.

Barnouin, M., "Remarques sur les tableaux numériques du livre des nombres," *Revue biblique* 76 (1969), pp. 351–64.

Barrett, J. C., "The Living, the Dead and the Ancestors: Neolithic and Early Bronze Age Mortuary Practices," in J. C. Barrett and I. A. Kinnes (eds.), *The Archaeology of Context in the Neolithic and Bronze Age* (Sheffield: Department of Archaeology and Prehistory, 1988), pp. 30–41.

Barthes, Roland, "Analyse textuelle d'un conte d'Edgar Poe," in Claude Chabrol (ed.), *Sémiotique narrative et textuelle* (Paris: Larousse, 1973), pp. 29–54.

Beccaria, Cesare, *Dei delitti e delle pene*, ed. Franco Venturi, 3rd ed. (Turin: Einaudi, 1973).

——, *On Crimes and Punishments and Other Writings*, ed. Richard Bellamy, trans. Richard Davies with Virginia Cox and Richard Bellamy (Cambridge: Cambridge University Press, 1995).

Bellamy, J. G., *The Law of Treason in England in the Later Middle Ages* (Cambridge: Cambridge University Press, 1970).

Bem, Jeanne, "Flaubert lecteur de Kafka, ou l'écriture de l'existence," *Revue d'histoire littéraire de la France* 81.4–5 (1981), pp. 677–87.

Benjamin, Walter, *Gesammelte Schriften*, eds. Rolf Tiedemann and Hermann Schweppenhäuser, 7 vols. (Frankfurt am Main: Suhrkamp, 1991).

——, *Selected Writings, Volume 2, Part 1: 1927–1930*, ed. Michael W. Jennings (Cambridge, MA: Harvard University Press, 2005).

Benveniste, Émile, "Le nom de l'esclave à Rome," *Revue des études latines* 10 (1932), pp. 429–40.

———, "Problèmes sémantiques de la reconstitution," in *Problèmes de linguistique générale*, 2 vols. (Paris: Gallimard, 1966–1974), vol. 1, pp. 289–307.

———, "Le sens du mot *kolossos*," *Revue de philologie, de littérature et d'histoire anciennes* 6 (1932), pp. 118–35.

———, *Le vocabulaire des institutions indo-européennes*, 2 vols. (Paris: Minuit, 1969).

Bettini, Maurizio, *Il ritratto dell'amante* (Turin: Einaudi, 1992).

———, *Voci: Antropologia sonora del mondo antico* (Turin: Einaudi, 2008).

Bewell, Alan, *Wordsworth and the Enlightenment: Nature, Man, and Society in the Experimental Poetry* (New Haven: Yale University Press, 1989).

Beyerle, Dieter, "Die Heimkehr des verschollenen Ehemannes bei Balzac, Zola, und Maupassant," *Romanistisches Jahrbuch* 27 (1976), pp. 129–51.

Bible: Authorized King James Version, eds. Robert Carroll and Stephen Prickett (Oxford: Oxford University Press, 2008).

Biblia hebraica, eds. Rud. Kittel and P. Kahle (Stuttgart: Bibelanstalt, 1949).

Billerbeck, Paul, and Hermann Strack, *Kommentar zum neuen Testament aus Talmud und Midrasch*, 4 vols. (Munich: C. H. Beck'sche Verlagsbuchhandlung, 1922–1928).

Binder, Hartmut, "'Der Jäger Gracchus': Zu Kafkas Schaffensweise und poetischer Topographie," *Jahrbuch der deutschen Schillergesellschaft* 15 (1971), pp. 375–440.

Blackstone, William, *Commentaries on the Law of England*, 4 vols. (London: A. Strahan, 1825).

Blanchot, Maurice, *L'espace littéraire* (Paris: Gallimard, 1955).

———, *The Space of Literature*, trans. Ann Smock (Lincoln: University of Nebraska Press, 1982).

Blecker, Paulin M., "The Civil Rights of the Monk in Roman and Canon Law: The Monk as *Servus*," *American Benedictine Review* 17 (1966), pp. 185–98.

Bleich, J. David, "Survey of Recent Halakhic Periodical Literature: A 19th Century *Agunah* Problem and a 20th Century Application," *Tradition* 38.2 (2004), pp. 15–48.

Block, Richard, "Queering the Jew Who Would Be German: Peter Schlemihl's Strange and Wonderful History," *Seminar* 40.1 (2004), pp. 93–110.

Boethius, Anicius Manlius Severinus, *Commentarii in librum Aristotelis Peri hermeneias*, ed. Karl Meiser, 2 vols. (Leipzig: Teubner, 1877–1880).

———, *In Ciceronia Topicis*, ed. and trans. Eleanor Stump (Ithaca: Cornell University Press, 1988).

———, *Liber contra Eutychen et Nestorium* (Turnhout: Brepols, 2010).

Bologna, Corrado, "Il linguaggio del silenzio," *Studi storico-religiosi* 2 (1978), pp. 305–34.

Bolton, Henry Carrington, *The Counting Out Rhymes of Children: Their Antiquity, Origin and Wide Distribution. A Study in Folk-Lore* (London: Elliot Stock, 1888).

Borgmann, Brigitte, "Mors Civilis: Die Bildung des Begriffs in Mittelalter und sein Fortleben im französischen Recht der Neuzeit," *Ius Commune* 4 (1972), pp. 81–157.

Bremmer, Jan N., *The Early Greek Concept of Soul* (Princeton: Princeton University Press, 1983).

Bretone, Mario, "Capitis deminutio," *Novissimo digesto italiano* 2 (1958), pp. 916–18.

Brillante, Carlo, "Metamorfosi di un'immagine: Le Statue animate e il sogno," in Giulio Guidorizzi (ed.), *Il sogno in Grecia* (Rome: Laterza, 1998), pp. 17–33.

Brod, Max, *Über Franz Kafka* (Frankfurt am Main: Fischer, 1974).

Brooks, Peter, "Narrative Transaction and Transference (Unburying '*Le Colonel Chabert*')," *Novel* 15.2 (1982), pp. 101–10.

Brückner, Wolfgang, *Bildnis und Brauch: Studien zur Bildfunktion des Effigies* (Berlin: Erich Schmidt, 1964).

Bruns, Carl Georg, *Kleinere Schriften*, 2 vols. (Weimar: Hermann Bölau, 1882).

Buckland, William Warwick, *The Main Institutions of Roman Private Law* (Cambridge: Cambridge University Press, 1931).

———, *The Roman Law of Slavery: The Condition of the Slave in Private Law* (1908; Cambridge: Cambridge University Press, 1970).

Buckley, Marjorie W., "Key to the Language of the Houyhnhnms in *Gulliver's Travels*," in A. Norman Jeffares (ed.), *Fair Liberty Was All His Cry: A Tercentenary Tribute to Jonathan Swift, 1667–1745* (London: Palgrave Macmillan, 1967), pp. 270–79.

Bur, Clément, *La citoyenneté dégradée : Une histoire de l'infamie à Rome (312 av. J.-C.–96 apr. J.-C.)* (Rome: École française de Rome, 2018).

Butler, Colin, "Hobson's Choice: A Note on 'Peter Schlemihl,'" *Monatshefte* 69.1 (1977), pp. 5–16.

Bynum, Caroline Walker, *The Resurrection of the Body in Western Christianity, 200–1336* (New York: Columbia University Press, 1995).

Byock, Jesse L., s.v. "Outlawry," in *Medieval Scandinavia: An Encyclopedia*, ed. Phillip Pulsiano (New York: Garland, 1993).

Caciola, Nancy Mandeville, *Afterlives: The Return of the Dead in the Middle Ages* (Ithaca: Cornell University Press, 2016).

Caillois, Roger, *Man, Play, and Games*, trans. Meyer Barash (New York: Free Press of Glencoe, 1961).

Campbell, Archibald, *The Doctrines of a Middle State between Death and the Resurrection* (London: W. Taylor, 1721).

Cancik-Lindemaier, Hildegard, "Corpus: Some Philological and Anthropological Remarks upon Roman Funerary Customs," in Albert I. Baumgarten, Jan Assmann and Guy G. Strousma (eds.), *Self, Soul and Body in Religious Experience* (Leiden: Brill, 1998), pp. 417–29.

Cardinal, Jacques, "Perdre son nom: Identité, représentation et vraisemblance dans *Le Colonel Chabert*," *Poétique* 135.3 (2003), pp. 307–32.

Carnochan, W. B., "The Complexity of Swift: Gulliver's Fourth Voyage," *Studies in Philology* 60.1 (1963), pp. 23–44.

Carriere, Jeanne Louise, "The Rights of the Living Dead: Absent Persons in the Civil Law," *Louisiana Law Review* 50.5 (1990), pp. 901–71.

Caruth, Cathy, "The Claims of the Dead: History, Haunted Property, and the Law," in Austin Sarat, Lawrence Douglas, and Martha Merill Umphrey (eds.), *Law's Madness* (Ann Arbor: The University of Michigan Press, 2003), pp. 119–46.

Chabalet, Gaston, *Droit romain de la capitis deminutio* (Cambrai: Deligne & Langlet, 1877).

Chadwick, N. K., "Norse Ghosts (A Study in the *Draugr* and the *Haugbúi*)," *Folklore* 57.2 (1946), pp. 50–65.

——, "Norse Ghosts II," *Folklore* 57.3 (1946), pp. 106–27.

Chamisso, Adelbert von, *Sämtliche Werke*, 2 vols., ed. Jost Perfahl (Munich: Winkler, 1975).

——, *Peter Schlemihl, The Shadowless Man*, trans. Joseph Jacobs (London: George Allen, 1899).

——, *Peter Schlemihls wundersame Geschichte*, with a commentary by Thomas Betz and Lutz Hagerstedt (Frankfurt am Main: Suhrkamp, 2003).

Chaniotis, A., et al. (eds.), *Supplementum Epigraphicum Graecum*, https://referenceworks.brillonline.com/browse/supplementum-epigraphicum-graecum.

Chantraine, Pierre, "Grec *kolossós*," *Bulletin de l'institut français d'archéologie orientale* 30 (1930), pp. 449–52.

Chartularium universitatis Parisiensis, ed. Henri Denifle and Émile Chatelain, 4 vols. (Paris: Delalain, 1889–1897).

Chin, Gabriel J., "The New Civil Death: Rethinking Punishment in the Era of Mass Conviction," *University of Pennsylvania Law Review* 160.6 (2012), pp. 1789–1833.

Chrétien de Troyes, *Le chevalier au Lion, ou le roman d'Yvain*, ed. David F. Hult (Paris: Librairie Générale Française, 1994).

——, *Le conte du graal, ou le roman de Perceval*, ed. Charles Méla (Paris: Librairie Générale Française, 1990).

——, *Lancelot, Le chevalier de la charrette,* ed. Mario Roques (Paris: Classiques français du Moyen Âge, 1958).

Cicero, *Topica*, ed. and trans. Tobias Reinhardt (Oxford: Oxford University Press, 2003).

——, *De officiis*, ed. Michael Winterbottom (Oxford: Clarendon Press of Oxford University Press, 1994).

——, *On Duties*, ed. and trans. M. T. Griffin and E. M. Atkins (Cambridge: Cambridge University Press, 1991).

——, *Tusculan Disputations*, trans. J. E. King (Cambridge, MA: Harvard University Press, 1927).

Code Napoleon, or the French Civil Code (London: William Benning, 1827).

Cohen, Marc S., "Hylomorphism and Functionalism," in Martha C. Nussbaum and Amélie Oksenberg Rorty (eds.), *Essays on Aristotle's De Anima* (Oxford: Clarendon Press of Oxford University Press, 1992), pp. 57–74.

Cohn, Max, "Zur Lehre von der capitis deminutio," in *Beiträge zur Bearbeitung des römischen Rechts 1* (Berlin: Weidmannsche Buchhandlung, 1878), pp. 41–400.

Coli, Ugo, *Capitis deminutio* (Florence: Vallecchi Editore, 1922).

Cook, Robert, "Reading for Character in *Grettis Saga*," in John Tucker (ed.), *Sagas of the Icelanders: A Book of Essays* (New York: Garland, 1989), pp. 226–40.

Cooperson, Michael, s.v. "al-Shanfara," in Michael Cooperson and Shawkat M. Toowara (eds.), *Arabic Literary Culture, 500–925* (Detroit: Thomas Gale, 2005).

Corngold, Stanley, *Complex Pleasure: Forms of Feeling in German Literature* (Stanford: Stanford University Press, 1998).

Corral Talciani, Hernán, and María Sara Rodríguez Pinto, "Disparition de personnes et présomption de décès: Observations de droit comparé," *Revue internationale de droit comparé* 52.3 (2000), pp. 553–80.

Craghan, John F., "The Gerasene Demoniac," *Catholic Biblical Quartlery* 30.4 (1968), pp. 522–36.

Crane, R. S., "The Houyhnhms, the Yahoos, and the History of Ideas," in Joseph Anthony Mazzeo (ed.), *Reason and the Imagination: Studies in the History of Ideas 1600–1800* (New York: Columbia University Press, 1962), pp. 231–53.

Crifò, Giuliano, "*Exilica causa, quae adversus exulem agitur*: Problemi dell'*aqua et igni interdictio*," in Crifò, *Du châtiment dans la cité: Supplices corporels et peine de mort dans le monde antique* (Rome: École française de Rome, 1984), pp. 453–97.

Cudini, Piero, "'Il Fu Mattia Pascal': Dalle fonti chamissiani e zoliane alla nuova struttura narrativa di Luigi Pirandello," *Belfagor* 6 (1971), pp. 702–13.

Danès, Jean-Pierre, "Peter Schlemihl et la signification de l'ombre," *Études germaniques* 35 (1980), pp. 444–48.

Davidsohn, Robert, *Storia di Firenze*, 5 vols. (Florence: Sansoni, 1956).

Davis, Natalie Zemon, *The Return of Martin Guerre* (Cambridge, MA: Harvard University Press, 1983).

Dayan, Colin, *The Law Is a White Dog: How Legal Rituals Make and Unmake Persons* (Princeton: Princeton University Press, 2011).

De Angelis, Enrico, introduction to Adelbert von Chamisso, *Storia straordinaria di Peter Schlemihl* (Milan: Garzanti, 1995), pp. vii–xxviii.

Degner, Uta, "What Kafka Learned from Flaubert: 'Absent-Minded Window Gazing' and 'The Judgment,'" in Stanley Corngold and Ruth V. Gross (eds.), *Kafka for the Twenty-First Century* (Rochester: Camden House, 2011), pp. 75–88.

DeKoven Ezrahi, Sidra, s.v. "Schlemiehl," in Dan Diner (ed.), *Enzyklopädie jüdischer Kultur und Geschichte*, 7 vols. (Stuttgart: J. B. Metzler, 2011–).

de la Mare, William, *Correctorium Fratis Thomae*, in Palémon Glorieux (ed.), *Le Correctorium Corruptorii 'Quare'* (Kain: Le Saulchoir, 1927).

Demolombe, Charles, *Traité de l'absence* (= *Cours de Code Napoléon*, vol. 2), 2nd ed. (Paris: Durand/Hachette, 1860).

Dent, J. M., ed., *Three Icelandic Outlaw Sagas: The Saga of Gisli, The Saga of Grettir, The Saga of Hord*, trans. J. M. Dent (London: University College, 2004).

De Rijk, L. M., "The Logic of the Indefinite Names in Boethius, Abelard, Duns Scotus and Radulphus Brito," in H. A. G. Braakhuis and C. H. Kneepkens (eds.), *Aristotle's Peri hermeneias in the Latin Middle Ages: Essays on the Commentary Tradition* (Groningen: Ingenium, 2003), pp. 207–33.

Derrett, J. Duncan M., "Spirit-Possession and the Gerasene Demoniac," *Man*, n.s., 14.2 (1979), pp. 286–93.

Des Chene, Dennis, *Life's Form: Late Aristotelian Concepts of the Soul* (Ithaca: Cornell University Press, 2000).

———, *Physiologia: Natural Philosophy in Late Aristotelian and Cartesian Thought* (Ithaca: Cornell University Press, 1996).

Desserteaux, Fernand, *Études sur la formation historique de la capitis deminutio*, 2 vols. (Paris: Champion, 1909).

Deutsch, Christina, "Zwischen Leben und Tod: Die Verschollenen und ihre Hinterbliebenen im Spätmittelalter," *Trajekte* 14 (2007), pp. 12–16.

Diels, Hermann, *Die Fragmente der Vorsokratiker*, 3 vols., 6th ed. by Walther Kranz (Berlin: Weidmann, 1951).

Dmitriev, Sviatoslav, "Athenian *ATIMIA* and Legislation against Tyranny and Subversion," *Classical Quarterly* 65.1 (2015), pp. 35–50.

Domat, Jean, *Les loix civiles dans leur ordre naturel,* 2 vols. (Paris: n. p., 1756).

Donati, Silvia, "The Notion of *Dimensiones Indeterminatae* in the Commentary Tradition of the *Physics* in the Thirteenth and in the Early Fourteenth Century," in Clees Leijenhorst, Christoph Lüthy, and Johannes M. M. H. Thijssen (eds.), *The Dynamics of Aristotelian Natural Philosophy from Antiquity to the Seventeenth Century* (Leiden: Brill, 2002), pp. 189–223.

Ducat, Jean, "Fonctions de la statue dans la Grèce archaïque: *Kouros* et *kolossos*," *Bulletin de correspondance hellénique* 100.1 (1976), pp. 239–51.

Ebbesen, Sten, "The Dead Man Is Alive," *Synthese* 40 (1979), pp. 43–70.

Edgerton, Samuel Y., Jr., *Pictures and Punishment: Art and Criminal Prosecution during the Florentine Renaissance* (Ithaca: Cornell University Press, 1985).

Eisele, Fridolin, "Zur Natur und Geschichte der capitis deminutio," *Beiträge zur römischen Rechtsgeschichte* (1896), pp. 160–216.

Epstein, Isidore, ed., *Hebrew-English Edition of the Babylonian Talmud*, various translators (New York: Soncino Press, 1960–).

Ernout, Alfred, and Ernest Meillet, *Dictionnaire étymologique de la langue latine: Histoire des mots*, 4th ed. (1932; Paris: Klincksieck, 2001).

Esch, Deborah, "A Jamesian About-Face: Notes on 'The Jolly Corner,'" *ELH* 50.3 (1983), pp. 587–605.

Ewald, Alec C., "'Civil Death': The Ideological Paradox of Criminal Disenfranchisement Law in the United States," *Wisconsin Law Review* (2002), pp. 1045–1132.

Faraone, Christopher A., *Talismans and Trojan Horses: Guardian Statues in Ancient Greek Myth and Ritual* (Oxford: Oxford University Press, 1992).

Felton, D., "The Dead," in Daniel Ogden (ed.), *A Companion to Greek Religion* (Malden, MA: Blackwell, 2007), pp. 86–99.

Ferguson, Frances, "Historicism, Deconstruction, and Wordsworth," *diacritics* 17.4 (1987), pp. 32–43.

——, "Malthus, Godwin, Wordsworth, and the Spirit of Solitude," in Elaine Scarry (ed.), *Literature and the Body: Essays on Populations and Persons* (Baltimore: Johns Hopkins University Press, 1988), pp. 106–24.

Ficker, Julius, *Forschungen zur Reichs- und Rechtsgeschichte Italiens*, 4 vols. (Innsbruck: Wagner, 1868–1874).

Finlay, Robert, "The Refashioning of Martin Guerre," *American Historical Review* 93.3 (1988), pp. 553–71.

Finley, M. I., *Ancient Slavery and Modern Ideology* (New York: Viking Press, 1980).

Fitzpatrick, Antonia, *Thomas Aquinas on Bodily Identity* (Oxford: Oxford University Press, 2017).

Flavius Josephus, *The Jewish War, Books I–III*, 2 vols., trans. H. St. J. Thackeray (Cambridge, MA: Harvard University Press, 1927).

——, *La prise de Jérusalem de Josèphe le Juif*, 2 vols., ed. V. Istrin, dir. André Vaillant, trans. Pierre Pascal (Paris: Institut des études slaves, 1934).

Flores, Ralph, "The Lost Shadow of Peter Schlemihl," *German Quarterly* 47.4 (1974), pp. 567–84.

Flower, Harriet I., *Ancestor Masks and Aristocratic Power in Roman Culture* (Oxford: Clarendon Press of Oxford University Press, 1996).

——, *The Art of Forgetting: Disgrace and Oblivion in Roman Political Culture* (Chapel Hill: University of North Carolina Press, 2006).

Floyd, Edwin D., "*Kleos aphthiton*: An Indo-European Perspective on Greek," *Glotta* 58 (1980), pp. 133–57.

Follis, Luca, "Of Friendless and Stained Men: Grafting Medieval Sanctions onto Modern Democratic Law," in Simone Glanert (ed.), *Comparative Law—Engaging Translation* (London: Routledge, 2014), pp. 173–90.

——, "Resisting the Camp: Civil Death and the Practice of Sovereignty in New York State," *Law, Culture and the Humanities* 9.1 (2011), pp. 91–113.

Forsdyke, Sara, *Exile, Ostracism, and Democracy: The Politics of Expulsion in Ancient Greece* (Princeton: Princeton University Press, 2005).

Fraenkel, Eduard, *Agamemnon*, 2 vols. (Oxford: Clarendon Press of Oxford University Press, 1950).

Frazer, James George, *Folk-lore in the Old Testament: Studies in Comparative Religion, Legend, and Law*, 3 vols. (London: Macmillan, 1919).

Freedberg, David, *The Power of Images: Studies in the History and Theory of Response* (Chicago: University of Chicago Press, 1989).

Fulda, Karl, *Chamisso und seine Zeit* (Leipzig: C. Reissner, 1881).

Fulkerson, Laurel, "(Un)Sympathetic Magic: A Study of *Heroides* 13," *American Journal of Philology* 123.1 (2002), pp. 61–87.

Gabrieli, Francesco, *Shànfara: Il bandito del deserto* (Florence: Fussi Editore, 1947).

Gaius, *The Institutes*, trans. W. M. Gordon and O. F. Robinson, with the Latin text of Seckel and Kübler (London, Duckworth, 1988).

Garland, R. S. J., "Geras Thanonton: An Investigation into the Claims of the Homeric Dead," *Bulletin of the Institute of Classical Studies* 29 (1982), pp. 69–80.

Garland-Thomson, Rosemarie, *Staring: How We Look* (Oxford: Oxford University Press, 2009).

Garnsey, Peter, *Ideas of Slavery from Aristotle to Augustine* (Cambridge: Cambridge University Press, 1996).

Garrett, James M., *Wordsworth and the Writing of the Nation* (Burlington: Ashgate, 2008).

Gaudemet, Jean, "Note sur l'excommunication," *Cristianesimo nella storia* 16 (1995), pp. 285–306.

Gellius, Aulus, *Attic Nights,* trans. J. C. Rolfe (Cambridge, MA: Harvard University Press, 2014).

Gernet, Louis, *The Anthropology of Ancient Greece*, trans. John Hamilton and Gregory Nagy (Baltimore: Johns Hopkins University Press, 1982).

Gerstein, Mary Roche, *Warg: The Outlaw as Werewolf in Germanic Myth, Law and Medicine*, PhD diss., University of California at Los Angeles, 1972.

Gioffredi, Carlo, "Caput," *Studia et documenta historiae et iuris* 11 (1945), pp. 301–13.

Gobi, Jean, *Dialogue avec un fantôme*, ed. Marie Anne Polo de Beaulieu, preface by Jean-Claude Schmitt (Paris: Les Belles Lettres, 1994).

Goffman, Erving, *Communication Conduct in an Island Community*, PhD diss., University of Chicago, 1953.

——, *The Presentation of Self in Everyday Life* (Edinburgh: University of Edinburg, 1956).

——, *Behavior in Public Places: Notes on the Social Organization of Gatherings* (New York: The Free Press, 1963).

——, *Stigma: Notes on the Management of Spoiled Identity* (Englewood Cliffs, NJ: Prentice Hall, 1963).

——, *Forms of Talk* (Philadelphia: University of Pennsylvania Press, 1981).

Gogol', Nikolai Vasil'evich, *Dead Souls*, trans. Bernard Guilbert Guerney, rev. Susanne Fusso (New Haven: Yale University Press, 1996).

——, *Polnoe sobranie sochinenii i pisem*, 23 vols., vol. 7, part 1: *Mertvye dushi* (Moscow: Nasledie, 2012).

Goldstein, Bluma, *Enforced Marginality: Jewish Narratives on Abandoned Wives* (Berkeley: University of California Press, 2007).

Goldstein, Kenneth S., "Strategy in Counting Out: An Ethnographic Field Study," in Elliott Oring (ed.), *Folk Groups and Folklore Genres: A Reader* (Logan: Utah State University Press, 1989), pp. 185–95.

Golinkin, David, "Does Jewish Law Permit Taking a Census?," *Modern Issues in Jewish Law* 3.4 (2008).

Gottfried von Straßburg, *Tristan: Text, Nacherzählung, Wort- und Begriffserklärungen*, ed. Gottfried Weber (Darmstadt: Wissenschaftliche Buchgesellschaft, 1967).

Grady, Sarah C., "Civil Death Is Different: An Examination of a Post-Graham Challenge to Felon Disenfranchisement under the Eighth Amendment," *Journal of Criminal Law and Criminology* 102.2 (2012), pp. 441–70.

Gray, Richard T., *Money Matters: Economics and the German Cultural Imagination, 1770–1850* (Seattle: University of Washington Press, 2008).

Greenidge, A. H. J., *Infamia: Its Place in Roman Public and Private Law* (Oxford: Clarendon Press of Oxford University Press, 1894).

Gregor, Walter, *Counting-Out Rhymes of Children* (London: David Nutt, 1891).

Gregory, Tullio, "Per una fenomenologia del cadavere," in *Speculum naturale: Percorsi del pensiero medievale* (Rome: Edizioni di storia e letteratura, 2007), pp. 121–50.

Grene, David, and Richmond Lattimore, eds., *The Complete Greek Tragedies: Aeschylus*, trans. David Grene and Richmond Lattimore (Chicago: University of Chicago Press, 1959).

Grettis Saga Ásmundarsonar: Bandamanna saga; Odds þáttar Ófeigssonar, ed. Guðni Jónnson (Reykjavik: Hið Íslenzka fornritafélag, 1936).

Grøn, Fredrik, "Über den Ursprung der Bestrafung in Effigie: Eine vergleichende rechts- und kulturgeschichtliche Untersuchung," *Tijdschrift voor Rechtsgeschiedenis / Revue d'histoire du droit* 13 (1934), pp. 320–81.

Gurevich, Aron, *Historical Anthropology of the Middle Ages* (Cambridge: Polity Press, 1992).

Halewood William H., and Marvin Levich, "Houyhnhnm Est Animal Rationale," *Journal of the History of Ideas* 26.2 (1965), pp. 273–81.

Hamesse, Jean, ed., *Les auctoritates Aristotelis: Un florilège medieval: Étude historique et édition critique* (Louvain: Publications universitaires, 1974).

Hansen, Mogens Herman, *Apagoge, Endeixis and Ephegesis against Kakourgoi, Atimoi and Pheugontes: A Study in the Athenian Administration of Justice in the Fourth Century B.C.* (Odense: Odense University Press, 1976).

Harðar saga, eds. Þórhallur Vilmundarson and Bjarni Vilhjálmsson (Reykjavik: Hið Íslenzka fornritafélag, 1991).

Haüy, René Just, *Traité élémentaire de physique*, 2 vols., 3rd ed. (Paris: Courcier, 1821).

Hawes, Janice, "The Monstrosity of Heroism: Grettir Ásmundarson as an Outsider," *Scandinavian Studies* 80.1 (2008), pp. 19–50.

Hawthorne, Nathaniel, "Wakefield," and "A Virtuoso Collection," in *Tales and Sketches*, ed. Roy Harvey Pearce (New York: Library of America, 1982), pp. 290–98 and pp. 697–713.

———, *The Scarlet Letter*, in *Collected Novels* (New York: Library of America, 1983).

Heine, Heinrich, *Complete Poems of Heinrich Heine: A Modern English Version*, trans. Hal Draper (Cambridge, MA: Suhrkamp/Insel, 1982).

———, *Romanzero*, in *Sämtliche Werke*, ed. Jost Perfahl and Werner Vordtrieder, 4 vols. (Munich: Winkler, 1969–1972).

Heller-Roazen, Daniel, *The Enemy of All: Piracy and the Law of Nations* (New York: Zone Books, 2009).

———, *No One's Ways: An Essay on Infinite Naming* (New York: Zone Books, 2017).

Herodotus, *Histories*, trans. A. D. Godley (Cambridge, MA: Harvard University Press, 1920).

Hertz, Robert, "Contribution à une étude sur la représentation collective de la mort," *Année sociologique* 10 (1905–1906), pp. 48–137.

———, *Death and the Right Hand*, trans. Rodney and Claudia Needham, with an introduction by E. E. Evans-Pritchard (Glencoe: The Free Press, 1960).

Heusler, Andreas, *Das Strafrecht der Isländersagas* (Leipzig: Duncker & Humblot, 1911).

Hiebel, Hans Helmut, "Parabelform und Rechtsthematik in Franz Kafkas Romanfragment *Der Verschollene*," in Theo Elm and Hans Helmut Hiebel (eds.), *Die Parabel: Parabolische Formen in der deutschen Dichtung des 20. Jahrhunderts* (Frankfurt am Main: Suhrkamp, 1986), pp. 219–54.

Higgs, Edward, *Identifying the English: A History of Personal Identification, 1500 to the Present* (New York: Continuum Books, 2011).

Hoffmann, E. T. A., *The Best Tales of Hoffman*, ed. E. F. Bleiler (New York: Dover, 1967).

———, "Die Abenteuer der Silvesternacht," in *Sämtliche Werke*, ed. Wulf Segebrecht et al., 6 vols. (Frankfurt am Main: Deutscher Klassiker Verlag, 1985–2004), vol. 2, part 1: *Fantasiestücke: In Callot's Manier, Werke 1814*, pp. 325–59.

Holmes, Brooke, *The Symptom and the Subject: The Emergence of the Physical Body in Ancient Greece* (Princeton: Princeton University Press, 2010).

Homer, *Iliad*, trans. Richmond Lattimore (Chicago: University of Chicago Press, 1951).

———,*The Odyssey*, trans. Richmond Lattimore (New York: Harper & Row, 1967).

Hübener, Rudolf, *A History of Germanic Private Law*, trans. Patrick S. Philbrick (Boston: Little, Brown, 1918).

Hubmann, Verena, *L'image de la mort: Über die mort civile und ihre Abschaffung im französischen Recht und ihre Nachbildungen in den Kantonen Waadt und Wallis* (Zurich: Schulthess, 1990).

Humbert, G. A., *Des conséquences de condamnations pénales relativement à la capacité des personnes en droit romain et en droit français* (Paris: Durand, 1855).

Hume, Kathryn, "The Thematic Design of 'Grettis Saga,'" *Journal of English and Germanic Philology* 73.4 (1974), pp. 469–86.

Hymes, Dell, *Foundations in Social Linguistics: An Ethnographic Approach* (Philadelphia: University of Pennsylvania Press, 1974).

Irwin, T. H., "Homonymy in Aristotle," *Review of Metaphysics* 34.3 (1981), pp. 523–44.

Isidore of Seville, *Etymologiae sive Originum*, ed. W. M. Lindsay, 2 vols. (Oxford: Clarendon Press of Oxford University Press, 1957).

———, *The Etymologies*, trans. Stephen A. Barney, W. J. Lewis, J. A. Beach, and Oliver Berghof (Cambridge: Cambridge University Press, 2006).

Itzkowitz, Howard, and Lauren Oldak, "Restoring the Ex-Offender's Right to Vote: Background and Developments," *The American Criminal Law Review* 11 (1973), pp. 721–70.

Jacobson, Howard, *Ovid's Heroides* (Princeton: Princeton University Press, 1974).

Jacoby, Michael, *Wargus, vargr 'Verbrecher', Wolf: eine Sprach- und rechtsgeschichtliche Untersuchung* (Uppsala: Almquist & Wiksell, 1974).

Jakobsson, Ármann, "Vampires and Watchmen: Categorizing the Medieval Icelandic Undead," *Journal of English and Germanic Philology* 100.3 (2011), pp. 281–300.

Jalet, Frances T. Freeman, "Mysterious Disappearances: The Presumption of Death and the Administration of the Estates of Missing Persons or Absentees," *Iowa Law Review* 54 (1986), pp. 177–252.

James, Henry, "Preface to 'The Altar of the Dead,'" in *The Art of the Novel: Critical Prefaces* (New York: Charles Scribner's Sons, 1934).

———, "The Jolly Corner," in *Complete Stories*, 5 vols. (New York: Library of America, 1996–1999), vol. 5, *1898–1910*, pp. 697–731.

Jeremias, Joachim, *Jesus' Promise to the Nations*, trans. S. H. Hooke (Naperville: A. R. Allenson, 1958).

Johnston, Sarah Iles, *Restless Dead: Encounters between the Living and the Dead in Ancient Greece* (Berkeley: University of California Press, 1999).

Jones, Alan, *Early Arabic Poetry: Edition, Translation and Commentary*, 2 vols. (Oxford: Ithaca Press Reading for the Board of the Faculty of Oriental Studies, 1992–1996).

Jousse, Daniel, *Traité de la justice criminelle en France*, 2 vols. (Paris: Chez Debure Pere, 1771).

Justinian, *The Digest of Justinian*, ed. Alan Watson, 4 vols. (Philadelphia: University of Pennsylvania Press, 1998).

——, *The Institutes of Justinian*, trans. J. B. Moyle, 2nd ed. (Oxford: Clarendon Press of Oxford University Press, 1889).

Kafka, Franz, *Briefe an Felice und andere Korrespondenz aus der Verlobungszeit*, eds. Erich Heller and Jürgen Born, with an introduction by Erich Heller (Frankfurt am Main: Fischer, 1967).

——, *The Great Wall of China and Other Texts*, ed. and trans. Malcolm Pasley (New York: Penguin Books, 2002).

——, *The Man Who Disappeared*, trans. Michael Hoffmann (London: Penguin Books, 1996).

——, *Nachgelassene Schriften und Fragmente*, ed. Jost Schillemeit, 2 vols. (Frankfurt am Main: Fischer, 1993).

——, *Oxforder Oktavhefte 1 & 2*, eds. Roland Reuß and Peter Staengle, 4 vols. (Basel: Stroemfeld / Roter Stern, 2006).

——, *Tagebücher*, 3 vols., eds. Hans-Gerd Koch, Michael Müller, and Malcolm Pasley (Frankfurt am Main: Fischer, 2002).

——, *Der Verschollene: Roman in der Fassung der Handschrift*, ed. Jost Schillemeit (Frankfurt am Main: Fischer, 1983).

Kahn, Charles H., *The Art and Thought of Heraclitus: An Edition of the Fragments with Translation and Commentary* (Cambridge: Cambridge University Press, 1979).

Kāsānī, al-, *Kitāb badā'i' al-ṣanā'i' fī tartīb al-sharā'i'*, 7 vols. (1402; Beirut: dār al-kitāb al-'arabī, 1982).

Kaser, Max, "Infamia und ignominia in den römischen Rechtsquellen," *Zeitschrift der Savigny-Stiftung für Rechtsgeschichte* 59 (1956), pp. 220–78.

——, *Römische Privatrecht*, 2 vols. (Munich: Beck'sche Verlagsbuchhandlung, 1955–1958).

——, "Zur Geschichte der 'capitis deminutio,'" *Iura* 3 (1952), pp. 48–89.

Kelling, H. D., "Some Significant Names in Gulliver's Travels," *Studies in Philology* 48.4 (1951), pp. 761–78.

Kelly, Ann Cline, "After Eden: Gulliver's (Linguistic) Travels," *ELH* 45.1 (1978), pp. 33–54.

Kelsey, N. G. N., *Games, Rhymes, and Wordplay of London Children*, eds. Janet E. Alton and J. D. A. Widdowson (Cham: Palgrave Macmillan, 2019).

Kenner, Hugh, *The Counterfeiters: An Historical Comedy* (Bloomington: Indiana University Press, 1968).

Killie, Kristin, "On the Source(s) and Grammaticalization of the Germanic -lik Suffix," *Neuphilologische Mitteilungen* 108.4 (2007), pp. 659–82.

Klare, Hans-Joachim, "Die Toten in der altnordischen Literatur," *Acta Philologica Scandinavica* 8 (1933–1934), pp. 1–56.

Knapp, Mary and Herbert Knapp, *One Potato, Two Potato . . . : The Secret Education of American Children* (New York: W. W. Norton, 1976).

Krasnopolski, Horaz, *Lehrbuch des österreichisches Privatrecht*, ed. Bruno Kafka, 5 vols. (Munich: Duncker & Humblot, 1910–1914).

Kristeva, Julia, *The Powers of Horror: An Essay on Abjection*, trans. L. S. Roudiez (New York: Columbia University Press, 1982).

Krüger, Hugo, *Geschichte der capitis deminutio*, vol. 1 (Breslau: Wilhelm Koebner, 1887).

Krusche, Dietrich, "Die kommunikative Funktion der Deformation klassischer Motive: 'Der Jäger Gracchus'. Zur Problematik der Kafka-Interpretation," *Textanalyse* 25.1 (1973), pp. 128–40.

Kuhn, Adalbert, "Ueber die durch nasale erweiterte verbalstämme," *Zeitschrift für vergleichende Sprachforschung* 2 (1853), pp. 455–71.

Kuzniar, Alice A., "Spurlos . . . verschwunden: 'Peter Schlemihl' und sein Schatten als der verschobene Signifikant," *Aurora* 45 (1985), pp. 189–204.

Lally-Tollendal, Trophime Gérard de, *Défense des émigrés français adressée au peuple français* (Paris: Chez Chochens, 1797).

Lambertini, Roberto, *La povertà pensata: Evoluzione storica della definizione dell'identità minoritica da Bonaventura ad Ockham* (Modena: Mucchi, 2000).

Laqueur, Thomas W., *The Work of the Dead: A Cultural History of Mortal Remains* (Princeton: Princeton University Press, 2015).

Lecouteux, Claude, *Fantômes et revenants au Moyen Âge*, postface by Régis Boyer (Paris: Imago, 1986).

Le Goff, Jacques, *La naissance du purgatoire* (Paris: Gallimard, 1981).

Levinson, Stephen G., "Putting Linguistics on a Proper Footing: Explorations in Goffman's Concepts of Participation," in Paul Drew and Anthony Wootton (eds.), *Erving Goffman: Exploring the Interaction Order* (Boston: Northeastern University Press, 1988), pp. 161–227.

Levy, Ernst, "Verschollenheit und Ehe in antiken Rechten," in *Gedächtnisschrift für Emil Secker* (Berlin: Julius Springer, 1927), pp. 145–93.

Levy, Yael V., "The Agunah and the Missing Husband: An American Solution to a Jewish Problem," *Journal of Law and Religion* 10.1 (1993–94), pp. 49–71.

Lévy-Bruhl, Henri, "Théorie de l'esclavage," in *Quelques problèmes du très ancient droit romain* (Paris: Domat-Montchrestien, 1934), pp. 15–33.

Liber Monstrorum (secolo IX), ed. and trans. Franco Porsia (Naples: Liguori Editore, 2012).

Liddell, Henry George and Robert Scott, *A Greek-English Lexicon*, 8th ed. (New York, Chicago, Cincinnati: American Book Company, 1901).

Lindow, John, review of Michael Jacoby, *Wargus, vargr 'Verbrecher', Wolf: eine Sprach- und rechtsgeschichtliche Untersuchung*, *Speculum* 52.2 (1977), pp. 382–85.

Lombard, Peter, *Sententiae in libri IV distinctae*, ed. Ignatius Grady, 4 vols. (Grottaferrata: Editiones Collegii S. Bonaventurae ad Claras Aquas, 1979–1981).

Lommel, Michael, "Peter Schlemihl und die Medien des Schattens," *Athenäum* 17 (2007), pp. 33–50.

Lo Vecchio Musti, Manlio, *L'opera di Luigi Pirandello* (Turin: G. B. Paravia, 1939).

Lyne, R. O. A. M., "Love and Death: Laodamia and Protesilaus in Catullus, Propertius, and Others," *Classical Quarterly* 48.1 (1998), pp. 200–12.

Maddoff, Ray D., *Immortality and the Law: The Rising Power of the American Dead* (New Haven: Yale University Press, 2010).

Mann, Thomas, "Chamisso," in *Gesammelte Werke*, 13 vols. (Frankfurt am Main: Fischer, 1960–1974).

Marchello-Nizia, Christiane, with Régis Boyer et al., eds., *Tristan et Yseut: Les premières versions européennes* (Paris: Gallimard, 1995).

Marcovich, M., ed., *Heraclitus, editio maior* (Merida: Los Andes University Press, 1967).

Masi, Gino, "La pittura infamante nella legislazione e nella vita del comune fiorentino (sec. XIII–XVI)," in *Studi di diritto commerciale in onore di Cesare Vivante*, 2 vols. (Rome: Foro italiano, 1931), vol. 2, pp. 625–57.

Masson, Charles, "Le démoniaque de Gérasa," in *Vers les sources d'eau vive: Études d'exégèse et de théologie du Nouveau Testament* (Lausanne: Payot, 1961), pp. 20–37.

Maupassant, Guy de, "Le retour," in *Contes et nouvelles*, ed. Louis de Forestier, 2 vols. (Paris: Gallimard, 1974–1979), pp. 206–12.

McCawley, James D., "Participant Roles, Frames, and Speech Acts," *Linguistics and Philosophy* 22.6 (1999), pp. 595–619.

———, "Speech Acts and Goffman's Participant Roles," *Eastern States Conference on Linguistics* 1 (1984), pp. 260–74.

Mendenhall, George E., "The Census Lists of Numbers 1 and 26," *Journal of Biblical Literature* 77.1 (1958), pp. 52–66.

Meritt, Benjamin D., "Greek Inscriptions," *Hesperia* 21.4 (1952), pp. 340–80.

Metcalf, Peter, "Meaning and Materialism: The Ritual Economy of Death," *Man*, n. s., 16.4 (1981), pp. 563–78.

Meyer, Elizabeth A., *Legitimacy and Law in the Roman World* (Cambridge: Cambridge University Press, 2004).

Meyer, Priscilla, *How the Russians Read the French: Lermontov, Dostoevesky, Tolstoy* (Madison: University of Wisconsin Press, 2008).

Miller, Andrew, *The Burdens of Perfection: On Ethics and Reading in Nineteenth-Century British Literature* (Ithaca: Cornell University Press, 2008).

Mirus, Christopher V., "Homonymy and the Matter of a Living Body," *Ancient Philosophy* 21 (2001), pp. 357–73.

Montaigne, Michel de, "Des Boyteux," in *Les essais*, eds. Jean Balsamo, Michel Magnien, and Catherine Magnien-Simonin (Paris: Gallimard, 2007), pp. 1071–82.

———,"Of the Lame or Crippel," in *The Essayes of Montaigne: John Florio's Translation*, introduction by J. I. M. Stewart (New York: Modern Library, 1933), pp. 928–37.

Motz, Lotte, "Withdrawal and Return: A Ritual Pattern in the *Grettis Saga*," *Arkiv for Nordisk Filologi* 88 (1973), pp. 91–110.

Muyart de Vouglans, Pierre-François, *Institutes au droit criminel ou principes généraux sur ces matières, avec un traité particulier des crimes* (Paris: Le Breton, 1757).

Nabokov, Vladimir, *Nikolai Gogol* (New York: New Directions, 1961).

Nagy, Gregory, *Comparative Studies in Greek and Indic Meter* (Cambridge, MA: Harvard University Press, 1974).

Nédoncelle, Maurice, "Prosopon et persona dans l'antiquité classique: Essai de bilan linguistique," *Revue des sciences religieuses* 22.3–4 (1948), pp. 277–99.

Negelein, Julius von, "Bild, Spiegel und Schatten im Volksglauben," *Archiv für Religionswissenschaft* 5 (1902), pp. 1–37.

Neubauer, Wolfgang, "Zur Schatten-Problem bei Adelbert von Chamisso," *Literatur für Leser* 9 (1986), pp. 24–34.

Nichols, Mary P., "Rationality and Community: Swift's Criticism of the Houyhnhnms," *Journal of Politics* 43.4 (1981), pp. 1153–69.

Nietzsche, Friedrich, *Human, Al Too Human: A Book for Free Spirits*, trans. R. J. Hollingdale (Cambridge: Cambridge University Press, 1986).

——, *Menschliches, Allzumenschliches I und II*, vol. 2 of *Sämtliche Werke: Kritische Studienausgabe*, eds. Giorgio Colli and Mazzino Montinari, 15 vols. (New York: De Gruyter, 1999).

Nilsson, Nils Åke, "On the Origins of Gogol's 'Overcoat'," in Elizabeth W. Trahan (ed.), *Gogol's "Overcoat": An Anthology of Critical Essays* (Ann Arbor: Ardis, 1982), pp. 61–72.

Norman, Arthur, "The 'Schlemiehl' Problem," *American Speech* 27.2 (1952), pp. 149–50.

Opie, Iona, and Peter Opie, *Children's Games in Street and Playground* (Oxford: Oxford University Press, 1969).

Orchard, Andy, *Pride and Prodigies: Studies in the Monsters of the Beowulf-Manuscript* (Cambridge: D. S. Brewer, 1995).

Oring, Elliott, "On the Tradition and Mathematics of Counting-Out," *Western Folklore* 56.2 (1997), pp. 139–52.

Ortalli, Gherardo, *La pittura infamante nei secoli XIII–XVI* (Rome: Jouvence, 1979).

——, "Pittura infamante: Practices, Genres and Connections," in Carolin Behrmann (ed.), *Images of Shame: Infamy, Defamation and the Ethics of Oeconomia* (Berlin: De Gruyter, 2016), pp. 29–48.

Orwell, George, *The Collected Essays, Journalism, and Letters of George Orwell*, eds. Sonia Orwell and Ian Angus, 4 vols. (New York: Harcourt & Brace, 1968).

——, *Nineteen Eighty-Four* (London: Penguin Books, 2013).

Ovid, *Heroides*, trans. Harold Isbell (New York: Penguin Books, 1990).

Oxford English Dictionary, 2nd ed., prepared by J. A. Simpson and E. S. C. Weiner, 20 vols. (Oxford: Clarendon Press of Oxford University Press, 1989).

Panagopoulos, Nicolás, "Gulliver and the Horse: An Enquiry into Equine Ethics," in Harold Bloom (ed.), *Jonathan Swift's Gulliver's Travels* (New York: Infobase, 2009), pp. 145–64.

Parker, Robert, *Miasma: Pollution and Purification in Early Greek Religion* (Oxford: Clarendon Press of Oxford University Press, 1983).

Partridge, Eric, *A Short Etymological Dictionary of Modern English*, 3rd ed. (London: Routledge, 1961).

Patterson, Orlando, *Slavery and Social Death: A Comparative Study* (Cambridge, MA: Harvard University Press, 1982).

Pausanias, *Description of Greece*, trans. W. H. S. Jones and H. A. Ormerod, 4 vols. (Cambridge, MA: Harvard University Press, 1918).

Pavlyshyn, Marko, "Gold, Guilt and Scholarship: Adelbert von Chamisso's *Peter Schlemihl*," *German Quarterly* 55.1 (1982), pp. 49–63.

Peace, Richard, *The Enigma of Gogol* (Cambridge: Cambridge University Press, 1981).

Péju, Pierre, "L'ombre et la vitesse," in Adelbert von Chamisso, *Peter Schlemihl*, trans. Hippolyte von Chamisso (Paris: Éditions Corti, 1994), pp. 99–166.

Pesch, Rudolf, "The Markan Version of the Healing of the Gerasene Demoniac," *Ecumenical Review* 23.4 (1971), pp. 349–76.

Picard, Charles, "Le Cénotaphe de Midéa et les 'colosses' de Ménélas. *Ad Æsch. Agamemn.* v. 414 sqq," *Revue de philologie, de littérature et d'histoire anciennes* 7 (1933), pp. 341–54.

Pieri, Georges, *L'histoire du cens jusqu'à la fin de la République romaine* (Paris: Sirey, 1968).

Pigeaud, Jackie, "La question du cadavre dans l'antiquité gréco-romaine," *Micrologus* 7 (1999), pp. 43–71.

Pirandello, Luigi, *Il fu Mattia Pascal*, ed. Giancarlo Mazzacurati (Turin: Einaudi, 1993).

Planiol, Marcel, *Traité élémentaire de droit civil*, 3 vols., 3rd ed. (Paris: Pichon, 1904).

Plato, *Plato in Twelve Volumes*, 12 vols. (Cambridge, MA: Harvard University Press, 1914–1921).

Pliny the Elder, *Natural History*, trans. H. Rackam, 10 vols. (Cambridge, MA: Harvard University Press, 1938–1963).

Politzer, Heinz, *Franz Kafka: Parable and Paradox* (Ithaca: Cornell University Press, 1962).

Polo de Beaulieu, Marie Anne, "Paroles de fantôme: Le cas du revenant d'Alès (1323)," *Ethnologie française*, n.s., 33.4 (2003), pp. 565–74.

Polybius, *Histories*, 6 vols., trans. W. R. Paton (Cambridge, MA: Harvard University Press, 1922–1927).

Pommeray, Léon, *Études sur l'infamie en droit romain* (Paris: Sirey, 1937).

Pradel, Fritz W., "Der Schatten im Volksglauben," *Mitteilungen der schlesischen Gesellschaft für Volkskunde* 12 (1904), pp. 1–36.

Preisker, Herbert, s.v. "Legiōn," in Gerhard Kittel (ed.), *Theologisches Wörterbuch zum Neuen Testament*, 10 vols. (Stuttgart: Kohlhammer, 1942–).

Radin, Max, "Caput et sōma," in Gabriel Le Bras (ed.), *Mélanges Paul Fournier* (Paris: Receuil Sirey, 1929), pp. 651–63.

Reising, Russel J., "Figuring Himself Out: Spencer Brydon, 'The Jolly Corner' and Cultural Change," *Journal of Narrative Technique* 19.1 (1989), pp. 116–29.

Renner, Rolf Günter, "Schrift der Natur und Zeichen des Selbst: *Peter Schlemihls wundersame Geschichte* im Zusammenhang von Chamissos Texten," *Deutsche Vierteljahrschrift für Literaturwissenschaft und Geistesgeschichte* 65.4 (1991), pp. 653–73.

Reuß, Roland, "Running Texts, Stunning Drafts," in Stanley Corngold and Ruth V. Gross (eds.), *Kafka for the Twenty-First Century* (Rochester: Camden House, 2011), pp. 24–47.

Richir, François, *Traité de la Mort civile, tant celle qui résulte des condamnations pour cause de crime, que celle qui résulte des vœux en religion* (Paris: Thiboust, 1755).

Riesenfeld, Conrad Ernst, *Verschollenheit und Todeserklärung nach gemeinem und preussischem Rechte, mit stäter Rücksicht auf die Vorschläge des Entwurfs eines bürgerlichen Gesetzbuchs für das deutsche Reich* (Breslau: Wilhelm Koebner, 1890).

Robbins, Hollis, "'We Are Seven' and the First British Census," *English Language Notes* 48.2 (2010), pp. 201–13.

Robert, Marthe, "Kafka et Flaubert," *L'Arc* 79 (1980), pp. 26–30.

Rochholz, E. L., "Ohne Schatten, Ohne Seele: Der Mythus vom Körperschatten und vom Schattengeist," *Germania* 5 (1860), pp. 69–94.

Rubin, David C., Violeta Ciobanu, and William Langston, "Children's Memory for Counting-Out Rhymes: A Cross-Language Comparison," *Psychonomic Bulletin and Review* 4.3 (1997), pp. 421–24.

Sadan, Dov, "Lesugia: Shelumiel," *Orlogin* 1 (1950), pp. 198–203.

Santillana, David, *Istituzioni di diritto musulmano malichita, con riguardo anche al sistema sciafiita*, 2 vols. (Rome: Istituto per l'Oriente, 1925–1938).

Saunders, Harry David, "Civil Death: A New Look at an Ancient Doctrine," *William and Mary Law Review* 11.4 (1970), pp. 988–1003.

Savigny, Karl Friedrich von, *Traité de droit romain*, trans. Charles Guenoux, 8 vols. (Paris: Firmin Didot Frères, 1840–1851).

Savoy, Eric, "The Queer Subject of 'The Jolly Corner,'" *Henry James Review* 20.1 (1999), pp. 1–21.

Sayers, William, "The Alien and the Alienated as Unquiet Dead in the Sagas of the Icelanders," in Jeffrey Jerome Cohen (ed.), *Monster Theory: Reading Culture* (Minneapolis: University of Minnesota Press, 1996), pp. 242–63.

Schanbacher, Dietmar, "Aqua et Igni Interdictio," in. Hubert Cancik et al. (eds.), *Brill's New Pauly*, Brill Reference Online: http://dx.doi.org/10.1163/1574-9347_bnp_e130020.

Schaub, Charles, *Dissertation sur la mort civile* (Geneva: A. I. Vignier, 1831).

Scheppele, Kim Lane, "Facing Facts in Legal Interpretation," *Representations* 30 (1990), pp. 42–77.

Schmitt, Jean-Claude, *Les revenants: Les vivants et les morts dans la société médiévale* (Paris: Gallimard, 1994).

Senn, Félix, "Des origines et du contenu de la notion de bonnes mœurs," *Recueil d'études sur les sources du droit en l'honneur de François Gény*, 3 vols. (Paris: Sirey, 1934).

Shakespeare, William, *Julius Caesar*, ed. Arthur Humphreys (Oxford: Clarendon Press of Oxford University Press, 1984).

Shokoff, James, "Wordsworth's Duty as a Poet in 'We Are Seven' and 'Surprised by Joy,'" *Journal of English and Germanic Philology* 93.2 (1994), pp. 228–39.

Simonin, Anne, *Le déshonneur dans la République: Une histoire de l'indignité* (Paris: Grasset, 2008).

Skeat, Walter W., *A Concise Etymological Dictionary of the English Language* (Oxford: Clarendon Press of Oxford University Press, 1901).

Snell, Bruno, *The Discovery of the Mind: The Greek Origins of European Thought*, trans. T. G. Rosenmeyer (Oxford: Basil Blackwell, 1953).

——, *Tragicorum Graecorum fragmenta*, 5 vols. (Göttingen: Vandenhoek & Ruprecht, 1977).

Sohm, Rudolph, *The Institutes of Roman Law*, trans. James Crawford Ledlie (Oxford: Clarendon Press of Oxford University Press, 1892).

Spieler, Miranda Frances, *Empire and Underworld: Captivity in French Guyana* (Cambridge, MA: Harvard University Press, 2012).

Starobinski, Jean, "Le démoniaque de Gérasa: Analyse littéraire de Marc 5. 1–20," in Roland Barthes, François Bovon, J. Leenhardt, Robert Martin-Archard, and Jean Starobinski, *Analyse structurale et exégèse biblique: Essais d'interprétation* (Neuchâtel: Delachaux & Niestlé, 1972), pp. 63–94.

Steinberg, Erwin S., "The Three Fragments of Kafka's 'The Hunter Gracchus,'" *Studies in Short Fiction* 15.3 (1978), pp. 305–17.

Steiner, Deborah, "Eyeless in Argos," *Journal of Hellenic Studies* 115 (1995), pp. 175–82.

——, *Images in Mind: Statues in Archaic and Classical Greek Literature and Thought* (Princeton: Princeton University Press, 2001).

Stoichita, Victor I., *A Short History of the Shadow*, trans. Anne-Marie Glasheen (London: Reaktion Books, 1997).

Stone, D., "The Presumption of Death: A Redundant Concept?," *Modern Law Review* 44.5 (1981), pp. 516–25.

Suchoff, David, *Kafka's Jewish Languages* (Philadelphia: University of Pennsylvania Press, 2012).

Sutton-Smith, Brian, *The Games of New Zealand Children* (Berkeley: University of California Press, 1959).

Swales, Martin, "Mundane Magic: Some Observations on Chamisso's *Peter Schlemihl*," *Forum for Modern Language Studies* 12 (1976), pp. 250–62.

Swift, Jonathan, *Gulliver's Travels*, ed. Claude Rowson, notes by Ian Higgins (Oxford: Oxford University Press, 2005).

Talandier, Firmin, *Nouveau traité des absens* (Limoges: Th. Marmignon, 1831).

Tarello, Giovanni, "Profili giuridici della questione della povertà nel francescanesimo prima di Occam," *Annali della Facoltà di Giurisprudenza dell'Università di Genova* 3 (1964), pp. 338–448.

Taylor, Aline Mackenzie, "Sights and Monsters and Gulliver's *Voyage to Brobdingnag*," *Tulane Studies in English* 6 (1956), pp. 27–32.

Taylor, C. C. W., ed., *The Atomists: Leucippus and Democritus, Fragments, a Text and Translation*, trans. C. C. W. Taylor (Toronto: University of Toronto Press, 2010).

Testart, Alain, *L'institution de l'esclavage: Une approche mondiale*, ed. Valérie Lécrivain (Paris: Gallimard, 2018).

Thomas, Julian, "Death, Identity and the Body in Neolithic Britain," *Journal of the Royal Anthropological Institute* 6.3 (2000), pp. 653–68.

Thomas, Yan, "Corpus aut ossa aut ceneres: La chose religieuse et le commerce," *Micrologus* 7 (1999), pp. 73–112.

——, "Imago naturae: Note sur l'institutionnalité de la nature à Rome," *Publications de l'école française de Rome* 147 (1991), pp. 201–27.

Thompson, Stith, *Motif-Index of Folk-Literature: A Classification of Narrative Elements in Folktales, Ballads, Myths, Fables, Mediaeval Romances, Exempla, Fabliaux, Jest-Books, and Local Legends*, 6 vols. (Bloomington: Indiana University Press, 1955–1958).

Thomson, George, *Æschylus and Athens: A Study in the Social Origins of Drama* (London: Lawrence and Wishart, 1916).

Tobias, Rochelle, "Writers and 'Schlemihls': On Heine's *Jehuda ben Halevy*," in Aris Fioretos (ed.), *Babel: Für Werner Hamacher* (Basel: Urs Engeler, 2009), pp. 362–70.

Todd, Dennis, "The Hairy Maid at the Harpsichord: Some Speculations on the Meaning of Gulliver's Travels," *Texas Studies in Literature and Language* 34.2 (1992), pp. 239–83.

Todeschini, Giacomo, *Visibilmente crudeli: Malviventi, persone sospette e gente qualunque dal Medioevo all'età moderna* (Bologna: Il Mulino, 2007).

Travers, Andrew, "Non-Person and Goffman: Sociology under the Influence of Literature," in *Goffman and Social Organization: Studies in a Sociological Legacy* (London: Routledge, 1999), pp. 156–76.

Treadgold, Warren T., "A Verse Translation of the Lamiyah of Shanfara," *Journal of Arabic Literature* 6 (1975), pp. 31–34.

Turville-Petre, G., "Outlawry," in Einar G. Pétursson and Jónas Kristjánsson (eds.), *Sjötíu ritgerðir helgaðar Jakobi Benediktssyni I* (Reykjavik: Stofnun Árna Magnússonar á Íslandi, 1977), pp. 769–78.

Tyan, Émile, "La condition juridique de 'l'Absent' (*Mafḳūd*) en droit musulman, particulièrement dans le Madhab Ḥanafite," *Studia islamica* 31 (1970), pp. 249–56.

Unruh, Georg Christoph von, "Wargus: Friedlosigkeit und magisch-kultische Vorstellungen bei den Germanen," *Zeitschrift der Savigny-Stiftung für Rechtsgeschichte* 74 (1959), pp. 1–40.

Usteri, Paul, *Ächtung und Verbannung in griechischen Recht* (Berlin: Weidmannsche Buchhandlung, 1903).

Vedder, Ulrike, "Die Figur des Verschollenen in der Literatur des 20. Jahrhunderts (Kafka, Burger, Treichel)," *Zeitschrift für Germanistik* 21.3 (2011), pp. 548–62.

Vernant, Jean-Pierre, *Myth and Thought among the Greeks*, trans. Janet Lloyd with Jeff Fort (New York: Zone Books, 2006).

——, *Œuvres*, 2 vols. (Paris: Éditions du Seuil, 2007).

Vestfirðinga sögur, eds. Björn K. Þórólfsson and Guðni Jónnson (Reykjavik: Hið Íslenzka fornritafélag, 1958).

Wagenbach, Klaus, *Kafka: Eine Biographie seiner Jugend* (Bern: Francke, 1958).

Wagenvoort, Hendrik, *Inspiratie door bijen in de droom* (Amsterdam: Koninklijke Nederlandse Akademie van Wetenschappen, 1966).

Walker, James A., "Gothic *-leik-* and Germanic **lik-* in the Light of Gothic Translations of Greek Originals," *Philological Quarterly* 28 (1949), pp. 274–93.

Ward, Julie K., *Aristotle on Homonymy: Dialectic and Science* (Cambridge: Cambridge University Press, 2008).

Ward, Thomas M., *John Duns Scotus on Parts, Wholes, and Hylomorphism* (Leiden: Brill, 2014).

Watkins, Calvert, *How to Kill a Dragon* (Oxford: Oxford University Press, 1995).

Weber, Sam, *Theatricality as Medium* (New York: Fordham University Press, 2004).

Weigand, Hermann J., "Peter Schlemihl," in A. Leslie Willson (ed.), *Surveys and Soundings in European Literature* (Princeton: Princeton University Press, 1966), pp. 208–22.

Weithase, Franz, *Über den bürgerlichen Tod als Straffolge* (Berlin: Ernst-Reuter-Gesellschaft, 1966).

Whinery, Andrew W., "Presumption of Death in New Jersey," *Mercer Beasley Law Review* 5.1 (1936), pp. 1–15.

Whiting, Jennifer, "Living Bodies," in Martha Nussbaum and Amélie Oksenberg Rorty (eds.), *Essays on Aristotle's De Anima* (Oxford: Clarendon Press of Oxford University Press, 1992), pp. 75–91.

Wieruszowski, Helene, "Art and the Commune in the Age of Dante," *Speculum* 19.1 (1944), pp. 4–33.

Wilamowitz-Möllendorf, Ulrich, "Heilige Gesetze: Eine Urkunde aus Kyrene," *Sitzungsberichte der Berliner Akademie* (1927), pp. 155–76.

Wilpiert, Gero von, *Der verlorene Schatten: Varianten eines literarischen Motifs* (Stuttgart: A. Kröner, 1978).

Winkler, John J., *Auctor and Actor: A Narratological Reading of Apuleius's "The Golden Ass"* (Berkeley: University of California Press, 1985).

Wolf, Joseph Georg, "Lo stigma dell'ignominia," in Alessandro Corbino, Michel Humbert, and Giovanni Negri (eds.), *Homo, caput, persona: La costruzione giuridica dell'identità nell'esperienza romana, dall'epoca di Plauto a Ulpiano* (Pavia: IUSS Press, 2010), pp. 491–550.

Woodward, James B., *Gogol's "Dead Souls"* (Princeton: Princeton University Press, 1978).

Wordsworth, William, *Poetical Works*, ed. Thomas Hutchinson, rev. Ernest de Sélincourt (New York: Oxford University Press, 1936).

Yaron, Reuven, "The Missing Husband in Jewish Law," in *Mélanges à la mémoire de Marcel-Henri Prévost: Droit biblique, interprétation rabbinique, communautés et société* (Paris: Presses universitaires de France, 1982), pp. 133–40.

Zeldner, Max, "A Note on 'Schlemihl,'" *German Quarterly* 26.2 (1953), pp. 115–17.

Žižek, Slavoj, *Tarrying with the Negative: Kant, Hegel, and the Critique of Ideology* (Durham: Duke University Press, 1993).

Zola, Émile, "La mort d'Olivier Bécaille" and "Jacques Damour," in *Contes et nouvelles*, ed. Roger Ripoll with Sylvie Luneau (Paris: Gallimard, 1976), pp. 803–30 and pp. 896–929.

Index

Zone Books series design by Bruce Mau
Typesetting by Meighan Gale
Image placement and production by Julie Fry
Printed and bound by Maple Press